MIKE CARR

WHAT DOESN'T KILL YOU...

CHAPTER 1
Tough Life

I'm about to share my deepest, untold secrets with you and promise this rollercoaster of intense highs and darkest lows is something that you will not want to miss. If you were to catch a glimpse of my life from the outside, without really knowing me, you'd believe that everything was going well for me and in all honesty, things are pretty good. However, you're catching my life at a point where things are about to take a dramatic twist and blow up in my face and there is only one person to blame, me!

Although life is good, I've consistently been in search of something better. Some may call me a dreamer, but there's no harm in that. Don't we all want to disappear from the real world occasionally, even if it is just for a day or two? It doesn't hurt anyone, or does it? Reality can be a tough place at times, especially when you've got responsibilities waiting for you. That's why I'm holding on to that desire of having the luxury lifestyle I've always dreamed of becoming a reality. It's etched in my mind, and I'm going to do whatever it takes to get it. Don't get me wrong, I'm not ungrateful for the things I've got now, as there's a lot of positives in my life, but I want something more.

My desire for something more has given me that drive, as I feel at this stage in my life I could be doing better. Something needs to excite me when opening my eyes in the morning! Who doesn't want that perfect life, even if it seems like a far-fetched idea that can only be dreamed of.

I've had to fight for everything in life and wasn't born with a silver spoon in my mouth. I'm from a close family, who didn't have a lot in life, but what little we did have my parents worked hard to get it. We managed with what we had and I'm truly grateful for all the sacrifices they made so that the life my brother and I had could be a little better. They did their best to ensure that we never wanted for anything, but I always had a plan of my own and that was to have more.

I grew up in the schemes of Whitfield, Dundee, where the crime rate was just as high as the peer pressure, and there was always the uncertainty of what tomorrow would bring. That's why it became important for me to take care of the people I valued most.

For all the boys my age living in Whitfield, being part of the crowd was a way of life. Image affected how you were treated by others in the scheme. Although a tough guy, I needed a sense of belonging, which came from my group of mates. We walked around thinking we owned the world and there wasn't anyone or anything that could stop us, or so we thought! Fights were inevitable. Most of the time I'd fight to stand up for someone who was being bullied. I'm not justifying my actions by any means, but it was the only way I knew how to help those who couldn't defend themselves. Bullies made my blood boil, and I fucking hated them in my younger years, and still do to this day! I viewed bullying as being unfair, but quickly learnt that life isn't fair and doesn't owe any of us anything. As my mum cleaned me up after another fight, as she always did, I remember her saying to me, "One day son you'll end up getting into proper trouble, you need to be careful. I don't understand what you are fighting for?"

She was right! One day I did get into trouble and my life turned upside down. It all started on a Sunday afternoon, one summer in 1984, when I was hanging out with a few of my mates. We quickly got bored knocking a football about the streets, until we remembered about the abandoned dark brown MK1 Escort that we'd spotted earlier in the week when walking home from school. We all agreed that we'd go and piss about in the car for

2

a laugh. It had no wheels and balanced shakily on bricks. All the windows were smashed except for the front one.

Jimmy, who was in our class at school, and had recently moved to Dundee from Glasgow, spotted us in the car and came over to hang out. We felt sorry for him because he hadn't really made any friends since moving to Dundee, so we let him join in.

We were having such a laugh, being typical boys, tops off in the scorching sunshine, thinking we were the dog's bollocks. We dared Shawzer, who was slightly smaller than the rest of our crowd, to climb into the boot of the car. As he climbed in, tucking his head into his chest, Davy slammed the boot shut. Shawzer shouted, "Right guys stop fucking about, let me out" as he banged hard on the inside of the boot.

It was only meant to be a prank, that was until things went wrong!

Unknown to us Jimmy had climbed into the back of the car and pulled a lighter from the pocket of his jeans, which he used to set the seat on fire. Within seconds the whole seat was engulfed in flames. I quickly ran around to the back of the car to let Shawzer out. Realising that the lock of the boot was fucked and couldn't be opened, panic filled my veins, as I frantically searched the ground for anything that could be used to try and open the lock. The only thing to be found was a long, sharp, piece of glass.

The other boys screamed desperately at me: "Quick Mike, get him the fuck out of there!"

The intensity of the heat from the fire was becoming unbearable as the flames began ripping out of the top of the car. The sweat stung my eyes as it dripped from my forehead, but I wasn't stopping for one second until he was out. My tight grip on the glass caused it to pierce my right index finger and thumb and blood dripped down my arm.

The sound of a police car's siren pierced the sky, even above the noise of the fire and the boys screaming at me.

As soon as it screeched around the corner to where we were, Hutchy shouted: "There's the polis, fucking run!" Without thinking I dropped the piece of glass, which shattered off the stones on the ground, before running as fast as my feet could carry me. We all split up, running in different directions, and the boys quickly disappeared out of sight. Running between the houses my heart almost stopped as a dog jumped out barking, bearing its teeth at me, but I never slowed my pace until close to my house. I then jogged past the kitchen window, where my mum was standing at the sink doing the dishes. What was I going to tell her, the truth wasn't an option, it would only hurt her. My mind was racing.

Lifting my hand to open the front door, I noticed the blood from the cut off the glass so quickly used my t-shirt to wipe it away before putting my hand into my pocket. "Mike go and get cleaned up son, tea will be ready soon," my mum shouted as soon as I'd shut the front door behind me.

Hurrying to the bathroom to clean up, I almost knocked my brother off his feet. When I was safely inside the bathroom, without anyone asking questions, I slid down the door onto the floor, trying to get my head around what the fuck had just happened. Had the police managed to get Shawzer out in time and was he okay? How could we have been so stupid?! I nearly jumped out my skin as my dad banged hard on the bathroom door. "Hurry up son I need in there."

Getting up from the floor and walking over to the sink, I caught a glimpse of my face in the mirror, it was black from the smoke of the flames. After washing my face and hands I bolted to my room before anyone could see me. The smell of the fire on my clothes was strong and made me feel sick so I got changed into my favourite tracksuit. Once ready, I lay back onto my bed staring at the ceiling, not having any idea what to do next, completely lost in my own thoughts.

After laying on the bed for what seemed like hours, my brother burst into my room. "Mum says tea's ready bro, you need to come down."

Following him sheepishly downstairs and into the kitchen, I decided not to say anything to my parents. Maybe they would never need to find out what we'd done.

We all sat around our square kitchen table. My family began talking about their day as they tucked into the feast that my mum had made for us as I stared, lost in the white and red squares of the kitchen wall paper. My appetite had disappeared and as I pushed food around my plate my mum asked in her soft, caring voice: "What's wrong with you son? You've hardly said a word and not touched your food!"

My parents always sat with their back to the window and me and my Brother sat looking towards it. Looking up, to make up some excuse for my mum, my face dropped at the sight of a policeman walking right past. "What is it son?" she asked again. My bottom lip started to tremble and before a word could escape my mouth there was a deafening thump on the front door. Everyone turned to look at each other, and the door, puzzled. "Who could that be at this time?" My dad asked as he stood up from the table to go and answer it.

As he stood at the front door talking for a few minutes, I sat staring down at the table, frozen, not knowing what to do. It was difficult to make out the conversation between the policeman and my dad as their voices were low and muffled and the kitchen door had closed slightly when the front door had been opened. Suddenly the front door slammed shut, which startled me. Hoping that the policeman had gone, I lifted my eyes up from the table, with my heart in my mouth, as the kitchen door opened. My hope was shattered as my dad walked in slowly with an anxious look on his face, closely followed by the policeman.

I was in deep shit, there was no escaping it. The policeman towered above me and reached out for my hand, snapping a cold, hard, metal handcuff against my wrist. "Michael Carr, I am arresting you for attempted murder. You do not have to say anything, but anything you do say may be used against you as evidence.

5

Do you understand?"

Tears filled my eyes, I wanted to speak, to explain what had happened but the words wouldn't come out. Within seconds my mum became hysterical, crying, trying to get to me, but my dad held onto her tightly. The thought of letting her down and seeing her in this state, caused the tears that had been welling in my eyes to stream down my face.

The policeman snapped the handcuff onto my other wrist and pulled me to my feet. My brother sat motionless, shocked, not being able to take it all in as I was led out of the kitchen towards the front door. Both my parents followed, my Mum was still hysterical. Just as the policeman was about to open the door I found my voice. "I'm sorry, it was a stupid accident," I whispered softly, looking back into my Mum's weeping eyes. This only made her cry even harder. My dad hugged her close to his chest, as the two of them stood looking at me, broken. The policeman opened the front door and pushed me hard in the back to walk through it.

"Your stupid accident nearly killed somebody son!" he said sternly. His words echoed through my mind. He said "nearly" which must have meant that Shawzer got out. At least I could take some comfort in knowing that.

"What happens now?" my dad asked.

"He will be taken to the police station where we will interview him. If you leave it for a few hours and come down to the station, will be able to give you further information about what will happen next," the policeman replied before stepping out the door.

A few of the neighbours had gathered in the street and watched intently as I was bundled into the police car. As the door slammed shut behind me, the realisation about how serious this was, hit me like a train. My life would never be the same again.

CHAPTER 2
Choosing a Path

After spending three weeks being remanded in custody, and
being found guilty at my trial, I was taken away from everything
I'd known and thrown into Rossie Farm, the toughest young
offenders institute in Scotland, located just outside Montrose.
I'd just turned fifteen, and because of a stupid prank that had
gone tits up, I was about to spend two of the longest years of
my life locked up. It wasn't my parents to blame for what had
happened, nor was it their fault for the punishment I'd now
have to endure, I'd brought this on myself.
That was my wake-up call, time to stop fighting others and start
fighting for myself and try to make sense of the life I was living.
Arriving at the young offender's unit, I struggled to get my head
around what was happening to me, feeling as though I didn't
deserve to be ripped away from my family. It was a confusing
time, not just for me, but for the other boys that were inside, as
we tried to figure out the purpose of our own lives now.
On my very first day, lost and vulnerable, I walked, with my
head hung low, in to the social area where all the other boys
were gathered. I didn't want to make eye contact with anyone.
Within a few seconds, a loud dominating voice sent shivers
down my spine as "I know you!" was shouted at me.
Fear washed over me, I didn't even want to turn around to
see who it was. "Hey, I'm speaking to you!" the voice shouted
again. Slowly turning, I was confronted by a tall, stocky built,
boy with jet black hair. He had a scar on his face that ran from
his right cheek to the top of his lip. He was obviously top dog
amongst the boys in here. There were two other boys poised

ready at his side, looking as though they would rip my throat out if he said the word.

"Do you?" I replied hesitantly, looking at him.

"I fucking knew it was you, Mike!" the boy said, recognising me. A huge smile spread across his face, stepping forward, he put his arm around my shoulder.

"I'm Davy Johnstone, Colin Johnstone is my wee brother. He came to your school a couple of years ago and was bullied because of his accent and for wearing specs. You took him under your wing and looked after him. My mum always said how grateful she was to you. You helped put her mind at ease because she knew you were there watching out for him. I owe you," he went on to explain.

"So now it's my turn to look after you. I'll make sure you're okay while you're in this shithole", he said as he pulled up a chair and climbed onto it.

Not having any idea what he was doing, I simply stood motionless, watching him.

"Mike's part of my crew now! If any of you fuckers go near him, you'll have me to deal with, understand?" he threatened.

Nobody said a word, or even looked directly at him, as they nodded in acknowledgement. From that moment it became clear that Davy ran things around here and that I'd be protected. Instantly I lifted my head and felt as though I'd grown about six inches. There would be nothing to fear with him fighting my corner.

Later that day I got into a fight with one of the other boys who thought he was tough enough to pick on the new guy. Although I was protected by Davy there was no way I'd let anyone think they could get the better of me. As soon as the fight started, it was stopped. Neither of us got the chance for a decent punch as we were quickly restrained by the screws. They were total bastards, bullies, the type of people I'd spent my young life fighting against. They dragged us apart and threw me into my cell, kicking the shit out of me, laughing as they punched and kicked me with their steel toe capped boots on. I could hardly walk for days after; my body was a mass of cuts and bruises. That was my introduction to this hardened place and was just a taste of things to come.

There were rules to be followed in the unit. We had a regime that needed to be adhered to, or there were severe consequences to be paid, we all learned that lesson very quickly. That lesson wasn't just with the screws but from Davy and his crew as well.

I'd only been inside for a few months when Davy came bursting into our room going off his nut. Eight of us shared our room and when Davy was pissed off we all sat up to pay attention. Paul, one of the boys, owed him money and hadn't paid it back. "Right guys this little fucker has to pay, follow me!" he instructed.

Davy stormed down to the kitchens where Paul was working, and we quickly followed. As soon as they spotted him, the boys were on him like a pack of wolves, tackling him to the floor. "Hold the prick still!" Davy shouted as he grabbed one of the milk crates off the floor and climbed up one of the solid metal shelving units, balancing right above Paul. Davy held the milk crate above Paul's head with one hand, whilst holding on with the other. He was stronger than any of us inside. Paul thrashed about, trying to break free, but the boys had him in a tight grip. "You have taken the piss for far too long you little bastard. No-one fucks with me and you need to be taught a lesson", Davy scowled, with a dark anger in his eyes,and with that, he let the crate go.

It smashed down hard. Paul let out a scream as the bones in his cheek cracked and his nose spread across his face. Blood splattered onto the clothes of the boys that were holding him down.

"Let that be your lesson you little cunt, now get me my fucking money!" Davy warned, as he jumped off the shelving unit and walked calmly out of the kitchen. We quickly fled before the screws caught us, leaving Paul writhing around in pain on the floor. He never told the screws what had happened to him and made up some bullshit story. Nobody grassed in here, especially on Davy and his crew.

Life went on like this for the next twelve months. It was a relentless cycle of fights and being battered by the screws. Even the strongest of boys were broken in here. I'd turned from a mummy's boy into a hard nut, not by choice, but for survival. Rebellion was second nature to me at this point in my life, but the unit gave me the discipline that was needed. The longer we spent inside, good behavior began to be rewarded, which gave me hope that I'd be able to make it out of this shithole and get back home.

As part of my rehabilitation, I needed to speak with counsellors and it was during these conversations the idea of joining the Army was first born. Everything would be different from that moment forward and I promised myself that I'd become a better person. It was time to start competing with myself and nobody else. I wasn't going to be influenced by others anymore, I was going to be a different person when I left.

We had all been sent to the unit to be reformed and turn our lives around, and that is exactly what I was going to do. Some of the boys didn't make any effort to become better people. They chose a different path from me, believing they had a point to prove.

Davy came to me one day to tell me about a plan he had. Him and five of the boys in our room were going to break out. The nightshift guard was a complete pisshead, so it would be easy to pull off. He gave me the choice to be part of their escape or not. With only six months to push there was no way I was going to fuck up my chance of getting out, so told him I'd stay and keep my mouth shut.

Sure enough Davy stuck to his plan and him and five of the boys fucked off one night. I didn't believe they'd get away with it but, fuck me, did we know about it when the screws realised they had gone. They beat us to an inch of unconsciousness before throwing us into solitary.

One by one the boys were caught and joined us. Weeks passed, and it must have been about a month since their escape that I heard Davy gobbing off at the screws as they dragged him kicking and punching down to solitary. He wasn't getting out of this place any time soon.

I often think back and wonder what happened to them. The unit wasn't perfect, it was a tough time for me, but honestly it made me a better person and the man I am today.

CHAPTER 3
A Different Life

As soon as I was free from hell, sticking with my plan for a better life, I joined the Army. This would be the start of something positive and a step closer to having everything I'd wanted. It made sense for me to be part of something selfless and that is exactly what I'd be doing. This would be the place for me to put my fight to good use.

Thriving on the routine that the Army provided, and the discipline that was instilled by those in charge, gave me a sense of belonging. This was my biggest turning point in finding out who I was and changing the path I'd been following. One of my fondest memories of being in the Army was getting my first of many tattoos. The pain I felt as the needle pierced my skin brought with it a strange sense of release. With my brother and I having such a strong bond, it made sense that my first tattoo mimicked him, a rampant lion holding a Scotland flag on my left shoulder blade. It was a symbol of the strength we shared and being there for each other.

Needing to be physically fit, brought with it a new-found passion for working out in the gym. With regular training, big changes happened to my physique. I'd always been a skinny wee guy before, but now I was stronger and more muscular than ever before, becoming known as "big guy." This was a great feeling and people soon learnt not to fuck with me.

After my two years was served, I went back home to my family, with no real plan of what to do next. It wasn't long before a job working in a local factory with my Brother came up. He showed me the ropes and I kept my head down and worked hard, which resulted in a promotion to Manager. My life was continuing to move in the right direction and I became even more determined to achieve everything I'd set my mind on. Whilst working in the factory I met Jenna, who became my fiancée after seven happy years. She was an amazing girl who never really complained and loved me unconditionally. A strong woman who was confident in herself, which is one of the things I loved most about her.

Being the manager was exciting to begin with, but after 15 years of living an ordinary life, the longing for something more returned, which brings me to the point where I'm at now, Spring of 2007, trying to create my own thrills.

The gym continued to be an important part of my life and I'd go at least three or four times a week. It was a good stress release and helped keep me calm when things got to me. Kick boxing became my passion and I became very good at it, winning many fights. The difference being I was winning fights in the ring this time and not on the streets.

I was in the gym one day kicking fuck out of the bag when one of the guys I trained with approached me. Jamal was an Asian guy who owned a well know restaurant in St Andrews, which he'd invited me to many times before. We ate lavish meals, drank plenty and had become close friends over the last few years.

"Mike, I was going to ask you something but I'm not sure if you'd want to get involved" he said. He had sparked my interest and had my full attention from that second. "What is it?" I asked inquisitively. "Will you come to my restaurant tonight, so I can explain?" he asked. "Of course, I'll be there for about 8pm is that okay?" I replied. "Perfect" he responded before giving the bag a hard-right jab and turning to walk out the gym.

After finishing my workout, I headed home to relax for the rest of the afternoon until it was time to meet up with Jamal. My mind raced with thoughts, wondering what could be so important that he needed me to get involved.

Walking into the restaurant I was greeted by the mouthwatering aroma of the Indian dishes that the chef had created for us. Jamal welcomed me with a warm handshake and led the way across the fish tank floor to a table in a quiet top corner of the restaurant. As we walked, flashes of colour flicked beneath my feet as the tropical fish darted about.

Our chef for the night was also one of the guys that trained with us in the gym. He looked up to me and liked to show off with the food he made. He certainly didn't let himself down, as he brought dish after dish of the finest Indian cuisine.

We were nearing the end of our meal before Jamal moved the conversation to why he had asked me to the restaurant that night.

"I've seen the way you train in the gym and I know you can handle yourself. So, when a friend of mine approached me about a job he needed help with, my thoughts turned immediately to you," he explained.

I nodded my head to show he had my attention but never spoke, letting him continue.

"He is looking for someone to help him out with debt collection" Jamal continued.

"Why don't you help him out J?" I joked.

We both began laughing. He was a 5ft 6 skinny guy who wouldn't put the fear into anyone. Not only that, Jamal was a family man and would never get involved in anything that could be dangerous.

"I'm joking mate, you don't need to explain why you've come to me with this, I get it." I replied. He went on to tell me that the debt was business related and nothing dodgy. It would be easy money for me and to be honest I needed my old spark back. Living the quiet life never suited me and this would be the escape from the norm I needed, so I agreed to get involved.

CHAPTER 4
A New Path

It was only a couple of days later that my Brother and I were driving down to Leicester. This would be the first debt collection either of us had done but we had no doubt it would be easy. We'd been told that a Scottish scaffolding company had completed a big job for a large company in Leicester who were now refusing to pay what was owed. Solicitors and other debt collection agencies had been involved but had got nowhere. There was a £30k debt to be recovered and we weren't going to fail with getting it back. I played it clever and made sure I did my research on the directors of the company before we left.

When we arrived, suited and booted, we walked straight into the head office of the company. There was a grand reception area with an immaculately polished marble floor. A small, attractive receptionist sat behind a huge desk frantically typing on her keyboard. Once she spotted us, she immediately stopped typing and peered at us over the top of her glasses.

"Can I help you gentleman?" she asked.

"We are here to speak to John" I replied in an authoritative voice. The girl looked us both up and down nervously.

"Do you have an appointment?" she asked cautiously.

"We don't need an appointment. Please can you tell him that we are here regarding a debt he owes, and we will not be leaving until he has spoken to us," I instructed.

"Oh, okay sir I will just go and speak with him" she replied shakily before getting up from her seat and scurrying away into a room only a few doors down from the reception desk, shutting the door behind her as she went in. She'd only been gone a couple of minutes before she returned with a flustered expression on her face.

"John will be with you in a moment, he is just in the middle of something. If you would like to take a seat while you wait," she asked politely before returning to her keyboard.

We took a seat in two huge arm chairs over by the window. After waiting for nearly 45 minutes I was beginning to get impatient and pissed off. Just as I was about to go and speak to the receptionist again, the door that she had disappeared behind opened. A small over weight gentleman dressed in an expensive suit stepped out and waved over for us to come into his office.

When I entered the office door John had already taken a seat behind his desk. He looked nervous, as my Brother followed in closely behind me, shutting the door.

"How can I help you gentleman?" he asked hesitantly.

"We are here to collect the debt you owe." I responded, moving closer to his desk.

"And who are you? You don't appear to be from a legitimate agency!" he replied with a cheeky tone.

"We are not here in an official capacity but simply helping out a friend, so the normal rules don't apply." I warned.

"Is that a threat?" John asked with a concerned look in his eye.

"Not at all my friend, but you will have the debt repaid within 7 days and we will be taking half the money you owe with us when we leave tomorrow. Do you understand?" I replied, putting my hands on the desk and leaning forward towards him looking directly into his eyes.

The colour drained from his face and I could sense his panic. He knew we meant business and he couldn't fuck us around the way he had with the solicitors and other agencies. We weren't leaving without getting what we'd come for.

"Please, I don't want any trouble. I'll do my best to get this resolved. Can you wait back in the reception for ten minutes whilst I make a few phone calls?" he begged, reaching for his phone.

"We will wait, but our patience is starting to wear thin," I forewarned him before turning and walking back into the reception.

Our ten-minute wait turned into an hour and there was still no sign of him. After a brief conversation with the receptionist, she scurried away again to find out what was happening. I'd lost all patience now and was sick of being fucked around.

Another few minutes passed before John came out of his office and walked towards me with his head hung low, dragging his feet. This was the demeanor of someone that didn't have good news.

"Sorry for keeping you so long. I've done everything I can but I'm not able to get your money until tomorrow" he whispered.

"That's okay we will pop by your house later tonight at 7.30pm to make sure you have everything in place for tomorrow. Do you still live at 27 Oak Crescent?" I asked with a dark look in my eye.

John's jaw dropped as fear filled his veins.

"How do you know where I live?" he stuttered.

Without answering his question, both my Brother and I turned and simply walked away. Just before we left the building, I shouted back without turning around:

"Catch you later!" leaving John standing motionless in the reception.

We went to a quiet local pub for some food and a blether for a few hours before it was time to go to John's. I'd put the fear of god into him that was for sure when I'd told him we'd come to his house that night.

As the clock turned 7.30pm we pulled up outside 27 Oak Crescent. John lived in a wealthy area and his huge five bedroomed detached house was positioned perfectly in the middle of a cul de sac. There were two top of the range Audis parked in the driveway and an expensive kid's bike propped against the steps to the house.

I knocked loudly on the front door. John's wife answered and behind, clutching her leg, hid their son.

"Can I help you?" she asked politely.

"I'd like to speak to John please. If you can tell him that Mike is here to discuss the matters we spoke about at his office today." I replied.

She opened the door wider, turning to shout.

"John, Mike's at the door for you!"

I was able to see John busily preparing dinner in the kitchen. He froze for a second at the mention of my name, but gathered himself quickly and rushed to the door, ushering his wife and son into the living room.

He stepped through the door and closed it behind him. His shaking hand was noticeable as he reached for the door handle. We had him right where we needed him. Knowing where he lived gave us the advantage.

"How did you get on this afternoon John?" I asked.

"I've managed to organise half the money as you asked, but the only problem is you will need to wait until the morning" he replied apologetically.

"We will be at your office tomorrow for 10am. John, just a reminder, you are better dealing with us and making sure the money is there on time as we are the good guys. The boys that I will send next, if you do not have the money, won't be as nice as we are!" I threatened.

"No, no, I understand. I'll not let you down" he replied with a tremble in his voice, before walking backwards inside the house and closing the door firmly behind him.

The next morning when we arrived back at the office, we were greeted by two heavies, standing guard at either side of John's office door. Both my Brother and I turned to look at each other and laughed. We could handle ourselves and weren't intimidated by these goons. They tried to act like hard men with their chat, but they quickly realised that they were out of their depth dealing with us, and after a heated conversation they left.

With a clenched fist I banged hard on John's door before walking straight in without waiting for a reply. He nearly jumped out of his skin when he saw us, not expecting us to get passed his heavies. His eyes darted passed me in search for his back up.

"If you're looking for your goons they have gone. That was stupid wasting your money on them when it could have gone towards paying off your debt" I said with a wry smile.

"If you've quite finished fucking around we want what we came for!" I added.

John knew he was out his depth and we weren't going to leave without the money. Within 30 minutes of us arriving he'd transferred £15k into the scaffolding company's account and assured us that the remainder of the debt would be paid within 21 days.

We headed back up to Scotland happy men that day as 25% of what we collected was ours, easy money, and that's where it all began.

Jamal came to me with at least one job a month after that. All similar work and I got the desired outcome every time. The trust continued to build and jobs on a larger scale came my way, which is how I was introduced to Goker.

Debt collection was now going to take me across international borders. Goker asked for me to visit him in his homeland of Turkey. He was a very prominent figure in Istanbul's underground world, a wealthy man. My flight was paid for me to visit him without even the blink of an eye. My reputation had proceeded me and Goker requested that I recover a £70k debt that he'd loaned a guy to set up business in Newcastle.

This would be the biggest job I'd been involved with and it wouldn't be a walk in the park like the other jobs had been. Failure was not an option and I'd not stop until the debt was recovered.

After 3 months my reluctancy to walk away from the job resulted in me recovering most of the debt. In that time, I returned to Turkey to visit Goker many times and our friendship evolved. He began treating me more like family and my bond grew not only with him but the people he cared most about.

I continued to do the odd job for him here and there over the next year, but business quietened down. Our bond continued to grow, however, as I visited more often, and we soon became more like brothers. My longing for the thrill returned and at the perfect time Jamal introduced me to Ishvara.

CHAPTER 5
The Search

My life had taken another turn of direction. In hindsight, I'm not sure whether I regret meeting Ishvara, or regret not being content with the life I had at that moment.

He introduced me to a different world and I became involved with another kind of debt collection closer to home. It was unpredictable, and I never knew what to expect from one moment to the next, which made this path appealing to me. It was more invigorating than what I'd been doing, meeting an array of new and exciting people from different backgrounds. Ishvara was a local businessman who had many properties in Scotland. I was in awe of the money he had, but later found out that some of this money was just an illusion.

In the beginning, when working for Ishvara, my main responsibility was to ensure that the tenants he had living in his properties paid their rent on time. If that didn't happen then it was down to me to forcibly remove them. It was too easy to become sympathetic to some of the tenants, which was a huge problem with this kind of work. I related to the situations that they faced as I'd been there before and knew exactly what it felt like to have nothing.

I have a big heart. To look at me you could easily assume that I'd be a trouble maker, but my smile could quickly erase this illusion. I'd take time to make sense of every situation during my work and if someone was genuinely trying to get together the money that they owed for rent, I'd find myself helping them. This is not a trait that was going to bode well for me as a debt collector.

Whilst at work, I remained even tempered and it took a lot for me to get angry, but whenever someone crossed the line, I'd instill the fucking fear of god into them. It was better to remain on my good side and not go up against me.

During a collection, I met a young girl who was three months behind with her rent payments and I still remember the fear in her eyes when she opened the door and saw me. I could see she was at her wits end and no matter how hard she tried, she had no way of getting out of the shit she was in. I tried to be friendly with her, but she knew what I'd come for.

"Please, give me one more day, I'll try my best to get you the money I promise," she begged.

Seeing the tears welling in her eyes, I really felt for her and the situation that she was in but knew that even if I'd given her a hundred more days, she wouldn't be able to raise the three months' rent that she owed. I remember standing at her door looking into her house to see if there was anything that could be used as collateral, but there was nothing. Although she had no money, she took pride in her home, it was immaculate.

Hearing a baby crying, made my heart sink. It was my job to evict her and her baby if she didn't pay, but how could I do that to them? She pleaded with me to let her go and tend to her baby, but before she walked away, I reassured her

"Don't worry you won't end up on the streets," whilst smiling. I think my words and smile made her feel better, even though it wasn't much.

Three months was too long to not have paid any rent, but she had a young baby and I couldn't stop imagining what life would be like for them both if they were out on the street. My conscience wouldn't let me do it, so I ended up helping her by paying her rent, I knew this wasn't a long-term solution, but it gave her the breathing space she needed and time for her to get things in order.

This wasn't the job I'd been paid to do and quickly realised that if I continued doing things like this then I'd end up being in debt myself.

Ishvara and I weren't very close at this point but spending time with him made me want to do better for myself and Jenna. He was younger than me, but he had a lot more to show for his life than I did. He seemed to be very wealthy, which could be seen by the way he presented himself. I was envious of the clothes he wore and the jewelry he had.

Ishvara wore one diamond earring stud in his right ear and I always wondered how much it was worth. When we met, I could never be sure which car he would roll up in. He had an array of flashy motors, one day he would be driving the Q7, the next day it would be the Range Rover, trying hard to fit into the stereotypical ideal of a gangster. To be honest I'm not sure if it was working for him.

Realising that debt collection wasn't for me, Ishvara asked me to become his bodyguard. I found this funny at first because he didn't really need protection, but he wanted to keep up appearances, and he was doing everything it took for people to perceive him as a dangerous man.

I thought about refusing the offer at first, but then after thinking about it further, I realised that this would be a cracking number. My hard man image made me the perfect choice as his bodyguard. Having me around would show people that he was a man not to be messed with. The idea of being responsible for his security was exciting, and the simple fact that he didn't really need any protection sold the idea for me. The attractive pay package was also a bonus. It was going to be an easy task, or so I thought!

Ishvara came from a very hardworking Asian family. He had a friendly, attractive wife and a few kids. We had the same drive in life, that's why I felt confident working with him. He too was searching for something more exciting. He was well-connected, in and outside of the UK. As well as owning luxurious cars, he ran a few businesses and it was through his businesses that most of his contacts came.

Becoming Ishvara's bodyguard brought the change and excitement that I'd been searching for, finally living in the fast lane, a life laced with a bit of danger. Not once was I fazed by our business even though I never knew what to expect from one moment to the next, which is probably what gave me the biggest thrill! I was drawn to this lifestyle and it came at exactly the right time for me.

I'd begun to wake up in the morning with a spring in my step. Being Ishvara's bodyguard was exactly how I'd imagined it would be and I was intrigued to see what each new day would bring. At least that is how it was at the start.

We spent most of our time in the Casino at first. The security guards manning the doors were always vigilant, they had to be. They were the key factor in ensuring that business remained steady and that there wasn't any trouble. The Casino was always infused with people of high stature and wealth and I was one of many bodyguards. It still felt a little awkward to begin with, following Ishvara around, but this feeling was short lived, and I soon became settled in my new role.

Ishvara remained low key on the Glasgow and Edinburgh Casino scene, and few people knew him. As we visited more often, and I became visual as his bodyguard, his reputation and perceived importance grew. This meant that when others were gambling at the same table as him, they would spend more money. It was my duty to handle the cash and as his winnings increased, Ishvara became more concerned about his safety and becoming a potential target. This was when he needed me the most and relied on me for his personal protection.

As there were always so many people on the floor at one time in the Casinos we visited, I had to be extremely vigilant and aware of everything that was going on in my surroundings and be conscious of any potential threats. I loved the buzz and feeling on edge, ready to go within seconds if needed.

Ishvara knew how to have fun, and nothing would dull his shine. If he won at the Casino it would be an amazing night of partying, but if he lost, we still partied. Either way he was never particularly up nor down.

I'd regularly put myself in his shoes and imagined how I'd feel losing the amount of money that he did at times, and if I'd be able to brush it off as easily as he could. The amount of money he lost some nights was insane, but his high energy level never faltered. I watched so many people end up in debt trying to regain money they had lost, but not Ishvara, once it was gone, we kept moving. Spending time with him was unpredictable which made this life addictive for me. I couldn't wait to experience more!

CHAPTER 6
Life Changing

We never really had a plan. A lot happened during my time with Ishvara. My new lifestyle allowed me to experience many new things, things that I'd only dreamed of previously. He invited me on a couple of foreign trips abroad with him and always treated me fairly, with respect. I was never made to feel like a lesser person because I was his bodyguard.

During my time off, trips to Turkey continued which only strengthened my bond with Goker and his family.

When I'd first met Ishvara I found him overbearing, due to his eccentric behavior. He was always dressed in a casual manor, no matter what the occasion. He had a shaved head and the one thing that made him stand out from the crowd was the amount of gold jewellery that he wore. I felt that it was excessive, but for him it was all about status. After time, I began to warm to his eccentric ways and we became friends. Ishvara seemed to have a split personality. One side was extremely business minded and focused on making as much money as possible. The other side of him, the side I liked the best, was fun fuelled! He was an organised risk taker, which fitted well with the business he was involved with. He was a thinker, who always considered the consequences of his actions, unlike me who was a thrill seeker. Consequences were irrelevant to me until they came and punched me in the face! We developed a friendship that I'd never known before and I came to appreciate it. I looked up to him, and even his theatrics started to grow on me. He was younger than me, but I still learnt a lot from him. I had his back and he had mine, we were a force to be reckoned with.

We had a good laugh together and he pushed me to become a better person. I'd grown so much in the time that I'd worked for him. We talked about the things we dreamed about, and how we wanted to improve our own lives. The more work we did together, the closer my dreams were getting to becoming a reality. Ishvara was to thank for this as I got to see life through his eyes.

A simple phone call on my day off, was about to take my life to another level. When I saw Ishvara's name appear on my phone I contemplated not answering. My plan was to spend the day with Jenna and go to the gym to train, but I was curious as to why he was phoning me, so answered.

"Hey mate, we need to meet. I need to run something by you about a potential job coming our way," he stated.

He sounded extremely excited, which was nothing unusual. Ishvara was an excitable character by nature, but I noticed something different in his voice, and knew that whatever he had to talk to me about, it was going to be big, bigger than anything we'd done before!

We had a lengthy conversation, as he talked me through what was on his mind. He went on to explain that he'd been approached by three guys from London who I didn't know. He never gave me the details about how he met them, which made me suspicious, because I'd come to know most of his business contacts by this time. I didn't ask for clarification though and continued to listen to him. Ishvara explained that these men weren't the types of people that you fucked with.

"They have an offer for us that we can't refuse. It's time Mike, this is what we've been waiting for. This will change our lives in ways that we have spoken about. We could have everything we've ever dreamed of!" he emphasised.

He reiterated further that this was a once in a life time opportunity. An opportunity that guys like us would probably look for their entire lives and it was right on our doorstep.

"It's a risky job, I know you thrive on that kind of thing, but you need to think long and hard before you make your final decision about whether you want to do this or not, okay?" Ishvara warned.

I nodded, then laughed remembering that we were still on the phone and he couldn't see me. I'd got so caught up with what he was saying that I'd forgotten where I was.

By this time my interest had already peaked, and there wasn't anything else he could have said from that point onwards that would have convinced me to change my mind. I was ready for any risk that was brought my way and wanted to get involved. Ishvara continued to warn me that the job would be difficult. It was obvious that he was excited and nervous at the same time by the tone in his voice. I'd already began telling myself that nothing in life comes easy, so whatever the job was, I was set for the challenges that would present themselves, and boy there were many!

He refused to give me all the details over the phone, so I'd have to wait until the next day to find out exactly what it was that would change my life forever.

CHAPTER 7
The Bonds

The next day I woke up slightly pissed off because I couldn't head to the gym as normal; keeping fit was an important part of my life and it was the drug that I needed before being able to function fully.

After showering, I got dressed in my usual outfit, Timberland boots, jeans and a Fred Perry polo shirt. Looking at myself in the mirror, I thought to myself that maybe I should start dressing a bit more like Ishvara, but quickly brushed that thought off as soon as it came into my mind. Mike Carr didn't need to be like anyone else! There was only ever going to be one of me in this world and I wasn't one for blending into the background. I ate a healthy breakfast then headed out for my meeting with Ishvara, eager to find out more about the offer the London Boys had for us.

I drove to our meeting place, arriving a few minutes early, so sat inside and waited for him. Thoughts about what the job might be were bombarding my mind. We were meeting at a local hotel, which overlooked a lake. My mind drifted as I watched the water lapping. There were many business men using the hotel for their own meetings that day, so this was the perfect place to meet. We weren't going to draw too much attention to ourselves in here.

When Ishvara walked in, I could see the excitement on his face, he looked as though he could burst. As he sat down, he greeted me with the biggest smile.

"Well, let's get straight down to business Mike. There is so much to discuss" he said eagerly.

We ordered two espressos and when the waiter brought them over, we asked him not to disturb us again unless we called for him. The smartly dressed waiter was unassuming and simply nodded in acknowledgement of our request. The staff were used to us by this point, as we used this hotel for many of our meetings. We would spend money, they could be certain of that, we always did.

From a distance, we looked like two friends having a catch up, but our conversation was a far cry from what the salesmen on the next table were discussing. Ishvara promised to blow my mind with the information he was about to share with me. My heart began to race with the excitement.

I was anxious to say the least and curious to know what he was going to say to me. I tried to be patient, but it seemed like an age before he got to the point, which only made things worse. He seemed to be chatting around in circles.

"Get on with it then! What is this life changing opportunity?" I urged.

"I don't have all of the details yet Mike, but the job is centered around bearer bonds," he replied.

He paused, taking a sip of his coffee, as he waited for me to digest the information. I didn't know what bearer bonds were, so I was beguiled by Ishvara's words.

"What the fuck are bearer bonds?" I asked, looking at him confused.

He confirmed that the deal would be focused solely around bearer bonds, but he didn't know exactly what we were meant to do with them.

I felt cheated and frustrated with his lack of information and was eager to find out more, but he couldn't answer my questions. I'd never heard about bearer bonds before and had no idea how they were going to change my life. The way Ishvara had built my interest over the phone, I'd have expected him to know more, but was disappointed in the lack of detail he could give me. He talked about it being risky, but he didn't back up what he meant by risky with any further detail.

This resulted in me becoming sceptical about the job. I didn't want to be sold on smoke and mirrors and if that was all the information he could give me, I wanted to walk away. Information truly is power, and I wasn't about to dedicate myself to something there was little or no knowledge about and at this point he'd given me nothing.

Ishvara could see the doubt in my eyes, so in a bid to salvage himself, he tried to explain exactly what he understood about the job. I learnt from him that a bearer bond is basically a document, a single piece of paper, that banks issue in place of money transactions.

"These pieces of paper are meant to make it easier for large amounts of money to be transferred from one person to another, you get me?" Ishvara asked while maintaining eye contact with me.

"I think I understand you, but you need to give me more information," I answered.

He went on to tell me that our niche was the fact that it was very difficult to get hold of bearer bonds. They were used by high rollers and large businesses to make instant, easy transactions. I started to relax as this was making much more sense to me; it seemed like a tangible idea.

"I admit that I don't know much about bearer bonds now, but I've got the basic idea. I'm telling you this will be a gold-mine for us if we can figure out how to work these bonds," he stated with conviction.

My interest in the job was restored because of the belief in his voice. When our meeting first began I thought he was overselling the idea, but there and then he had me back on board with his plan. I was bit sceptical about how it was going to work. It all sounded very official, but I was willing to get stuck into it and wanted to see how far we could progress with this. If we could compile a successful plan it would mean huge changes for both of us. We had to at least give it a try.

"What I need from you, is information. Mike, I need you to go and find out everything you possibly can about bearer bonds

and then we can decide where we go from there," he said.
There was a lot of work to be done. Ishvara insisted that I
needed to be on my A game as my research was going to be
crucial for the next step of the plan.
"The information will help us have the upper hand during
negotiations and I cannot be side-tracked, I'm trusting you with
a lot here," said Ishvara.
Even though our friendship had developed, I was still Ishvara's
bodyguard which meant I needed to look after his interests and
do whatever the job required.
I'll be honest, I felt frustrated that I'd be the one doing all the
hard graft and Ishvara would be the one to sit back and reap
the rewards, taking the credit for it all. But I said to myself, yes
it was true that Ishvara would look good in front of the men
we were meeting, but it would put him in a good light. He was
giving me a seat at the table and that was the bigger picture
I needed to focus on. My motivation was the money we were
expecting to make!
After the meeting with Ishvara was over, I headed home with
one mission on my mind, to find out exactly what bearer bonds
were and how we could use them to change our lives forever.
'Bearer bonds can be termed as a bond or debt security,
issued by a business entity such as a corporation or a
government.'
These were the first words I read about bearer bonds. I wasn't
one for reading but when Ishvara gave me the task of
gathering the information about bearer bonds, I had to do my
best. There was immense pressure to get this right and Ishvara
trusted me to get the job done. He expected results, which I'd
have to work hard to get.
Ishvara's simple definition of bearer bonds got me going in the
right direction, and the internet was a life saver. I questioned
how these simple pieces of paper, of different sizes, each
carrying a different value, would make me rich. Bonds were
meant to make transfers easier, especially with large sums
of money. They were also good for anonymity, which I knew

would work in our favour. Investors who would like to remain anonymous, would jump at this opportunity and I could see this as our way forward.

It soon became apparent that if I had a bond in my hand, I'd be the one deemed to own it at that moment. The thought of holding something so valuable made my heart race. There was a great risk with bonds because if they were lost or destroyed, recovery was impossible!

Continuing with my research, I found that on the black-market, bearer bonds were the financial investment method that people used for money laundering, tax evasion and concealed business transactions. It was evident that through bearer bonds individuals could transfer large amounts of money amongst themselves easily and discretely, without a trace of where the money had come from or who it went to. I gained much more clarity.

These pieces of paper were extremely valuable and could be sold at twice their face value. The potential and opportunities for us were endless. This is exactly the kind of money that would change our lives, and that's what I'd spent my entire life dreaming about. I wasn't sure of a precise plan to make it work, but knew it was vital that Ishvara understood the information I'd gathered. We couldn't afford for him to make a mistake with this.

I couldn't wait to share the information I'd found out with Ishvara and was eager for him to learn what I had. Although the internet was a good place to start, I needed more from someone who was in the industry, someone who could give me real time information. I knew exactly who to speak to!

CHAPTER 8
Decision Time

I reached out to a good friend of mine, Steve. He was ex Special Forces, always smartly dressed in designer suits and he didn't beat around the bush. His straight talking was exactly what was needed for this situation. Steve was very confident within himself and was a highly successful business man. I wanted to hear his thoughts and valued his opinions. After working with him numerous times previously, I knew that he was a man who knew what he was talking about and he had the experience within the financial sector that I was lacking. Steve was very intelligent, and any guidance he could offer me would be invaluable.

Speaking to Steve about the bearer bonds, he confirmed what I'd already learned during my own research. He also added that the key to bearer bonds were that they had authentication marks and codes on them. Once authentication was confirmed it would then be checked at the bank. The bank would check the description of the bond against the original draft to make sure all authentication points matched up, which made it near impossible to create a forgery. To gamble with a fake bond would be crazy. There had been many scandals surrounding bearer bonds in the past which had resulted in the banks being more concerned with forgery, so they would take strong measures to ensure that they were not duped.

I was grateful to Steve for the further insight he'd given me into bonds. Once our chat regarding the bonds was over, I felt more at ease and we went out to a local pub for a few drinks so that we could catch up.

An attractive waitress, wearing a short black skirt and tight white top, approached us as soon as we sat down.

"What is your poison mate?" Steve asked.

"Whisky of course," I stated.

We laughed as we both ordered a whisky. Chat flowed as we waited for the waitress to return with our drinks. I asked Steve how business was going, and I was glad to hear that he couldn't have been happier with how things were working out for him right now.

During the evening I could sense that Steve wanted to ask me something, but he was holding back because he was unsure of how I'd react. Once we had finished a few more drinks though the environment became freer and he spoke openly.

"So, what's with all the questions about bonds Mike?" Steve enquired.

I took a minute to get my thoughts together before finding the story that would work best, before speaking. I knew that the only way to keep Steve away from the truth, and to protect him, was to say as little as possible, so I kept it simple by saying that my questions were for a friend. I could tell that he wasn't convinced but he didn't push the subject.

Steve and I had a cracking night, catching up and reminiscing about the good old days. We both agreed that it had been too long, and we promised to catch up more often in the future.

We headed our separate ways and for once I was home early enough to spend some quality time with Jenna.

The next day the time was right. With all the information I'd gathered, I arranged another meeting with Ishvara to bring him up to speed with all I'd found out up to this point. He was impressed with my research and I could tell by his body language that the information I'd brought to him was going to be a step in the right direction. However, I still had no idea about what the job involved, so my frustration grew.

"I've done my bit and brought you all of the information you needed. It's driving me nuts not knowing what the job involves. Are you going to give me the heads-up boss?" I asked Ishvara.

"Honestly, I don't know mate. There is a meeting scheduled in London and hopefully this will shed light on it for both of us. I wish there was more to tell you, but there isn't." Ishvara stated. My frustration only grew at the thought of having to wait for the meeting in London to find out more, but I kept my mouth shut and just went with it, there was nothing else that could be done.

Ishvara went on to say that he wanted me to attend the meeting with him as I'd done all the research and knew more than he did about bearer bonds. He wanted me there not only as his back-up, but so that I could give my opinion about how we should move forward once all the details about the job had been revealed.

Just as I thought our meeting was over, he dropped a bombshell on me. Ishvara went on to explain that we needed money for the meeting in London, which I didn't think much of to be honest. I'd half expected it, what with the cost of flights and accommodation, but then he hit me with it.

"We need £70k to sit down at the table with these guys, to show them that we mean business" he stated.

What the fuck! Was he off his head? 70 thousand pounds just to sit at a table with a bunch of London Boys. I thought Ishvara was losing it! I couldn't understand how £70k showed our interest. We were already prepared to travel to London to meet with them, how much more interest were they fucking looking for? Who did these pricks think they were?

"I can see in your face that you think I'm crazy Mike. You're the one that's done the research and you know everything there is to know about bearer bonds. I think we can do this, but I'm going to leave it up to you to decide whether we go or not," he exclaimed.

I stood motionless for a second trying to take in the enormity of what he'd just said. Did I hear him right? Did he just say he was going to leave this huge decision up to me, his bodyguard?! Surely not!

My head was all over the place and it was too much to take in.

I needed time to think, time to sit and process everything properly. It was a massive decision to make and one neither of us could afford to get wrong. Researching bearer bonds was one thing but Ishvara had just taken this to a whole new level. There was a lot of money at stake here and I wasn't about to make a hasty decision. Ishvara agreed to give me time to think and I walked away from the meeting in a daze. What the fuck was I going to do?

The next few days I spent running through everything in my mind and just couldn't reach a conclusion. Ishvara then called me to say that the London Boys were ready.

"They want our meeting scheduled for tomorrow!" he informed me.

I was taken aback, not realising how quickly they would want to move with this. The pressure was pushing down on me, it was too quick, I wasn't ready and still didn't know what to do!

"Are we in or out Mike?" asked Ishvara directly.

The words echoed in my head. He wanted me to make my decision right there and then. Without even thinking, I threw all caution to the wind and told him to go for it. I'd been saying to myself that I needed a thrilling, exciting life, that was full of taking risks, and here it was, punching me right in the face.

Ishvara paused, I think it was shock. After my initial reaction, I don't think he expected me to say that we should go for it.

"Really? That's certainly not the answer I'd been expecting from you Mike, but I'm thrilled. Let me call you right back," he said before hanging up the phone.

And that's how one decision, would shake my whole world. I was the one to make the decision. Ishvara would spend £70k to meet the London Boys and then they would decide whether we would get the chance to be part of a deal we had few details about. This was certainly the biggest risk I'd ever taken. Ishvara was not as wealthy as he wanted people to believe. This was a big decision for both of us. I thought about exactly how much this meeting was costing and it made me feel uneasy. For me to earn £70k I'd need to graft for two years.

I couldn't get my head around the amount of money Ishvara was willing to sacrifice. He had lost a lot of money in the Casino before but nothing like this, this was different. Whatever happened, I had to make this work.

After an anxious wait, Ishvara called me back to tell me that the meeting was set. We were going to London!

The next day we were on our way. It was only right that we travelled in style in one of Ishvara's flashy cars, the big black Audi Q7. The location of the meeting was in Mayfair; often referred to as one of the most expensive districts, not only in London, but in the world.

The drive to London was intense. Ishvara and I were both away in our own different worlds. We didn't speak very much during the first part of our journey. I was lost in my own thoughts about what to expect at the meeting, so I asked Ishvara what he thought, to try and help me gain some clarity. "Mike, just be open minded" was his advice.

We went on with the drive and opted to discuss anything other than what would happen when we arrived in London.

It took us two days to get there as we had other business to deal with on route. It was strange, but I felt like the pressure had been taken away from me now. I'd already made the decision that brought us to this point and now I could go back to my official role of being his bodyguard. It was Ishvara's time to shine, whatever happened next was up to him!

CHAPTER 9
Out Our Depth

As we arrived, I realised that we were in a different world. £70k to people that were from Mayfair was simply pocket change. Growing up in the schemes, I'd never seen anything like it. The streets were lined with luxurious mansions, with huge driveways hosting at least two top of the range cars. There were designer shops as far as the eye could see. The place was dripping with money.

We pulled up outside the most sophisticated hotel I'd ever been to in my life. Surely this couldn't be happening to me? I pinched myself, I must be dreaming and am going to wake up at any minute. But I didn't wake up, this wasn't a dream and was really happening!

Inside the hotel we were escorted to a room behind huge oak doors, the sheer size of which amazed me. The ceiling was easily 12 feet high and the doors extended all the way up. As the doors were opened, an office like I'd never seen before was revealed. The smell of expensive leather, coffee and designer fragrances hit me as soon as we walked in.

There was an antique oak table in the middle of the room, behind it sat three stern faced men in leather seats. They were all dressed in designer suits and each wore an over stated designer watch. Their body language was not very receptive. Towering behind them were two beastly monsters. Their bodyguards were scar-faced, huge man-mountains, making me appear tiny. They had an evil emptiness to their eyes that gave me chills.

I began to feel uneasy as the realisation of the enormity of what we were about to get ourselves involved in started to sink in. We were in a room with three big time London gangsters and their heavies and no-one had a clue who we were. For the first time I felt like we might be out of our depth.

One of the men summoned Ishvara to the table with his index finger and told him to sit down. I stood behind him near the door, ready for what was about to go down.

"Hello gentlemen," Ishvara said.

They simply nodded at him and no-one verbally responded to his greeting. I thought that Ishvara would have introduced me, but he didn't. I didn't let it bother me though as I understood my place as his bodyguard.

He had given me the responsibility of keeping hold of the bag which contained the money. I could feel my hands sweating and my heart began to beat faster. I'd never held this amount of money in my hands at one time before.

"We need your 70 thousand before we continue!" one of the men stated brashly.

Ishvara beckoned me to come forward. The bag containing the money was an expensive, brown leather Luis Vuitton, which was symbolic of wealth. It represented the start of mine and Ishvara's prosperous future.

I felt like handing it over to them would relinquish some sort of power. We had no idea what we would get in return for the money and they could easily take it and tell us to fuck off. Shit became real at that moment. If that did happen, we couldn't do anything about it.

One of the bodyguards, who was built like a brick shithouse, stepped forward and came to take the bag from me. I didn't want to let it go, feeling beads of sweat forming on my forehead. Had I made the right decision about coming here or had I just made the biggest mistake of my life?! He looked at it's contents then handed it to the other bodyguard, who remained expressionless and fearless as he headed into another room.

At that point I started to question what direction this meeting was taking. The money had gone and there had been no discussion at all about what the job involved. Maybe we should have demanded a conversation first, before handing the money over so easily. The silence in the room was deafening. These people were out of our league and we had no chance against them. They had the upper hand, we were in their territory and playing with the big boys now.

I'd already spotted the butt of a pistol showing in one of the bodyguards' jackets and felt like a fish out of water, starting to lose my cool. I couldn't get a read on Ishvara as I was unable to see his face from where I was standing. All that I could do was hope that everything would go to plan, and we would come away from this meeting with the outcome we desired.

I found my focus again and realised that they had probably gone to check the money we'd given them wasn't forged. Then the strangest thing happened. They began talking, but not about what they had brought us to London for. They started talking about football, asking which team Ishvara was rooting for and whether he watched the match on the previous day. "What's your take on Chelsea this season?" one of them asked.

Maybe this was their way of breaking the ice, but I couldn't help feeling like I was in an episode of You've Been Framed! They continued to talk about day to day stuff, which started to piss me off. We hadn't spent £70k, and driven all the way to London, to chat about football! I feared that we might have wasted our time coming here, but the worst thought was that I'd just lost 70 thousand pounds of Ishvara's money.

Everything about this day hadn't been as I'd expected. We were served tea, coffee and biscuits. I'd have thought that strippers, vodka and cocaine would have been more up the street for London gangsters.

Finally, the conversation shifted to what brought us to London, the bearer bonds! About fucking time! One of the men, who had the demeanor of being the boss, spoke. Everyone listened intently to every word as he presented us with the information we had travelled all this way for. When he spoke, he stated that they had sixty-two separate bearer bonds.

"The value of the sixty-two bonds being 300 thousand dollars each at face value" he informed.

I quickly recalled my research and determined that we could double the face value price of these bonds, and if they were sold the amount of money in discussion was unbelievable. This would take us into the major league and Ishvara and I could finally have the lives we had been searching for. We were way out of our depths without a shadow of a fucking doubt. Did Ishvara realise what this meant for us and did he remember what I'd told him about bearer bonds? I wished I could have spoken to him, even just for a second.

As everything was unveiling itself it puzzled me, what exactly did they need us for? If they have the bonds what did they want us to do with them? It was as if they had read my mind.

"Your job would be to turn these bearer bonds into cash in the bank. This needs to be a clean operation. Any fuck ups would have serious consequences!" he stated.

Ishvara turned to look at me for the first time during the meeting. I realised that he was uncertain about how we could turn these bonds into cash and he was looking at me for answers, but the truth was I didn't have any! This was one aspect of bearer bonds I'd never went into detail about during my research. One simple shake of my head and he knew that I didn't know what to do.

I could see in his face that he was starting to panic. He sat for a moment and never said a word, trying to compose himself. He knew that one wrong word at this point could have cost us everything. I wanted the ground to swallow me when he ended up asking the London Boys how we could turn the bearer bonds into cash. What was he doing?! The three of them looked at each other, surprised by his utterances. You could see by the expression on their faces they were pissed off and that they felt as though we had wasted their time.

For the first time since we'd come into the room, I looked closely at all three of the men individually. One of them was sharply dressed in a pinstriped suit and tie. He presented himself on a different level to the other two. He wore an overcoat and had an expensive silver gripped cane at his side. There was an air of importance about him. He looked like the Boss Man to me and it turned out that I was right. He had jet black hair with a slim build and spoke softly but had a dominant Russian accent.

"You figure it out, that's your fucking problem. We were told you could handle this job," he attacked.

Ishvara tried to speak but the Boss Man lifted his hand arrogantly to quieten him, as a master would silence his slave. He continued speaking and asked whether Ishvara still wanted the job or not.

Ishvara sat motionless. He was sitting there with barely enough information about bearer bonds. All he had was the information I had given him and we both knew that there was nothing about how to turn bonds into cash. How could we possibly agree to the proposal on the table now? You would need a good reason to have bonds in your possession and if you wanted to deposit them into the bank and withdraw the cash, this was going to be a near impossible task. My heart sank as my dream began slipping away.

Ishvara finally spoke, speaking directly to the Boss Man to ask him for time to seriously consider the proposition. I thought he was going to laugh in his face and tell him to get out there and then, but after muttering with the others he reluctantly agreed. Ishvara was given fourteen days to make his decision, not a day more. The Boss Man warned him not to discuss the offer with anyone else and if he didn't contact them within the time agreed then there would be consequences. Ishvara looked worried and I couldn't help feeling to blame. I should have been more thorough with my research and maybe we would be sitting in a totally different position to what we were now. I couldn't stop thinking about the £70k and if I hadn't agreed to the meeting then Ishvara would not have lost it all.

Ishvara stood up and shook hands with the Boss Man assuring him that he would be in touch and the two of us turned to walk through the huge doors out of the office. They were quickly slammed shut behind us. My presence wasn't even acknowledged.

We walked through the corridors of the hotel for what seemed like an age. I felt as though we were walking away from our dream as we left the lavish hotel into the dark and back to the car. There wasn't a single word spoken between the two of us. The silence was intensely deafening, and it was the first time I'd felt awkward in Ishvara's company. His head was down, and he never made eye contact with me. I felt like I'd let him down and could sense his hostility but couldn't be sure who it was directed towards. I couldn't blame him if it was towards me, he had every right to be angry. My research into bearer bonds was incomplete and he ended up looking foolish in front of three of London's hardest gangsters.

As we got closer to the car Ishvara began slowing his walking pace. He was slightly in front of me and had been since we left the hotel. Stopping he turned to look at me. It was almost as if our thoughts synchronized.

"What the fuck just happened?" we said at the same time.

We laughed as we got back into the car.

"Can you tell me what we have just spent 70 thousand pounds on Mike?" he asked with a hint of humour in his voice.

He was right! What had we spent, what would take me two years to earn, on? A two-minute conversation with tea and biscuits that's what!

We were crazy to even meet with the London Boys but the desire for a better life was our driving motivation. The confusion about what had just happened made it a struggle to process the finer details of their proposition. I felt lost, with no idea which way to turn, or how we could achieve what they were asking. The pressure was on. We only had fourteen days to come up with the answers otherwise our dream would be crushed, and I couldn't let that happen!

CHAPTER 10
Many Faces

"Do you think we will be able to do this?" Ishvara asked.

As I was about to answer, he interrupted me by saying that he had asked me the wrong question and continued to say.

"What I should have asked is do you know how we can do this?"

Ishvara's change of question gave me hope that he wasn't about to walk away from this, as I'd first thought. He'd switched his negativity and was more like the Ishvara I had got to know, the man who never let anything dull his energy. He wasn't going to give up on our dreams without a fight.

I wished I could have replied in a different way but couldn't, not without the answers he was looking for. I wasn't about to bullshit him, there was too much respect for that.

"I haven't got a fucking clue Boss," I answered honestly, explaining that I'd not done any research on how to turn bearer bonds into clean money. With no clue on where to find the information we needed either, I felt like I'd failed him.

Ishvara started the engine of the car and we drove back up the road to Scotland. We talked on the way, avoiding the subject at the forefront of our minds, the bearer bonds. Our conversation helped to dissolve the tension that was apparent between us directly after our meeting. I got lost in my thoughts a couple of times but concluded that if we decided to go ahead with this proposition, and the worst came to the worst, Ishvara would have my back.

Neither of us wanted to talk about the meeting because it had resulted in a loss like neither of us had experienced before.

The money Ishvara lost was not pocket change and much greater than any amount he'd lost in the Casino. It was gone and there wasn't a thing we could do to change the fact. The toughest part for me was knowing that I'd made the decision to go to the meeting in the first place and the uncertainty of what would happen next brought with it an unbelievable low.

We had to move forward, but I had no idea in what direction, I felt totally done in and as if we had bitten off more than we could chew. It was clear that this was way above our heads. I started to feel foolish as I truly believed that we were ready for this, even though we knew nothing about this kind of life.

I began questioning how far I'd be willing to go to fulfill my desire for a more exciting and thrilling life. This meeting had put a lot into perspective for me. I didn't know where my mind was at that moment. Was I giving up too soon on everything I'd ever wanted, just because of the fear of uncertainty?

We had been on the road for about six hours and as we got closer to home, we started discussing the bonds and what our next move would be. Our conversation went around in circles and never resulted in a conclusion, which was frustrating for both of us. We did make one decision however, to come together after we had both had some head space.

Ishvara pulled up outside my house to drop me off. The two of us sat for a moment without speaking. It was dark outside now and I stared into the blackness, lost in my own thoughts, unable to shake the feeling that the failure of this meeting fell on me and I'd let Ishvara down. I owed him and had to make this right. With only fourteen days I'd need to do whatever it took to fix this!

"I'll do everything I can to fix this Ishvara, just give me a few days to figure it out," I reassured him climbing out of the car. He didn't say anything to me as I closed the door behind me, keeping his eyes forward, not looking in my direction. He just waved at me as he drove off.

I watched him drive away until the lights of his car had disappeared into the distance. With no clue where to start with fixing this, I was exhausted and unable to think straight. One thing was certain, I couldn't do this on my own and needed to speak to someone who could be trusted, to help answer my questions.

I walked slowly up the driveway, taking a minute to compose myself before going into the house. It was a relief to get home and be greeted by Jenna's smile. She was my rock and always supported me with whatever direction I chose to follow. She gave me the biggest cuddle as soon as I walked through the door, not even realising how much it was needed.

My night was restless, I stayed awake for hours trying to figure out how this situation could be resolved. Who was the best person to speak to? Who could be trusted to give me the information that was needed? Finally, I managed to fall asleep, but my thoughts remained on what could be done to make things up to Ishvara. The guilt of being the one responsible for him losing such a great amount of money, and the disappointment that surrounded the meeting with the London Boys, was plaguing me. The look in the bodyguards' eyes kept haunting my mind, making it harder for me to get any sleep.

I woke up early the next day, with the sun beating through the bedroom window. My mind was still racing, so decided I'd head to the gym to see if that would help me gain some clarity. Kicking fuck out of the bag was just what I needed, and it helped me to forget everything. I started to feel myself relaxing, even if it was only for a short time. I found a new focus and was determined that I'd find a solution before the deadline we'd been given. I'd make this up to Ishvara and would not let him down again.

As I thought long and hard, one name kept coming into my mind, Steve. I'd gone to him before to ask his advice about the bearer bonds and knew he was the one person I could turn to for help. Steve was a true friend and could be trusted, knowing I could tell him anything and it would stay between us. He could keep things to himself and that was the level of confidentiality that was needed with this. He had a vast knowledge concerning matters of business and whether it was banking or bearer bonds I was confident he would have the answers.

I was sceptical about involving Steve and knew that if this situation went tits up there would be serious implications, but this was a desperate time and I felt like there was no other choice. Not wanting to do anything to jeopardize our friendship, but being in too deep, there weren't any other options.

The 70 grand that was wasted on our bullshit meeting was a constant reminder of why it was Steve I needed to speak to. Something had to be done but I'd no idea what. There was no way I'd stand by and watch Ishvara's credibility go down the drain on my account.

Feeling on edge, I finally made the call to Steve, not knowing how much information would be safe to disclose to him about what was going on at this point. Calling him under the pretext that I wanted to go for a few drinks with him, I was gutted to find out that he was unavailable for a few days as he was away on business. He agreed that he would meet up with me when he got back. Frustrated, there was no other option than to wait. Knowing that I'd drive myself crazy if I didn't keep busy, I threw myself into the gym and trained like fuck, waiting for him to return.

Everything returned to normality between Ishvara and I. We desperately needed our daily routine and business to keep our minds distracted from anything other than thoughts of the fucking bearer bonds. I did my best to focus on the jobs at hand but found myself drifting away from time to time determined to find a solution.

We went back to hitting the Casino scene and staying out until the early hours of the morning. My schedule and routine had become predictable, getting home at around six in the morning, taking a shower then going to sleep. I'd wake up in the afternoon, head to the gym and then go back to the Casino in the evening. The routine repeated itself day in day out. In as much as I now found it a bit tedious, it was what the norm had become for me.

Ishvara was living large and at the back of my mind I'd question his spending habits. He was spending around six grand a night, on good days he would win back the money, on bad days he would lose around four grand. He wasn't shaken even for one second. I was the last person to question his decisions, especially with it being my responsibility for him blowing 70 grand.

The monotony was taking its toll, but I had no other choice but to dig in and get on with it. My only chance at redemption was fixing the mess I'd created. With six days of the fourteen already passed, the clock was ticking.

One night as we headed into the Casino as usual, Ishvara turned to me to tell me that he felt like tonight would be a good night for him. I just nodded in acknowledgment, no-one could ever be sure of what to expect at the table, but I admired his positivity.

It felt like the first night at the Casino with him every time, he reminded me of a kid in a sweet shop. He would easily forget about the losses or wins from the previous nights. I could never gamble away my money the way he did but I enjoyed watching the players. Each person had a different reaction depending on the outcome of the game. There were individuals who gambled away money that they didn't have and losing destroyed their world, and there were those who didn't give a fuck whether they won or lost, they were just playing for the buzz. It was difficult to place Ishvara, looking in you would think he was just looking to enjoy himself.

While we were heading home from the Casino one night, Ishvara said to me.

"I need you to do something for me."

"Yeah sure Boss what is it?" I asked.

He went on to explain that he needed me to go to Birmingham on business. Without hesitation I was ready to go, even though he hadn't even told me what it was for at that point. Anything to escape the monotony.

"There are a group of shops for sale that I want to buy but the gentleman selling them is not willing to sell them to me. That's where I need you Mike." he explained.

"Why is he refusing to sell them to you?" I asked.

"Ah it's an Asian thing I guess. The guy is Asian, and he doesn't want to finalise the deal with me," he stated.

From the conversation, I gathered that what Ishvara needed me to do was to pose as the buyer. Although the gentleman didn't want to sell the shops to Ishvara it was apparent that he would sell them to a white person. He was unhappy selling to another Asian because of him being from a different family or area. I didn't understand but liked the idea of doing something different. It was going to be straight forward with no complications and the reward would be a good bonus.

I had to get up to speed with the situation quickly before travelling to meet the gentleman. There was no way I'd be making a mistake with this, once arriving to meet him. I found out that the Asian man selling the shops, who was from Birmingham, had eight bakeries for sale throughout the North of England and Scotland.

Ishvara told me that he had been trying to purchase the shops for the past four months and he already had a buyer lined up once the deal was finalised. Every time Ishvara made any progress, something else would happen to cause the deal to fall apart. He was extremely frustrated, and this would be my chance to start making amends for what happened in London.

CHAPTER 11
Making Amends

It was not an elaborate plan, it was simple and all that was needed of me was to pose as the buyer. The most important part of my plan was to convince Ahmed, who was the owner of the shops, to sell all eight of them to me as part of one deal. I didn't want to cheat an honest man out of his money and reminded myself that this was not a con, it was just a means to an end for both parties. Everyone would end a winner.

Firstly, the idea that I was a wealthy business man who could afford to purchase eight shops, needed to be presented. I asked Ishvara to hire a luxury car for me. This car would be an invaluable part of my plan, which will become clear.

Ishvara did as I asked, with no questions, and delighted me with his car of choice, a convertible DB7. It was a dream, with a supercharged straight–six engine. I felt like a million dollars driving the beautiful beast.

Perception is everything, particularly when it comes to the world of business. How a person perceives you will directly reflect how they will treat you. You must look like you have money to make money. Looking the part at my meeting with Ahmed was paramount and I decided that a few wardrobe alterations would be needed. My usual look of boots, jeans and polo shirt was not going to cut it. I was playing a character and had to pull it off.

Everything was put into motion, making my first contact with Ahmed to set up our meeting for the following day. We had a brief conversation over the phone, but it was enough for me get to know him a little better. He sounded like a nice guy who I could easily get along with. He invited me to his home to share a meal together, which surprised me.

Cruising in the Aston Martin DB7, I felt like the dogs' bollocks, never thinking there would come a day that I would be driving such an expensive motor. By the grin on my face, and the confidence oozing out of me, you would have thought that I owned the car myself. I began thinking about all the wealthy people I knew and wondered whether they sometimes exaggerated the things they had in life, just to keep up appearances and impress the big boys.

On the way to Ahmed's house, I deliberately phoned him to ask for directions. This was part of my plan. I didn't really need directions but wanted him to look out for me and see me pull up to his front door in my DB7. As I arrived, I could see that he was a man of wealth, he had a huge house and he too had a high-end car parked in the driveway. Ahmed came out of the house to greet me and I could see by the expression on his face, and the way his eyes lit up, that my plan with the car had worked a treat.

The DB7 was the perfect icebreaker, conversation about cars flowed freely. I could see by the way he was observing me as we spoke that he was trying to determine how wealthy I was. The topic of conversation was predominantly about my car to start with. He asked about its performance and what were its highlights. Knowing a fair bit about cars, made me comfortable with our conversation. We remained outside for a good while as Ahmed walked around the car checking it out, running his fingers across the bonnet.

He then invited me into his house. It had a traditional feel and was extremely lavish, the kind of house that most people could only dream of living in. The foyer was beautifully furnished with polished wooden floors and a huge elegant banister. As we walked into the house Ahmed told me that he had a request that may seem a bit odd. To which I replied that he could ask me anything as he had so courteously invited me into his home.

"We usually take off our shoes when we come into the house and I would like for you to do the same?" he requested.

I was not surprised by his request, aware that this was an Asian tradition. I bent down and started by taking off my left shoe, as I slipped off my right shoe, I realised that there was a hole in my sock. Fuck! I'd worked so hard to present myself as a wealthy man and I'd forgotten to check my socks.

Working so hard to portray the correct image to Ahmed, I couldn't believe that I'd been so careless. The irony made me laugh inside, even the best laid plans can sometimes have hiccups.

Looking to see if Ahmed had noticed, but luckily, he was not paying any attention to me, I quickly tucked the hole in between my toes to hide it and thought "Fuck, that was close, too close for comfort."

"Welcome to my home," he said as he smiled.

We walked towards the sitting area where he proceeded to introduce me to his wife and his two daughters. I took the time to look around his home. There was a dark brown sofa set with heavy oak arms, which I imagined would be where Ahmed would choose to sit. He had a large bookcase, which was neatly stocked with paperbacks. The house looked clean and everything had its place, even the family pictures were neatly arranged on the wall.

"We shall eat first before we get down to business," he said, directing me to the dining area.

Upon taking our seats, a banquet of food was served to us by his wife and daughters. The table was filled with a variety of dishes. I felt like a king who'd had a feast arranged in his honour. I opted to have a pick of all the various dishes as I love Asian food. The nan bread was cooked to perfection, nice and crispy, just the way I like it.

Ahmed and I were seated at the table and it surprised me that his wife and two daughters took a seat on the floor, once they had brought in all the food.

"Are they going to join us?" I inquired as they just sat there.

I felt guilty because as we started tucking into our food they simply looked on.

"You are a guest in my home today, we will eat first and when we are finished the women may eat," he stated casually.

It made me feel uncomfortable that the women would eat after us, but I didn't voice my opinion, not wanting to upset him. This was their culture and they were used to it.

The food was deliciously prepared, so focused on my meal I could have easily forgotten that I'd come on business. Our conversation was like that of old friends, for the first hour we steered clear of any business talk and chatted about family and our life experiences.

Ahmed shifted our conversation to the Quran. I knew a little bit about Islam and didn't feel nervous about discussing it with him. My knowledge came from the time I'd spent with Goker and his family in Turkey. I was able to recite a few passages of the Quran in English, which I'm sure impressed him.

I waited for Ahmed to shift the direction of the conversation again, not wanting to seem too eager and spook him.

"Okay onto serious matters my friend," he stated.

We moved to the sitting area and discussed in detail the sale of the shops. I convinced Ahmed that it was in his best interest to consider me as his only buyer. We talked for hours and by the time we concluded I had a written signed agreement.

"I'll have my solicitors sign over ownership of all the properties to you as soon as payment is received," he said as we shook hands, before adding that the deal could be sealed as soon as the next day if the money was in his account.

Feeling totally delighted that I'd finalised the deal, I couldn't wait to share the news with Ishvara. In one night, I'd achieved what others couldn't in the last four months. It was a good feeling. At least this would help the current situation with Ishvara and I hoped he could see some light at the end of the tunnel. Maybe this was the kind of thrill I'd been looking for over the past few months, I felt more like myself.

I thanked Ahmed for his hospitality.

"It was a pleasure doing business with you," I said, giving him a firm handshake before leaving.

His handshake was notably more welcoming than when I arrived as he placed his second hand on top of mine. Both of us acknowledging a new friendship.

The final stage of the plan was to meet with Ishvara. I headed to the Lowry Hotel in Manchester, where we had agreed to meet. He was anxiously waiting for me when I arrived. I wanted to brag about how amazing I'd been and how I'd convinced Ahmed to sell all the shops in just one night, but instead, simply pulled out the paperwork that Ahmed had drawn up and placed it on the table in front of him. Ishvara's eyes light up as he stared in disbelief at the paperwork.

"How did you do it Mike?" he asked, whist reading over the documentation.

I explained that Ahmed just needed the right person to sell to.

"We should celebrate this moment," Ishvara said as he gestured to the waiter. I made five grand that night, it was easy money! If only all jobs could run as smoothly as this.

We returned home, both in a better mood, which lifted my hopes in terms of the bearer bonds. Tonight made me eager to meet Steve and keen to move forward as the deadline the Boss Man had given was fast approaching.

CHAPTER 12
What Next?

I was relieved when Steve texted to tell me he was back, and free to meet me the next day. We opted to meet during his lunch hour, meeting at a local restaurant so that we could grab a quick bite to eat.

Our conversation immediately moved onto the bearer bonds. I tried to be discreet by changing some of the details regarding the proposition to protect Steve.

"I've met a business man who has in his possession some bearer bonds. He wants to know the best way to turn these into cash and I knew you were the man to ask," I stated.

I reassured Steve that the information he had given me in our conversation previously had been helpful, but it didn't give direction on how to turn the bonds into cash. He emphasised that bonds were valuable, especially in the open market.

"If they are legitimate, and from a reliable source, then you can do anything you want with them. They are an international currency and on the black market the opportunities are endless. You're onto something good here Mike," he stated.

I could sense the excitement in his voice but chose not to tell Steve the detailed background about exactly where the bonds were coming from, for his own protection.

He began explaining that if one of the bonds was issued by a corporation, contact would need to be made through a bond agent, before continuing to tell me he had a couple of good contacts in this sector and he would try and set up a meeting with them.

It was at this point I realised just how detailed this process would be, which brought doubt into my mind about whether we could pull this off. We were expected to cash in bonds that didn't even belong to us and turn them into clean money. It seemed an impossible task.

 "So why isn't it possible to just go into the bank and cash the bonds?" I questioned.

Steve sat with his hand up to his chin, slowly stroking it for a moment. I could tell that he was beginning to question whether what I was telling him was the truth. With all my questions, it didn't take him long to realise that I was out my depth and was involved in something risky.

"What are you involved in Mike?" Steve queried.

We had been friends for a long time and he knew something wasn't right. I had no other choice and had to explain everything to him. After weighing up my options carefully and realising if Steve was going to give me the information and trust me, I needed to be honest with him. This was the only way I could gain all the facts needed about how to turn the bonds into clean money. Without the facts there was the chance of making a serious mistake, and that wasn't an option. After I'd explained the full story to Steve, he stayed silent for a while. His silence worried me as I thought he was going to walk out. He was the only person that I knew who could help me with this and I needed him on my side.

"Okay, I'll pretend that I didn't hear all of what you have said, and I'll help you out," he stated.

I felt relieved, if there was any chance of this happening, it wasn't going to be without Steve's help. Before he left, he asked me to give him a few days to talk to a couple of people and make some enquiries, then he would get back in touch. Unsure whether to say thank you, I remained silent hoping that he wouldn't change his mind.

After Steve left the restaurant I chose to stay for a while, in need of some time to myself. I sat and had a couple of drinks, taking time to think about everything that had happened in the last few weeks. It was all down to Steve now. I just hoped that

I'd done enough, and he'd come back to me with good news. It was back to work with Ishvara, whilst waiting for Steve to make the enquires he needed to. Back to the Casino and being his bodyguard, but it was constantly at the back of my mind that time was ticking away. The deadline given to us by the London Boys was fast approaching.

One night at the Casino, Ishvara didn't seem his usual self. It was obvious that there was something on his mind bothering him. He was normally low key but tonight he seemed to be deliberately aggravating people at the tables. I had to put a few people in their place and intervene when they took his bait, which didn't faze me at all. It felt good to release my aggression on some jumped-up-prick who thought they could take on Ishvara.

As the night was coming to an end, he asked me to join him for a drink. We sat and chatted for a few minutes before he said. "Mike I've got a separate problem I need your help with, as my bodyguard."

I knew that there had been something on his mind and was glad that he was ready to confide in me. Without even knowing what it was that he needed me to do, I was already eager to help him. It would be good to do something different and take my mind off waiting for Steve.

"Of course, Boss, anything you need just say the word!" I replied.

Ishvara shook my hand and thanked me. He was grateful that I had his back.

CHAPTER 13
Roughed Up

"There's a guy in Edinburgh giving me shit and I need it sorted. I'm fucking sick of him Mike," he explained.

Because he'd come to me with this, I knew that this guy must have been a heavy. To be honest I'd become complacent in my new job and this would be the very first time that I'd be put to the test. I couldn't wait for it!

Ishvara explained that the guy owed him money for an advance he had given him when they were gambling, and he was now refusing to pay it back. That was his first mistake; you never mess with a man's money. His second mistake was bad mouthing and threatening Ishvara. He obviously had no idea who he was fucking dealing with.

I told Ishvara to arrange to meet him the next day just off Leith Walk, one of the longest streets in Scotland. It was the ideal public place to meet. It would be busy and there would be nowhere for anyone else to hide. We could easily be friends meeting for a drink and not arouse any suspicion.

That night I went to bed buzzing for tomorrow. It was finally time for some action.

At about half four the next day Ishvara and I went to meet the prick that was giving him bother. As we walked along Leith Walk, Ishvara spotted him and pointed him out to me. The guy was about 6ft and had a stocky build. My heart skipped a beat when I laid eyes on him. This was going to be fun! I'd never been the type to back down and was well known for my lack of fear when growing up, so taking him on would be a walk in the park. I wouldn't go down without a fight if he was stupid enough to cross me. He was dressed in a cheap tracksuit and trainers and had a swagger like a wannabe hard man.

I wasn't going looking for a fight and was prepared to give him the benefit of the doubt, but he had other ideas. As soon as he set eyes on the two of us, he instantaneously became aggressive. Screaming at Ishvara for bringing me with him. He obviously thought Ishvara would be alone and he'd be able to intimidate him, but not today!

Sensing his aggression, I told Ishvara to return to the car. If this was about to get messy there was no need for him to get involved, that was my job. Ishvara agreed and quickly left. With him out the way I hoped that we could get this over with quickly, but the guy had other ideas. Before he could say another word, I quietly whispered in his ear

"Shut the fuck up," pushing him into the lane we were standing beside to get away from prying eyes.

"Listen, let's just talk about this so that we can get it sorted," I advised. I wanted him to remain calm and not cause a scene, but it was clear he was up for a fight. It was obvious that he was off his nut as we got closer and stood only a few feet apart. He kept shouting and I felt like smashing him in the mouth there and then to shut him up, he was drawing too much attention from passers-by and that was the last thing I needed. I tried to reason with him, but he didn't want to listen, and it only took a couple of minutes before the situation turned physical. He pulled a baseball bat from behind him, which he had hidden in the waist band of his tracksuit. At the exact same moment, I slipped on the knuckle duster in my pocket. I'm not one for weapons but came ready, just in case things got nasty. He swung the bat at my head, which I side-stepped, feeling the air against my face as he just missed me. Throwing a punch, I hit him square in the jaw. He fell back, swinging the bat again, this time smashing me in the ribs. The pain rippled through my body, almost knocking the wind out of me.

Anger raged inside me and I lost it. Grabbing him and throwing him to the floor like a rag doll. Holding him down, putting my hand across his throat instilling fear in the bastard. As he lay on the floor, I knelt next to him pressing my thumb hard into his eye socket, feeling it bulge underneath as though it was going to pop. He fought against me trying to get up. When I finally let go, he began coughing, holding his throat.

As I stood up to step away from him, he grabbed my ankle, but I quickly swung my other leg around, kicking him hard in the arm. He let out a piercing howl and within a second, he let me go. I felt like stamping on his head there and then but feared I wouldn't stop. He had crossed the line and had taken me to my dark side.

Towering over him as he cowered on the ground, in a very calm, intimidating manner, I told him exactly how much money he was going to repay to Ishvara, and exactly when he would pay it. I warned him that if he dared cross me, I'd be back. Struggling to his knees, his face all blooded, he accepted my terms.

As I was walking away, still buzzing with adrenaline, I noticed my surroundings. I'd not really paid much attention to them before as everything kicked off so quickly. There was a fucking police station only a couple of meters up the road from where we had been fighting. If one of the officers had walked out at any point I'd have been in deep shit. Luck was on my side today. I got out of there rapid.

Heading back to the car to meet Ishvara, I could feel my ribs throbbing where the prick had hit me with the baseball bat. Ishvara was watching me intently as I walked towards the car. He had an anxious look on his face. The second I'd got in he asked, "How did it go?"

The details weren't important, and it was probably best he didn't know what happened, but I assured him that everything was sorted, and he would get back the money he was owed. The drive back from Edinburgh was quiet until we were just outside Dundee. "How are things progressing with the bearer bonds?" Ishvara asked whilst keeping his eyes on the road.

I told him that things were moving forward but we needed a

little more time.

"We are running out of time Mike, but I trust that you have the situation in hand," he said with worry in his voice.

There wasn't anything else to say so we didn't chat about the bonds any more.

When we got back to Dundee Ishvara had other business to deal with that he didn't need me for, so he took me straight home.

"See you later. I'll call you!" He said before driving away.

The second he left, my mind was back on the bearer bonds. I still had no clue what could be done. The pressure was mounting as the clock was ticking. Fourteen days seemed so much longer when we were first given the deadline, but we only had six days remaining and were still no further forward. I'd had no word from Steve either and I was becoming impatient.

It was as if Steve read my mind as I'd not been home for long, when the phone call came. I was elated, it had been a long wait but at least he was calling now. Surely, he had some positive news? After chatting briefly, we agreed to meet the same day.

Feeling a little awkward, I sat down with him, still unsure of how he felt about the whole situation.

"There is a way this can be done!" he exclaimed.

I couldn't believe the words that had just come out of his mouth. I'd been waiting for this moment for what seemed like a lifetime. Steve explained that one of the options was the direct sale of the bonds, which meant selling the bonds to others involved in money laundering.

He continued to explain another option for which I'd need to pose as his client. We'd then need to use a broker to progress this second option further. The broker would sell the bearer bonds on our behalf. Obviously, it would be crucial that they perceived this as a legitimate business transaction and they'd expect to be paid commission from the sale of the bonds.

Finally, there was something to work with. 24 hours ago, I had nothing but now Steve had played a blinder and helped me to find a tangible plan. It wasn't without risk, and by fuck it was going to be complicated, but I believed that it could be done. Nothing worthwhile was done without ever taking risks and I was ready for it.

We organised our meeting with the professional brokers quickly as time was running out: they were eccentric, with outgoing personalities who oozed confidence and seemed legitimate. I'd been around enough people in my time to know that they lived life in the fast lane.

There was no messing around and we quickly got down to business.

"We're not interested in anything illegal. Our company has a long and unblemished record," one of them stated.

The fact that they felt the need to tell me that made me question how legitimate they really were.

"I assure you gentlemen that everything is totally above board," I told them in a bid to guarantee their business.

They had already drawn their own conclusions about my character, so I left most of the chat to Steve. This was his field not mine. The brokers tried to remain straight faced as Steve explained what we needed, but their eyes lit up at the lucrative deal that was on the table in front of them.

The meeting lasted for most of the day and was very detailed. They listed their terms of service and that the bearer bonds would need to be insured, transferred and authenticated before any transactions could begin. This part of the deal made me feel uneasy as I was unsure about the history of the bonds and how the London Boys had got hold of them in the first place. I'd many doubts but was in too deep and there was no way to back out now.

We were advised that the best place to authenticate, transfer and insure the bonds would be in Switzerland, the financial capital of the world.

The meeting finished on a high. The progress excited me, but I needed more help as we would need to cross international borders. It was time to play the ace I had up my sleeve and contact my trusted friend Goker.

CHAPTER 14
No Turning Back

It was time to visit Turkey for a few days to discuss my plan with Goker and to find out if he could help me out with the finer details. If he agreed, this would certainly give me peace of mind. He'd become like a brother to me and I not only trusted him, but also his family, with my life.

My confidence in being able to pull this off had grown over the last few days, as had the belief in myself to make this work. Having Goker's support would only have a positive effect. Goker's family were very wealthy, but they always treated me as one of them. I'd visited their mansion villa in Istanbul many times over the past years which was in the picturesque countryside. Words can't describe how stunning it was, it perched on the hillside, surrounded by breathtaking views. During my time there I'd grown accustomed to the luxurious lifestyle they lived and felt comfortable living here. Security at the villa was always highly visible and I was treated better than a VIP guest.

Goker had a passion for guns and we spent a lot of time in his armoury choosing from an array of weapons to fire. This family isn't one that you would fuck with and when they were around, I felt protected.

I called Goker to arrange to visit for a few days. He was delighted that he was going to see me again. The pieces of the puzzle were all beginning to fall into place. I booked my flight and took time to reflect about how far things had come and how close we were to making this happen.

Before leaving for Turkey, Steve and I returned to see the

brokers. The deadline from the London Boys was fast approaching and we had to act now. After a few long conversations and much deliberation, they agreed that they would help us. All the boxes were slowly but surely being ticked off and my belief that this could happen couldn't have been stronger.

Everything was planned, and it was time to meet with Ishvara again to explain it all to him. I was convinced by the plan but if Ishvara wasn't, then we wouldn't even get started. I had to make him share my vision and get him on board.

Telling him my Turkish family would be our international connection and that they would help establish other connections abroad would be the icing on the cake to having two brokers in place ready. This was a winning formula and I'd have expected him to be excited, but I was devastated when he played his cards close to his chest and insisted on having a day to think before making his final decision.

That night was one of the longest of my life. But when he called me the next day and said

"Go for it mate, let's do this!"

The wait was worth it. That was all he said before hanging up the phone, leaving me stunned, unable to believe he had finally agreed. All my hard work had paid off, the deal was on and I was completely buzzing for it!

Ishvara organised a meeting with the London Boys for the following day. I couldn't believe it when he told me that they expected £20k just to sit down with them again. They were piss taking bastards!

"It's going to be difficult for me to find another 20 grand. Are you 100% sure about this Mike?" he asked.

I told him my honest opinion, and that was we'd regret it if we didn't go for it. If everything went as we'd planned, then it would result in the biggest pay day of our entire lives. My passion convinced him, and he agreed. The meeting was set for the next day. Ishvara decided that we would fly to London this time because we were heading straight to France immediately after to deal with some other business.

London was worlds apart from the first time we were there. It felt different, we were different. We knew what to expect and had a better understanding about bearer bonds. Our connections had given us a better insight about what needed to be done to make this plan a success. There was a sense of confidence, but it was mixed with an air of caution. There was a lot at stake and we couldn't afford to make any mistakes. There was an eerie silence in the hotel where we were meeting the London Boys. I wasn't ready for another round of tea and biscuits, and just wanted to get straight down to business. Walking hesitantly into the room, it was just how I remembered it from the first time. The palms of my hands starting to become clammy as I gripped the bag containing the £20k. Ishvara looked me in the eye. We both knew what the other was thinking without even speaking. The time was now, decision time!

"I hope we won't be wasting each other's time today!" the Boss Man's number two said sarcastically.

Ishvara was summoned to the table by the Boss Man, who never spoke but simple clicked his fingers arrogantly and pointed at the chair for him to take a seat. Ishvara quickly followed the Boss Man's command and sat down whilst I stood behind him near the door. Neither of us were sure how the meeting would proceed and simply had to wait for their lead. It was only a short nervous wait because there was no small talk this time. It was straight down to business.

The Boss Man stated that before the meeting would proceed further the next payment needed to be paid, so without hesitation I stepped forward, placing the bag containing the money on the table in front of them. One of their heavies snapped it up and took it away into the other room as before. My heart sank as I watched him disappear. Another small fortune gone! This meeting needed to go as we anticipated then at least it would have been money well spent.

To the London Boys I was insignificant, and they never even

acknowledged me as someone other than Ishvara's protection but to Ishvara I was the brains behind the operation. I'd provided him with the detailed information he needed for this meeting to be a success. The conversation was very quiet, and it was a struggle to catch what was being said. The large room didn't help either.

Determined to hear the conversation, I stepped a little closer to Ishvara without anyone noticing, just in time to hear him say something wrong.

"He's going to fuck the whole thing up! He should have let me do the talking, I knew the finer details of the plan!" I thought to myself.

As he continued to speak, panic washed over me like a wave. If he didn't stop talking now, he was going to make a mistake. I wished that he'd get to the point without messing this up.

The Boss Man looked directly at Ishvara

"Do you have a plan?" he enquired.

"Yes!" Ishvara answered confidently.

"And will it work?" the Boss Man asked directly.

"Yes!" Ishvara answered again, with conviction.

Suddenly everything fell silent and no-one moved. I looked around in search for what had triggered the silence, then one of the heavies burst in through the double doors with a large brown envelope grasped in his hand. The Boss Man gestured for him to step forward, which he did, promptly sitting next to Ishvara. I watched intently as the Boss Man opened the envelope and spread what looked like the bearer bonds across the table. My heart began to race, fuck there they are!

I remembered what we'd been told in our previous meeting. They had sixty-two bearer bonds in their possession, the face value of each being a massive 300 thousand dollars.

Seeing the bonds right there in the flesh, spread across the table made everything seem so real. We were being given a taste of what to expect. The bonds were quickly snapped up and placed back in the envelope. Once exchanged for money, they would be worth millions. I could hardly believe my eyes, all that money contained within one simple brown envelope. Starting to let my thoughts drift, I began imagining what we could do with all the money. I'd become lost in my thoughts for a second and when I came back to the room, things had fallen silent again. The Boss Man was holding the envelope firmly in his hand. Everybody's eyes drawn to it as if it were a magnet. He shifted in his seat so that he was looking Ishvara straight in the eye.

"You take these out of my hand, and they become yours!"

My heart began beating faster at the thought. I felt beads of sweat forming on my forehead as his words registered in my mind.

Ishvara never said a single word, sitting completely motionless, staring at the envelope as if in a trance. We had walked into this room with a plan, but I'd no idea what Ishvara's next move would be.

"If you have the balls to follow this through, you will be a very rich man," The Boss Man stated, and for the first time I saw a small smirk appear on his face. Ishvara was like a rabbit caught in head lights, not knowing which way to turn.

CHAPTER 15
Stepping Up

There would be no way that they'd simply hand over the envelope and let us leave. The Boss Man turned to look at the others sitting at the table. He never even said a word, but his look prompted them both to nod. They knew what he was thinking, even if I didn't. He continued to present a list of warnings to Ishvara if he chose to take the envelope. Stating that if the envelope was misplaced, if the police got a hold of it or the bank were to seize the bonds, then it would fall to him to replace what was inside to the equivalent value. Basically, if anything happened to the bonds, they didn't give a shit about excuses, it was entirely down to Ishvara. The Boss Man strongly reiterated that if the envelope left his hands, any problems going forward lay solely with him. Fuck! This was bigger than anything we'd been involved with before.

Still, there was no reaction from Ishvara. Maybe he couldn't take it all in, but he had to say something! The Boss Man leant forward over the table, pushing the envelope closer to Ishvara, close enough for him to touch.

"Here, take the envelope!" he said with a glint in his eye. Ishvara was starting to frustrate me, why wouldn't he just get on with what we had come here to do? Still, he never moved, he didn't reach for the envelope or say anything to indicate whether he was in or out. Every single second felt like hours. The London Boys began looking at each other and I could see the frustration in their faces too.

Sweat began rolling down Ishvara's face and I knew he was panicking. Something had spooked him. Why the hell was this happening here and now? The only thing I could do was stand and watch, thinking about what they would do to us both for wasting their time if Ishvara didn't do something, all the time wishing I could have stepped forward and shaken him out of his trance.

The Boss Man banged down hard on the table with his clenched fist, he was getting angry, and I couldn't blame him. He leant further across the table so that his face was now right in front of Ishvara's. He looked at him with an evil stare.

"Do not waste my fucking time! Are you taking the bonds or not?" he growled.

Ishvara snapped out of his trance.

"Sorry, I can't do it!" he whispered.

What?! He couldn't be serious? We had come this far, surely, he wasn't about to walk away? But he was serious, and he'd changed his mind!

The whole room fell silent, you could have heard a pin drop. All I could think was that this was going to be the day that I die. We'd fucked them around too much. They had a reputation to uphold and couldn't let us get away with this. Why would Ishvara do this to us? The Boss Man's face was turning red with anger.

The heavies were shifting on their feet, more alert, as if they were getting ready to kick off. I wouldn't go down without a fight but couldn't help thinking what I'd do if they pulled a gun. That would be a fight I'd never win.

I felt like killing Ishvara myself at that moment. Why was he just giving up? Why didn't he tell me what he was thinking before we came into the room? I wish I knew what was going on in his head.

The heavies stood strong, eyes looking towards their boss, waiting in anticipation for instructions, but nothing happened! It was as if time had stood still. I think everyone was just as confused as me by Ishvara's words. We were all expecting to discuss the way forward and how the rewards would benefit us all, not this! My mind kept replaying Ishvara's words, which was making me angry with him. I'd put in all that work and he simply dismissed our plan without even consulting me before he spoke.

"What?" the Boss Man asked finally, with an angry tone.

"I can't do this anymore!" Ishvara repeated, with more conviction this time. He was standing firm with his decision.

"Why have you changed your mind?" he snapped.

We all wanted to know the answer to that question. After everything we'd discussed and the plan that we had in place, what valid reason did he have to walk away?

I was left stunned when he said he was "scared". We were in a room with three of the toughest gangsters in London, surrounded by their heavies and he just admitted that he was scared! What the fuck was wrong with him? Had he forgotten everything he knew about this lifestyle?

They all started laughing, a loud sarcastic laugh, which made me nervous and angry.

"What do you mean you are scared?" the Boss Man laughed.

"If this doesn't work, I cannot afford to take on this kind of debt," Ishvara exclaimed.

I totally understood his concerns, but he already knew the consequences. Why didn't he back out before paying 90k and travelling all the way to London? He was making himself look fucking stupid!

"That's the risk you take. If it doesn't work, then you'll not be here to worry about that!" the Boss Man threatened.

"Your money is non-refundable, you do realise that, don't you?" the Boss Man's second in command snapped.

Ishvara took a deep breath and looked towards me. He looked hopeless and ready to breakdown. He was not a tough man and he was not handling this situation very well.

Surprisingly the Boss Man dropped the envelope containing the bonds onto the table and slumped back into his chair.

"Okay," he said angrily.

This should have been our cue to leave but I couldn't do it. This was a once in a lifetime chance to change my life forever, and it was an opportunity that couldn't just be passed up. The hard work that had gone into ensuring that we had all the information we needed to make this plan work wasn't about to be thrown away, just because Ishvara bottled it.

I had to say something and take the risk to do this, even if it meant going it alone. Mike Carr wasn't going to be invisible any longer. Everyone was preparing to leave, and still wasn't sure what to say. I knew I'd be crazy to go ahead with this, especially since Ishvara had already pulled out, but being a risk-taker there was no other option but to stand up. Without any more thought I blurted out

"I'll do it!". Instantly thinking, shit what have I done?

Everyone in the room turned to look at me, then they looked at each other thinking who the fuck is this?

"What did you just say?" the second in command asked as he leant forward, putting his hand on the table.

"I will take the bonds," I replied with an air of confidence. The words were out my mouth and there was no going back now. He turned to look at everyone else at the table giving them a smug smile.

"And who are you?" he asked, with a hint of disgust. Taking a step towards the table.

"I'm Mike, Ishvara's bodyguard." I stated proudly.

"I cannot hear you man, come closer," he added.

I knew he'd heard me perfectly well but was just being a prick. I'd had enough of him, he wasn't going to intimidate me. Taking a deep breath, lifting my chest, I took the few steps towards the head of the table and slowly and confidently walked right up to him. Looking him directly in the eye as I approached, bending slightly forward into his personal space.

"I'm Mike, Mike Carr!" I repeated.

There was a shocked expression on Ishvara's face. He looked at me as if to say what are you doing, you are making a big mistake! His eyes begging me to be quiet, but it was too late it was done!

"What makes you think you can do this?" The Boss Man asked

as he leant forward in his chair, now interested in what I had to say.

Not wanting to disrespect Ishvara, he'd done everything for me and I had learned so much from him, I thought that it was only right to speak to him before going any further. So, I asked for a couple of minutes to speak with him before giving my answer, to which they hesitantly agreed.

Ishvara and I walked to the back of the room to talk in private. His first instinct was to yell at me.

"What the fuck are you thinking?" Ishvara asked, whilst trying to control the tone of his voice.

I needed to make him see that we could do this and if anyone could make it happen it was me. Reminding him that he was losing 90 thousand pounds, and I wasn't prepared to walk away without attempting what we had planned. This would be our only chance to get his money back.

"Boss it's not your neck on the line anymore, it's mine, trust me I can do this!" I reassured him.

"Are you sure? You do know they will kill you if this goes tits up Mike?" Ishvara asked worriedly.

Looking at him, I replied

"Fuck it! If I don't do this, we will regret it for the rest of our lives. This could bring us everything we've ever wanted."

He nodded and gave me a reassuring slap on the shoulder and we turned to walk back towards the table.

CHAPTER 16
Changing Hands

Approaching the table, the London Boys' impatience quickly became very apparent. I understood their frustration, but I'd just agreed to take the bonds so there was still the chance for them to win big. I stood strong behind the chair Ishvara had been sitting in and began to explain the plan.

"Believe me, I know what I'm doing. I'm the one that has done all the ground work and the research for Ishvara, and I've all the right contacts set up waiting to kick things off. Give me the go ahead and I'll make us all very rich men!"

I tried to get a feel for what they were thinking, but they gave nothing away, as they sat with blank expressions on their faces. I'd have expected a bit more enthusiasm from them. The Boss Man stared at me:

"Go and wait outside and we will call you back when we are ready!" he said coldly.

Both Ishvara and I did as we were asked and moved outside the room.

"Fuck sake mate, I hope you know what you are doing!" Ishvara said as the door closed behind us.

"Don't worry this will work, I'll make sure it does. Let's just hope they go for it. There is no way I'm letting you lose 90 grand!" I replied.

Ishvara looked at me and smiled, and at that moment I knew there was no bad blood between us. It was an anxious wait. There was a huge grandfather clock in the hallway where we were waiting and the only noise that could be heard was the ticking of its hands. It felt like forever before they called us back inside.

The doors opened and one of the bodyguards signalled for us to come back into the room. I could feel my palms becoming clammy, everything was riding on the decision they made.

"Good luck mate!" Ishvara whispered as we walked back inside.

Luck was needed, but at the same time I felt like I had this under control.

When we were only a few steps into the room, the second in command gestured for me to take a seat at the table.

"Fuck me they are actually taking me seriously now, I'm getting a chance to sit down with them." I thought to myself.

This was a big deal, especially considering they had never even acknowledged me the first time I'd been here. To be allowed to sit at the table with them showed me that they respected me, and they were interested in what I had to say. This realisation brought with it a new-found confidence.

The Boss Man leant across the table towards me as he had done with Ishvara. He had the envelope grasped tightly in his hand. I couldn't take my eyes off it and desperately wanted a piece of this. He began the same speech, reinforcing the consequences.

"If you take this envelope and you lose it…"

Before he could even finish his sentence, I whipped the envelope from his hand without even braking his stare. My heart was racing like a train.

"Confident little cunt aren't you!" The Boss Man said.

I nodded, replying

"Would you want it any other way?"

With a straight face, he turned to his number two and said

"I like this guy's attitude!"

Then he turned back to face me.

"Well let's make some fucking money then!" he said, reaching out to shake my hand.

The second I'd shook the Boss Man's hand, his second in

command stood up and snatched the envelope back from me. I didn't like him, he was a cocky fucker.

"I'll look after this and put it in a safe place until you need it," he said with arrogance.

"I hope it's a very safe place, my balls are on the line now," I jokingly replied.

"Not your balls my friend, your life!" he replied smugly. I wanted to punch him.

As easy as that, it was done. The meeting was over, and I'd agreed to take the bonds. The second in command continued to explain what would happen next, but I'd stopped taking anything in. We were told to stay in London that night, and we would be contacted first thing in the morning.

This was the biggest risk I'd ever taken, but it felt good. This was going to be the beginning of a change for me. I knew it wasn't going to be easy, but I was ready for the challenge. Before leaving the room, I leant across the table and shook each of their hands. Ishvara followed my lead and did the same. Now I was the one taking control and with that responsibility came a heavy burden. We left the meeting and headed to the nearest hotel.

"Fuck me Mike, we are actually going to do this. We are completely crazy, but if we get it right, we're going to be fucking rich!" Ishvara stated.

I took a deep breath before replying

"I can't believe we have pulled this off. This is an opportunity of a life time and we are so going to smash it."

Little did I realise what was ahead of me.

We had a quiet night in the hotel that night and both went to sleep after a meal in the hotel bar. The next day I was called to a meeting as expected, where I was introduced to my handler. He was now my direct contact and anything concerning the bonds would go directly through him. My meetings with the Boss Man were now over. I had to keep my handler informed about every move that was made. At least there was someone who was going to be looking out for me.

My handler introduced himself to me as J. As we discussed the next step, he asked how long I imagined the job would take to complete.

"If everything goes as planned, then in six months we could have the money," I told him. This was only an estimation because every little detail mattered with this plan.

One of the first things that we needed to do was to create fake identities. J took me to a dodgy housing estate. The place was crawling with gang members and junkies. We went into a block of high-rise flats at the back of the estate; the lift was broken so we had to use the stairs. The stench of piss climbing the stairs made me boke. I saw a dirty needle left in the stairwell. This was not a place any of us wanted to be.

When we got to the flat, J banged hard on the door. We were met by a big 6ft Nigerian guy. He didn't say anything, he just took us into one of the back rooms in his flat. I couldn't believe my eyes, there were computers, laser printers, credit card machines, the whole shebang, you would never have believed that this amount of technology could be embedded in a shitty little flat like this. We spent a few hours with him, putting together a whole array of fake credentials and left with all the documentation I needed for my new identity.

Our next step was to set up a safety deposit box. This would be where the bearer bonds would be kept for the time being. We chose to use one of the most prominent banks in London; to give us a bit more credibility. Opening an authorised signature account with two signatories, J and me, I knew that the Boss Man would never let me walk out with the bearer bonds without a contingency plan in place.

We deposited the bonds into the safety deposit box for safe keeping. Neither of us could access it without the other one, which was probably to ensure that I didn't do a runner with the bonds. After that I gave J a rundown of the plan that was in place for the bonds, which he seemed to approve of. Not that it mattered what he thought, he was just the eyes and ears for the London Boys.

After we had the fake identity documents and the safety deposit box was opened, there was nothing more to do in London at that stage, so I decided to take a few days and go back home to be with Jenna. I'd been away from her a lot over the last few weeks and was missing her. I had to be back in London in three days to start putting things into motion, so going home at this point was perfect timing. On the way home, I felt a sense of relief that we were finally getting the break we'd been looking for, all thanks to my balls of steel.

I couldn't discuss any of this with anyone, even though I felt like shouting it from the roof top. If too many people knew what I was up too this could have blown the whole plan. What was important right now, was to ensure that we didn't fail, which seemed simple, right?

Arriving back home, it was time to chill. The past few days had been a complete rollercoaster, which left me feeling drained. It was great to see Jenna and I wished that I could tell her everything, but my only gift for her was that I was home and that I was excited about our future. Not wanting to put her in danger, there was no way I could tell her what was really happening. It was up to me to protect her. The less she knew about what was going on, the better for her sake.

CHAPTER 17
A Taste of Luxury

I met up with Steve whilst home because he was the brains behind the plan and I needed his perspective on how to handle things to ensure that everything ran smoothly. We decided to meet at a local bistro. It was a popular place and busy as always. I arrived first, so found a quiet corner and took a seat. This gave me time to sit and absorb all that had happened over the past week and to plan in my mind my next trip to London. When Steve arrived, we ordered a late lunch and we caught up on what each other had been up to. We didn't dive straight into conversation about the bonds, because although that was why we were meeting, we were friends, so we chatted around the subject for a while.

"Tell me what went on in London? I've been waiting to hear from you since you left," he eventually asked.

I explained that I'd not even had the time to process all the information properly myself yet.

"I've got big news for you mate. I'm now the point man for the project now!" I stated.

Steve was perplexed. The first time we'd spoken about the bonds he was under the impression that I was asking questions for somebody else.

"How the fuck did that happen?" he asked surprised.

We ordered a drink before I continued telling him the whole story, right up until the point I told the London Boys I'd take the bonds. Relaying everything to Steve, it sounded like an exaggerated story that someone would only have written about, but it wasn't a story, it was happening to me and I was the one in charge now.

"This is a huge deal! Are you ready to handle this kind of pressure Mike?" he asked.

Without hesitation I told him that I'd die trying to make this work, which was ironic because if it went tits up that's exactly what would happen. As we continued chatting, my self-confidence grew and my belief that I could pull this off couldn't have been stronger.

After a long conversation we went our separate ways, agreeing to take time to go over the details separately for the next couple of days and then meet again.

Steve was a great asset and my personal encyclopaedia when it came to the bearer bonds. It wasn't my intention, but I'd brought him into becoming part of the deal. I would have preferred it if he was out of the loop, but it was too late for that. I promised myself to ensure that his involvement would be on a need to know basis, to ensure that his safety was guaranteed. We arranged to have a further meeting with the brokers to ensure that we were still on the same page. To continue business with the brokers they needed money, which I didn't have; twenty thousand pounds to be exact. Even though I was the point man, I'd very little pull, especially when it came to funding. Ishvara was the only one who could get his hands on this amount of cash, and he needed to find the twenty thousand pounds. The amount of money we'd spent up to now was £100,000 and it was up to me to ensure that he got every penny back and more.

When I approached Ishvara for the money, my thought was that he'd be a little cautious, especially after the money he'd lost in London, but he never blinked. We were working together to ensure that the plan was going to succeed. The tables had turned. I'd be the one to face the consequences if anything went wrong and the pressure was off him. Yes, it was true that he might lose his money, but my life was at stake here. Ishvara had the money, whilst I had the key to the safety deposit box, it was a partnership that was going to go places.

Once the meeting with the brokers was confirmed, the plan continued to take shape. My confidence was growing at every stage, which was important to keep moving forward. The reality of this situation was enormous. It was the biggest job of our lives, not just for Ishvara and I, but for everyone involved.

The next step was to head to Turkey. During my time there I'd meet up with the Turks and Cypriots, who would be the important element in bringing the whole plan together. Discussion needed to be face to face, to ensure that nothing was lost in translation. Goker would be essential for me crossing borders and would be my trusted contact abroad.

I was looking forward to going to Turkey because every time I'd visited Goker and his family they made me feel like a king. They treated me like an important member of their family. Goker also wanted to discuss with me the possibility of involving the Greeks in our plan. I wasn't entirely convinced about involving them and felt that minimizing the number of people who knew what was going on, was a safer option.

The Turks had many contacts who had experience of working high risk jobs in the past, as well as the man power to pull off a job like this. The decision to make Turkey my base until everything was over was an easy one.

Goker presented me with different options regarding how the bonds could be turned into hard cash. We discussed contacts he has in Germany and Athens that could help. I'd gone from not having a clue about what to do with the bonds to being spoilt for choice with options. I didn't want to make any rushed decisions that would leave me, or any of the people involved in this plan, exposed. As the point man it was my responsibility to think everything through thoroughly. There was risk-taking to be made, but these risks needed to be calculated ones.

As I stepped out of the airport in Istanbul there he was, standing larger than life. My good friend who was going to be a vital part of the army I was building, to protect me in case anything went wrong. Goker had his grey hair swept back into a ponytail. I truly respected a man who could rock a ponytail.

Communicating with him was a little difficult because his English wasn't the greatest, and my Turkish was limited. He never dressed in anything other than a suit. It would need to be an important event to get me into a suit! Goker had a commanding air around him, which he never let go to his head. He was a gentleman in all sense and purpose, legendary to some extent. Everyone called him the General in Turkey, which was a symbol of his importance.

He'd come to pick me up in a beat-up old silver Clio which made me laugh, considering his wealth. We greeted each other like brothers as always, which was a comfort. Being around him made me feel like I had an army around me. I didn't expect him to pick me up in such a shitty car, especially with it being so small and him being so tall, but he seemed to like it. We headed straight to his flat in Taksim Square in Istanbul. Taksim was well known for its busy nightlife, shopping and amazing dining. It made sense that he would live in a place like this and it suited his personality perfectly. I'd been there a few times before and loved it. His flat was something else and always thought about how much Jenna would love to live in a place like this when I visited. It was truly stunning.

White was the signature colour in the flat. I'm a messy guy so that would never have been my go-to colour, but it seemed to work for Goker. There was white marble everywhere and there were expensive white leather seats in the sitting area. The view overlooking the Square was magnificent.

We decided to stay in the flat that night, catching up and drinking chai, we would head to the mansion on the outskirts of Istanbul the next day. Goker was not materialistic, but he still liked the finer things in life. Being in his world made me want to finish this deal more than ever, I wanted this kind of life for me and Jenna. It was the kind of life we both deserved.

We woke early the following day and drove to the mansion, just on the outskirts of the town. The scenery was breathtaking. I'd forgotten exactly how big the house was and was taken aback as we drove up the driveway. There were two huge dogs at the gate alongside two security guards. His armed security guards were professionally trained, which was extremely apparent. Goker asked me if I remembered the dogs' names from the last time I'd visited, but for the life of me I couldn't, so told him I'd rename them Tyson and Bruno, which made him laugh, "I like that," he said, with his strong Turkish accent.

The dogs were fucking massive, strong, and not to be messed with, just like their handlers were.

Goker gave me a tour of the mansion and its grounds, he wanted to show me some of the changes he had made to the place since I'd been there last. He wasn't showing off but was proud to have me back in his home.

Part of his estate included stables, where he kept around ten horses. During our tour we met the stable keeper who was working. They exchanged pleasantries and Goker asked about specific horses and how they were doing. I didn't understand their conversation, so stood and took the time to have a look around. His land was divided by a river flowing across it, which I thought would be the perfect place to go to be alone to think, it looked so peaceful. Goker told me that we could go horse racing when we had free time, which would be great as I'd a passion for horse riding. The sheer power of horses always amazed me.

As we continued our tour, we went through the garage to get back to the house. The cars he had in his garage were out of this world, Ferraris, Porsches, you name it, and yet he chose to drive a beat-up Clio. This showed what a down to earth kind of guy he really was. I started to let my thoughts wander and began to think about what kind of man I'd be if we managed to pull off the deal with the bonds and I came into the same kind of money he had. I was experiencing a different kind of world, one that I liked and one that I wanted to become part of.

Back at the house we headed to the sitting area where we were served reiki. The reiki was accompanied by beetroot juice, which was meant to complement it and keep the alcohol content low. I didn't particularly like the beetroot juice, but the reiki was something I could easily get used to.

It was a great evening, full of drink, laughter and chat about old times. Going to bed that night I hoped I'd wake up hangover free the next day so that I could make the most of my time in Turkey. It was a totally surreal experience.

CHAPTER 18
The Book

I woke up early the next day, thankful not to be too hungover from the previous night. While we were having breakfast, we reminiscented about the night before, laughing just as much as we had then. It felt good and I thought to myself
"If only everyday was like this, what a life that would be to live."
"It's time to play with the guns my Brother! I've some new ones for you to try!" Goker said as we finished breakfast.
The range had an array of guns from shotguns to machine guns, semi-automatic rifles, and automatic pistols. Since this journey had begun, I'd the chance to experience so many new things and this was by far the most exciting for me and I couldn't wait to get my hands on some of these bad boys.
My eyes lit up at the sight of the guns laying on the table in front of me when we got to the range. Spoilt for choice with the weapons he had, Goker gave me the opportunity to use any of the guns that I wanted. I was in my element and choosing to fire a pump action shotgun, was an awesome experience. The shotgun was beautifully polished. It had a laser sight, which was something I'd never seen before. Goker had a barrel set up at the bottom of the open field that was sitting at the end of the range. I watched in awe as Goker fired a few sweet shots, which ripped right through the barrel. When it was my turn, I picked up the shotgun, putting it on my shoulder to fire it. Goker quickly intervened before I could take my shot.
"You have to go slow with her, she is a very powerful weapon," he warned. He added that if I wasn't careful, I'd rip my shoulder off and recommended firing from my waist. Goker was very experienced when it came to guns and I enjoyed soaking up

his knowledge.

With my heart racing, I took the shotgun and shot it from my waist. The loud echo of the gunshot scared the birds out of the trees. On my third shot, a huge recoil caused the butt of the gun to smash me in the mouth. The initial impact was painful but not as bad as the embarrassment I felt as blood ran down my chin from my lip, but we laughed it off.

I had so much fun that day. My visit to Turkey wasn't meant to be for fun but for business, but I'd let myself escape for a few hours, which is exactly what was needed.

When we got back to the mansion that evening, it was straight down to business again. We discussed going to Athens followed by Cyprus. I was a bit sceptical about going to Athens as I wasn't sure what they could do to help but after chatting with Goker he convinced me to go and see where our meeting would take us. I was also unsure how the Turks and Greeks would work together, especially with a job like this. Goker was positive about the outcome and tried to convince me that everything would go to plan. I trusted him, so after much thought I agreed that I'd go to the meeting in Athens and then make my final decision about whether to involve them.

I quickly organised the meeting so that we could move onto other things. Once everything was in place, I flew to Athens. The first meeting was uneventful, in fact it was borderline boring. I met with Antonio who seemed disinterested and it felt like he didn't even want to be there. I struggled to hold a conversation with him, firstly because of his disinterest and secondly because of his limited English.

Antonio asked what I'd brought for him to look at, and I went on to explain about the bonds. We discussed what he would expect from the deal and he explained that he wanted four of the bearer bonds, which would have a face value of 1.2 million dollars, but he'd be willing to pay 1.5 million. He asked to see the bearer bonds, to confirm their authenticity. I had to be careful with how I handled the situation because showing him the bonds wasn't possible as they weren't in my possession and to be honest, I didn't trust him. My safety was paramount, and I'd not be blinded by my want for money.

During our meeting it became obvious that he wasn't the main man in their operation. I chose to cut our meeting short, explaining to him that if his boss wanted to meet with me, I'd be willing to oblige.

After my disappointing meeting in Athens, I headed back to London to speak to J for an update. When J told the London Boys about the possibility of selling four of the bonds to the Greeks, they didn't seem very impressed. Reluctantly they were willing to go ahead if I thought the deal could be finalised. It was a difficult choice for me, but I enjoyed being at the heart of every decision. From a business perspective this deal would create some cash which would be useful for other transactions still to come, so it was decided to go ahead.

During my time in London I spent a lot of time together with J and we started to get to know each other better. I was beginning to get on with him much more and saw him as a friend. It was important for me to learn about the people I'd be working with, so after doing some digging on J, I found out that he was Russian. That explained where the big scar going down the left side of his cheek came from. He looked like he could handle himself and I was glad to have him on my side.

We both agreed that the time had come to go and pick up one of the bonds. We needed the bond to show my credibility to potential buyers in any further meetings.

Shit was about to get real and I was going to be in possession of one of the bonds. This was going to be extremely dangerous for me and would make me a target if anyone knew. I was taking my life in my hands, but it didn't faze me one bit.

Before going to pick up the bond with J, there was one stop I needed to make first. We headed into the local book store. I loved Andy McNab books, and with that in mind, I chose one of his books to be my hiding place for the bond once we had taken it from the security deposit box. To most people this would probably sound crazy but what better place to hide it! I'd be able to carry the book around with me and no-one would suspect a thing.

Book in hand, J and I went back to the bank where we had deposited the bonds. The staff were very meticulous, and security was tight in the bank, which gave me confidence. This was a safe place for the bonds to be without a shadow of a doubt. Once we had both opened the security deposit box, I nervously picked up one of the bearer bonds and tucked it safely between the pages of my newly purchased book. This would now be the proof of the bonds for potential clients.

I couldn't take my eyes off the book for a second. Its value had just increased by 300,000 dollars and had my life attached to it!

Chapter 19
Too Close for Comfort

Before leaving for Turkey I wanted to spend some quality time with Jenna. Once I got back to Scotland, we planned a big night out for us. We got dressed up and headed out for a meal. I'd be away for at least six weeks and wanted us to enjoy each other's company for the evening, wanting a conversation that ran longer than hello and goodbye. We had both been missing each other and I really missed our chats. I wanted to spend our evening sitting and talking about seemingly meaningless stuff, which would be a great escape away from the pressures of the bonds. There was a realisation that we had taken these precious moments forgranted in the past. She had always been supportive of me and stood by me no matter what. We'd been together for too long and there was not a chance that we were going to throw away what we had.

Jenna always looked stunning when we went out and tonight was no exception. We headed to one of her favourite restaurants in town. I would do anything to make her smile and desperately wanted this night to be special, to forget about all the negative conversations we had been having recently and enjoy ourselves together.

As we sat down, telling her that she looked beautiful made her smile. I could see in her eyes that this was forced and not the happy smile that I'd been used to seeing from her. If she was having to try to be happy, that would make me feel shit.

When the waiter came to our table to take our order, I encouraged her to order anything that she wanted. Money was not going to be an issue tonight and it was my mission to show her that the time we'd spent apart was at least starting to pay off. Tonight was important for me. I'd be away from Jenna for a long time and wanted to go to Turkey with great memories of this night.

It was obvious that she wanted to say something, but was holding back, so I urged her to tell me what was on her mind.

"I was just wondering how long your business abroad will be going on for, because I miss you and feel like we never get any time to spend together anymore," Jenna said, as she took a sip of her vodka and coke.

There was not a definite answer to give because I didn't have any idea myself. I'd been away for long periods of time and was just as frustrated as she was, but it was in the bid to make our lives better. Not being able to give Jenna all the details about what was going on made the situation harder and I hated the thought of not being 100% honest with her.

"Things will get better babe," I said placing my hand over hers, squeezing it tight. She looked away from me as tears filled in her eyes. I hoped that Jenna understood that this was for us and that she could stand by me through the tough times.

Jenna turned to look at me. She squeezed my hand tighter and a tear rolled down her check as she looked deep into my eyes.

"I don't want the fairy tale lifestyle if you're not in it babe" she said with a teary voice.

She went on to say that she didn't care about the big house, the fancy cars or luxury holidays. All she wanted was for us to be together, even if it was in a cramped one bedroom flat.

Jenna was speaking from her heart and her eyes told me that she really meant what she was saying. Maybe I was being too materialistic, but I wanted us to have more than we have now and never wanted to have to struggle for anything in life.

"I know that you are happy with the little we have now Jenna, but we deserve more!" I told her.

Not wanting the conversation to turn negative, I tried to change the subject to something cheerier, to see her laughing again.

I hadn't seen her laugh for a while. We'd been together for a long time and raised two children together, so there was no way we could throw that away. My plan was to give her the world and my determination was to make this work for all our sakes. From the outside it may have seemed as though I was only interested in the excitement of the high life, but what was most important, was for my family to have a good, happy life. We put everything aside and had a great night together. When heading home, all I hoped was that I'd done enough to reassure her and that she could see that what I was doing was to benefit all of us. A life without Jenna was not an option.

I was leaving for Turkey very early the next day and Jenna was going to drive me to the airport, so we went to bed early. We were closer than we'd been for a long time and it felt like we were a team again, holding her close as we fell asleep together.

The morning came quickly and as we were getting ready Jenna saw my unzipped folder on the kitchen counter. She was curious to what it was and opened it to have a look inside.

"What are these diamond brochures and business cards for?" Jenna asked.

I wished I'd been more careful with my folder and she hadn't seen it. The documents were part of my cover story for my Turkey trip. I told her that over in Turkey you needed to be perceived as being wealthy when buying and selling large properties, which is what I'd told her I was doing. This cover would help me be viewed as a high-powered business man. My last intention was to lie to her, but unable to tell her the truth I had to protect her.

"Was I going to lose myself doing this job?" I thought to myself. I'd already had to pretend to be a business man involved with buying and selling property and now I'd have to pretend to be a diamond broker. What the fuck was I doing?

My identity as a diamond broker needed to appear realistic, that's why the business cards and brochures had been made. The brochure was going to be used for the transportation of the bearer bond. It was illegal to enter another country with a

300,000 dollar bond without first declaring it. If I were caught, I'd need to answer a lot of questions about how I came to have it in my possession.

Having to travel on a fake passport was risky but there was no other option. Using my real identity was too dangerous for obvious reasons and I needed to make it difficult for anyone to trace my movements.

I finished getting dressed and, in the rush never had enough time to have a proper breakfast. Jenna drove me to the airport and we talked about silly things on the way, which was good for us both. I felt sad as we kissed goodbye but left her with the promise of flying her out later for us to spend time together.

I didn't have any luggage, so going through customs would be quicker and not present any challenges, well so I assumed! My cover was that I'd be flying back the next day as I was only going away on business.

My first stop was London to meet J. He needed a play by play account of my every move to report back to the bosses. One of the other key factors for meeting with J was to figure out the best and safest way for me to carry the bond when meeting potential clients. We were working towards a deadline and J continued to remind me that time was of the essence.

The longer we waited to get things moving, the higher the chances were of getting caught. He warned me against being a sitting duck, but I explained to J that the main plan was to try and move the bonds through the banking system, which could take months rather than weeks. There were deals set up with the Greeks, and the Germans, separately through my Turkish connections, but he simply had to get it through to his boss that none of this was easy and would take time.

He agreed and assured me he would relay the information the best he could up the chain of command. He told me that I'd be given a spotter. These guys were not messing around and were doing everything in their power to protect the bonds. Because I was going to have one of them in my possession, it was vital that someone was always watching me. The spotter would have eyes on me every step of the journey, until I was safely in the car in Istanbul.

I wasn't given any information about the spotter and had no idea what he looked like, or whether I'd met him before. According to J this was the safest way for everybody concerned. In simpler terms the spotter was put in place to ensure that I didn't fuck up and if that did happen, the Boss Man would know instantly. It was strange to think that someone would be following my every move, but it was also a relief to know that someone was watching my back.

After my meeting with J, I went to the hotel at the airport where I spent the night before travelling onto Istanbul the next day. My mind was full of thoughts about the bonds, which was driving me crazy. As I sat alone at the bar in the hotel, all I could think about was how perfect it would be if the job paid off. I could finally live the life I'd always imagined and could be care free when it came to money.

I'd never been one for giving up and wasn't about to start now. Things were about to get tougher and I was under no illusion about that fact. It was time to dig in and get on with it. There was a voice in my mind constantly reminding me that this was heavy shit and how dangerous it would be for me if things went tits up.

As I sat sipping my beer, the negative thoughts kept coming into my mind, so I thought that it would be best to go and try get some sleep before the big day ahead of me tomorrow. It was a very restless night.

CHAPTER 20
A Lucky Escape

The next morning, I checked to see if the bond was still tucked safely away in the brochure. The safety of that piece of paper was crucial. After checking, I headed into Heathrow Airport. On the way I kept looking around myself to see if I'd be able work out who the spotter was but couldn't see anyone that looked like a potential, but that was the way it was meant to be. The airport was busy, and everyone was consumed in their own little worlds.

I gripped the folder tight in my right hand, knowing how important its contents were. I was beginning to feel a little nervous, especially when approaching security. If I got caught with the bond it would undoubtedly mean a prison sentence for me. That was not my biggest fear though, my biggest fear was that I'd have also lost 300,000 dollars of the Boss Man's money and the consequences of this would be far more severe than prison!

This was my moment of truth, walking up to the security check. It was make or break time. I didn't have any luggage, so it should have been an easy walk through. I took off my jacket, belt and watch, putting them along with my phone and folder into the grey tray provided as was protocol. I held my breath and confidently walked through the metal detector. I wasn't stopped by security which surprised me because the metal plates in my jaw, from a run in with a couple of prick bouncers' years ago, usually set it off. I thought I'd nailed it.

Suddenly my heart skipped a beat as I saw the tray my things were in being pulled to the side.

"What the fuck! Were they able scan through a folder and see what the paper contained?"

The security officer told me to step aside and asked me what was in the folder. This was about to fall apart, and it hadn't even got started. Shitting it but trying so hard not to show it and remain calm, I had no idea what to say. It was only paperwork in the folder, the way they had pulled me aside you would have thought they'd spotted a bomb.

"Look at the screen sir, what is that?" he asked as he pointed to a thick highlighted block.

"What the hell was it?" I asked myself, feeling sweat running down my back, with no idea what was showing on the scanner.

"Unzip your folder!" the security guard demanded.

Doing as instructed and to avoid drawing too much suspicion, I hesitantly unzipped the folder, not sure of what was about to be revealed. Then I caught sight of what it was that had caused security to become suspicious. It was a fucking protein bar! Remembering back to the previous morning and Jenna telling me that she had put something in my folder in case I got hungry. I could breathe again, feeling completely relieved. Thank fuck they didn't notice the bearer bond.

My celebration was premature. I assumed that because they had discovered what the block was, they would simply let me go, but that was my mistake! A female security guard was watching me put my jacket and belt back on and as I tried to pick up my folder and walk away, she gently held me back. I wondered what was going on.

"Excuse me sir you cannot leave just yet. We have to look at everything inside your folder," she said politely.

She went on to explain that once there had been an issue with somebody's possessions, they had to check them in their entirety. My plan was about to blow up all because of a fucking protein bar.

Believing I was only seconds away from being caught, I thought there was no way out of this. The bond was lodged in between the folds of the diamond brochure. There was no reasonable explanation as to why it was in my possession. I watched her every move, at the same time scanning for all the exit points to see if I could make a break for it but knew that it would be pointless.

She picked up my note pad that I'd been using to write a few Turkish phrases in. She inquired about it and I told her I'd been trying to learn a few phrases to help with my work whilst I was in Turkey. She didn't say anything but simply nodded with a smile. She flicked through the pads pages, scrutinizing every single page to see if anything dropped.

As soon as she picked up the diamond brochure, I knew that this was the end and there was no rational explanation as to why I had the bond. My shirt collar started to feel tight. It felt as though it was cutting off my air supply and was stopping me breathing. She slowly opened the first section of the brochure, then holding it at the top corner gave it a shake. Nothing fell out! I couldn't believe it! Why the fuck did the bond not fall out? I should have been in deep shit but for some reason luck was on my side.

I tried to rationalise what was happening, but it just didn't make any sense. How could I have been so lucky? She must have pinched the top of the bond whilst shaking it, which held it in place. None of that mattered now as I was free to go. She thanked me for my time and told me to have a nice day. That was a very close shave and too close for comfort.

As I finally cleared security and started to calm down after my near miss, I wondered if the spotter had seen what happened and if he would have reported back to London. I'd been lucky today but what would happen the next time?

CHAPTER 21
Foreign Mix Ups

Waking up, regardless of what happened the day before, today I needed to get on with things. There was work to be done! People expected results and there was no choice but to deliver, even if it was stressing me out. Goker had sparked the interest from the Greeks and Turks, which I wasn't too sure about. But since he'd put the effort in to speaking with them and getting them to agree to a speak with me, I was willing to set up a meeting and see what came from it. Not knowing any of them made me a little cautious but at least one of Goker's men would be with me for protection.

The first thing on the agenda was to plan where to hold the meeting. I couldn't have it in either Turkey or Greece because I didn't want to appear biased towards one or the other, so we settled for Switzerland. Mainly because it was on neutral ground and Goker had some good contacts there. Everybody was happy on that front; however, I still wasn't sure about the Greeks. They seemed hot headed to me and what was needed in this situation was for everyone to be calm to allow it to run smoothly.

Both the Turks and Greeks were accustomed to luxury and I had to ensure that part of the package was catered to accordingly. We arranged to meet in a high-end Swiss hotel in the centre of Basile. Walking into the hotel, the first thing I noticed was the huge crystal chandelier hanging in the centre of the large reception area and the expensive marble floor was perfectly polished, you could see your reflection in it.

One Turkish and two Greek gentlemen attended the meeting.

The main purpose was to prove to them that the bonds existed. I had to be clever with negotiations and had to figure out a way of carrying the bond without anyone knowing it was in my possession.

The Greeks wanted to see the bearer bonds before they would participate in any negotiations, but I wasn't prepared to show it to them for my own safety. They could have easily pulled out a gun on me and fucked off with it. The bond was worth 300,000 dollars but that was just its face value and if sold on the black market it would be worth much more. I couldn't afford to lose a single bond; the consequences were too high a price to pay.

The meeting started off well and we were making good progress but there was some bad blood between the Greeks and the Turks. The situation then began to get too aggressive for my liking. To the point that they started to push each other around physically. One of the Greeks grabbed the Turk by the lapels of his jacket and shoved him so hard into the wall that he nearly knocked a painting down. The Turk retaliated by slapping him in the face with an open hand. They were like a pair of school kids in the playground trying to prove who was stronger than the other. I pulled them apart, not wanting things to get out of hand.

None of them thought the bearer bond was in my possession at that moment and were under the illusion that there was a third party waiting outside, who would come in once I gave the signal.

The truth was they were already charged and looking for a fight, constantly trying to get at each other. I'd spent the whole meeting so far trying to keep them calm and we weren't getting anywhere. To the point that letting them fight it out seemed like a better idea, so that they could get it out of their system. The situation was starting to piss me off.

"I know you have the bond with you, so get out of here!" Goker's man whispered to me.

The fighting was beginning to escalate and attracting attention from the hotel staff. There was no time for me to ask him to explain how he knew I had the bond. The bottom line was I needed to get out of there and quickly!

Making a sharp exit was my best option. This was only a side line deal that couldn't fuck up the bigger plan if it went tits up. Making an excuse, I left the hotel. Walking at a fast pace down the street it didn't take long for the two Greeks to follow. What the hell would they do to me if they caught up with me? They wanted the bond, that was certain.

Quickening my walking pace, trying to figure out how to get rid of them, I had to get away, and fast. If they caught up with me, I'd need to fight with the two of them. Although confident in my ability to handle myself, I started running, there was no way I was losing the bond.

I was running along a busy street in Basile, but was drawing too much attention to myself, so thought it'd be best to slow down. Glancing back, I saw the Greeks were close behind, they had angry and determined expressions on their faces. There was no doubt that they were only interested in the bond and would do whatever it took to get it. The street was busy and there were too many people around as witnesses for them to grab me. I wasn't the type of person that would just hand the bond over without a fight, even if they had a gun, and they knew it.

I kept scanning the area to see if there was a place to hide or lose them. Out of the corner of my eye I noticed a police station, which should have been the last place on my mind to go, but this was a life or death situation and there was no other choice. Walking into the police station guaranteed that they wouldn't follow me inside.

There was no more time to think, so without giving it a second thought, I opened the door. Before stepping inside, not having any idea what my reason for being there would be, I took one final look over my shoulder to see the utterly bemused look on their faces.

Approaching the reception desk, I had to think quickly on my feet. The police would ask me why I'd come in today without a doubt. My excuse needed to be a feasible one.

"Could you tell me where the train station is please?" I asked the officer seated at the front desk.

The officer was friendly and spoke perfect English. He even went the extra mile, came from behind the desk and stepped out of the station with me to show me. As we walked outside, I spotted the Greeks at the bottom of the street. When they caught sight of me with a police officer their faces dropped, and the colour drained from them in panic. We hadn't even crossed the street before they made their sharp exist.

I felt like laughing out loud but kept up the pretense of being a lost foreign businessman. The officer gave me clear directions, pointing out the best way for me to get to the train station. It wasn't very far from the police station, only a short walk. Following his directions, I was there within a few minutes and jumped onto the first train at the first platform. Once the train pulled away from the station, I had a quick look around to double check that the Greeks hadn't followed me. There was no sign of them, which was a relief.

I didn't have any idea what happened at the hotel after leaving but all that mattered was that I'd protected the bond from being taken. With no phone with me I couldn't call anyone either to find out if they knew what had happened.

Not concentrating when jumping onto the train, I didn't realise the destination was Amsterdam, Schiphol Airport to be precise, until they announced it over the train tannoy. Having been in Switzerland, now heading to Amsterdam, that was an unexpected detour.

On the train, I began thinking about my next more. With only a small amount of cash, no credit cards, and travelling on a dodgy passport, options where limited. My conclusion was the best thing for me to do would be to settle down in a hotel for the night near the airport and contact J in the morning.

It was a long night in my room that night, spent reflecting on my shit day.

CHAPTER 22
Dirty Business

The next day after a brief conversation with J, I took a flight back to London. On my arrival we met at the airport and I explained what had happened in Switzerland and how it was a huge fuck up, not giving him all the details because he wasn't too keen on me going in the first place.

After staying in London overnight I headed back to Turkey and arranged to catch up with Goker to give him an update on the bullshit that had happened in Switzerland, and to find out if there was any progress with the bank. Goker met me at the airport and was excited to see me. He was expecting good news from my trip.

"The Greeks are a no go!" I disappointedly told him, going on to explain what had happened.

He defended his thoughts on why it was a good idea to meet with them in the first place but we both agreed that this option was no longer available to us.

"Are you okay?" Goker asked.

I was touched that he was concerned for my safety, he was a true brother. After telling him all was okay, I gave him a little sarcastic smirk and continued to tell him about walking into the police station to get rid of the Greeks.

"You have certainly got a pair of balls on you don't you!" he laughed.

This was a dirty business and I was beginning to learn that quickly. The only way to survive was to take whatever came my way and deal with it. I'd learnt a valuable lesson whilst in Switzerland and that was to only work with people I trusted, who were the Turks and the London Boys.

I waited in Turkey for Steve to sort everything out back in Scotland and decided to take a few days break to relax a little bit before having to be on the move again. Steve was dealing with the brokers who were an integral part of the plan. They wanted to see legitimate paperwork, proving that I was the director of a legitimate company before they agreed to progress further with helping us. It was becoming complicated because there was no company, but I trusted Steve and knew that he had everything under control. He knew what he was doing, so I left him to it.

My plan to take a few days to relax was never going to happen, especially with all that was going on at the minute. My phone was constant with questions about how things were progressing. There was ongoing pressure from the London Boys to get things moving.

Ishvara called me, he needed to know what was going on. He'd invested a lot of money and needed to be certain that he would get a return on his money. I explained to him that the deal with the Greeks was off because of what had happened in Switzerland. He could hear in my voice that times were tough right now.

"Keep going and it will all be worth it in the end." It wasn't much but what he did say helped me to refocus and not let one setback get to me.

After the failed meeting in Switzerland the pressure was on for Steve to come up with the goods, but I had to be patient. He was the ace up my sleeve, and without him the whole plan would have remained a dream rather than a reality.

When his call finally came, I hoped that it would be good news.

"You don't know how happy I am to hear from you," I said picking up the phone.

He laughed, and I tried to gauge whether his laughter was laced with good or bad news.

"So, tell me!" I asked anxiously.

A wave of relief washed over me when he explained that he'd

done what was needed his end and that we could move onto the next stage. Finally, the green light I'd been waiting for. This was one of the most crucial parts of the plan.

Authentication of the bearer bonds was our next step. Authenticating them would require close examination, which could be done through a broker or at the bank. Steve went on to tell me that the brokers had made their decision and were in! To authenticate the bonds, we had to prove that they had come from a legitimate business and not won in a poker game. This would mean setting up a couple of companies solely for this purpose. I'd need to be the named director of these businesses which would mean having multiple fake identities. I'd need to be in possession of many forged documents to match my identities, making me a ticking time bomb. It would only be a matter of time before suspicions would be aroused so we'd have to move quickly with the next stages. Opening multiple bank accounts for my fake companies, I'd then be able to deposit the bonds in these accounts.

Every part of our plan required money and Ishvara and Goker were now funding every stage. I certainly didn't have any ready cash and wouldn't have been able to fund this kind of job myself. My sole purpose for getting involved with this in the first place was so that I could create a better life for me and Jenna. I owed Ishvara and Goker everything for trusting in me.

It would take at least six to eight weeks before the bonds could be authenticated by the bank. During which time I was becoming slightly impatient, but what kept me going was the thought of a better life.

Keeping a low profile was important, so I rented a villa in Kyrenia in the North of Cyprus with the help of Ishvara and Goker. I owed them both so much, which made me even more determined to succeed.

Cyprus was split into two parts, the North being predominately Turkish and the South being Greek. My villa was surrounded by breathtaking beaches. It was a peaceful place, somewhere that I could think and clear my mind. Its beauty made me think of Jenna and how much she would love to live somewhere like this. The villa was total luxury, but it was missing something. For me it didn't have that touch of home. Even though it overlooked the beach and it was an amazing place to be, I never felt settled.

I shared the villa with Sancar and Berkof, who were Turkish friends of Goker. They were originally from London but had come with me to Cyprus to support me with any complications that I may face.

Sancar was in his late forties. The first thing I noticed about him was his grey goatee and his flamboyantly coloured shirt. He was a friendly, likeable character, ready to help anyone that needed it. He was a great cook and the meals he prepared for us were out of this world.

He smoked thin cigars and always offered me one even though I didn't smoke and constantly refused. His persistence had to be admired. He made me laugh, always saying that one day he would convince me to smoke. I was grateful that Sancar spoke good English because the time we had in Cyprus would have been lonely otherwise.

Berkof was huge, just looking at the sheer size of him would be enough to intimidate you. He had a deep voice that simply commanded respect, but you would rarely hear him speak. He kept himself to himself so much so that you could easily forget that he was even there.

Sancar and Berkof organised a small barbeque to welcome me to the villa on my first day. The food they prepared was amazing. As we were enjoying our meal a guy appeared from the next-door villa, shouting and screaming in Turkish across the fence.

With no clue what he was shouting about I just ignored him. Then another couple of guys appeared and began shouting too. They were starting to piss me off. I felt like they were directing their anger towards me. I only understood a small amount of Turkish, so I asked Sancar what they were shouting about.

"He is shouting at you and is saying that you slept with his wife a few months ago." Sancar replied.

 "I've never been here in my life. It is my first time in Cyprus, so he must be mistaking me for someone else. I know my cock's big, but it doesn't span two countries!" I laughed.

Sancar laughed loudly at my comment, which made the guy angrier as he must have thought we were laughing at him. I tried to calm him down and explain that I'd never been to Cyprus before. He obviously didn't understand English and continued to shout and make gestures to get me to come and fight him.

I saw red and don't know what came over me, jumping over the fence and punching the guy straight in the face. He fell to the floor looking stunned. Sancar and Berkof didn't want any trouble and they quickly jumped over as well to hold the other two guys back. After a brief conversation with Sancar the guys calmed down and went back inside and we continued to enjoy our barbeque.

Later that day the guy sheepishly appeared again and came to apologise to me. He went on to explain that he had mistaken me for somebody else. I respected him for coming back to sort things out. I'd been beating myself up since everything kicked off because it's unlike me to be so hot headed and quick tempered. The pressure was obviously getting to me. I didn't want Sancar and Berkof to think I was a loose cannon but to be honest it probably did my reputation some good. We had a laugh about it later that night and they gave me the new nickname "Tyson".

That night I couldn't get it out of my mind that I still had one bearer bond with me and needed to find a place to store it safely whilst travelling around.

The next morning it was arranged that I'd meet Mustafa, a friend of Goker. He found a solution for me and took the bond and put it into a hotel safe, far away from where I was, in case anything went wrong. With the bond no longer in my possession, it put me at less risk and if I needed it, my contact at the hotel would ensure access to it whenever needed.

CHAPTER 23
The Waiting Game

Things had been stagnant for about four weeks, waiting for the companies to be set up and the forged identities to be completed. During this waiting period I was summoned to London for a meeting with J. Because he was my handler, I had to make an appearance whenever he asked. There was nothing new to tell him and my visit was going to be a waste of time but there was no other choice.

"You need to get things moving quicker, the boss is not happy!" J stated. There was no change in the situation from the last time I'd seen him, but he still insisted on a full run down of what had been happening. It was frustrating, but there was nothing else that I could do. I wasn't in control and bureaucratic procedures took time.

"We need results!" J stated. There was a hint of anger in his voice as he spoke, but I knew he wasn't a bad guy and was undoubtedly under pressure from the Boss Man. My frustration ran as deep as everyone else's, but it was vital to get every part of this plan right, otherwise there was a high risk of being caught and none of us wanted that.

In a bid to give him a ray of light to take back to the Boss Man, I told J that I'd push a meeting with the Germans, who Goker had also put me in contact with, to discuss a potential deal with them to purchase an individual bond. This should be straight forward!

Reminding myself that my cut of the deal, if everything went as planned, was going to be £900,000, kept me focused.

Tolerating a bit of bullshit from J and the London Boys was a small sacrifice to make. I'd invested a lot of my time and had put my neck on the line countless times for this to work, but it would all be worth it. I wished that everyone would just let me get on what had to be done. Travelling back and forth to London for pointless meetings wasn't benefiting anyone.

After my visit to London, it was the perfect opportunity to go back home to see Jenna. From the second I saw her she appeared different, pissed off at the time I'd been spending away from her. It was shit seeing her like this, but I needed her to be patient.

"I'm probably sounding like a broken record right now babe, but I don't want to let you down," I reassured her, pulling her close. Wanting her to feel safe in my arms.

Things were tough, but we'd get through them together and I needed her to believe that.

It was Jenna's belief that my work with Ishvara involved buying property and selling it on at a higher price and in my time away I travelled between the properties to make sure there were no problems.

Hating not being able to tell her the truth and trying to be as honest as possible with her, I explained that there was something illegal I needed to do. Naturally she was worried about my safety but remaining true to the promise I'd made I told her as much as possible. I sensed she was beginning to lose faith in me and no-one could blame her for that.

Only being home for a day, before having to head back to Cyprus, didn't help the way things were between us.

My patience was wearing thin. Each day I checked the progress of the documents, and every day I was told they would be ready the next, but they never were.

Contact from the Germans came at exactly the right time and was the perfect distraction for me. They had somebody interested in meeting with me to have a look at the bond and went on to explain that if the meeting was successful, they'd be interested in purchasing a huge chunk of the bonds for cash; finally, the break that was needed!

There was no time to waste so the meeting was quickly set up. Heading to Germany I needed people who could be trusted by my side. Turkish Tamas and George the Greek would be the perfect companions for this visit.

Turkish Tamas had long black hair, which he always wore in a ponytail. He was very eloquent with his speech and had a very strong Turkish accent when he spoke English. I'd met him when working in London a few years before and we'd remained friends ever since.

George was in his late fifties, a typical father figure, who never spoke much. He always dressed in a suit that was far too big for him, which made me laugh. I was glad to have them both by my side on the way to Germany.

On the trip over to Germany I found my buzz that had been missing again. I'd become bored with all the waiting and was relieved to finally be doing something other than sitting about in Cyprus.

On the flight to Germany it was good to catch up with Tamas. He told me that George, once a wealthy man, had lost everything and he was helping him get back on his feet. Intrigued to find out how George had lost everything, but not wanting to offend him by asking, I thought it best not to ask.

We travelled to a local hotel in a town called Barin, where we had arranged to meet the German. It was a small town and the hotel was its main focal point. It was a bleak place to be, in the middle of nowhere, and there was little else in Barin other than a shoe shop and garage.

Once we settled into the hotel, all that was left to do was wait until our contact arrived.

After being in Germany for five days, there was still no sign of him. With frustration being at a high, we were getting ready to leave when he finally made an appearance.

A powerful man with the run of the whole hotel, with his own private smoking room in the basement where all business meetings were conducted. When summoned to his room, I took Tamas along with me, but George stayed in our room.

Arriving at the door, I knocked hard!

"Come!" A voice from inside shouted.

Opening the door, the first thing to hit me was the smell of stale smoke. It was fucking disgusting, enough to take my breath away.

The German was sitting behind the only table in the room. As we approached, he looked up and peered over his glasses at us, but never spoke a word. He had muscular bodyguards towering at either side of him, who were part of his security team; I later found out that they were ex Israeli secret service and were part of Mossad, which was part of the Israeli intelligence unit.

It was apparent he was an extremely important man to have this kind of protection. When it transpired that he was in fact the cousin of a prominent General in the Bosnian army, it made me feel a little uneasy. I felt in over my head dealing with people of this stature. The situation dwarfed anything that I'd been used to.

Crossing different lines, I couldn't show that they intimidated me. The bonds were my power and I'd be the one calling all the shots in this meeting.

During conversation, the German asked to see the bearer bond. After the incident in Switzerland I'd learnt my lesson and there wasn't a fucking chance he'd be getting to see the bond until I knew he could be trusted.

"The way this will work is, you show me the cash and I'll show you one of the bonds!" I stated, with an air of confidence.

There wasn't going to be a repeat of the previous incident with the Greeks, so I took control of the meeting quickly, insisting that he made his intentions clear. I needed to see proof of the cash before we went any further. Seeing the cash was the guarantee that I needed to show they were ready to do business. There was no time to fuck around, the London Boys were getting impatient and were expecting results.

As our meeting progressed, the German kept pushing to see the bond. As a good will gesture I agreed to show him a picture on my phone, which he could analyse. Standing firm with my decision, no bonds without proof of funds. They weren't going to fuck me around!

One of the bodyguards continued to look at me in disgust throughout the meeting and I knew what he was thinking: "Who the fuck did I think I was?"

He'd have killed me in a second if he got the chance, but I never felt threatened by him. The bond was my insurance policy, for as long as it was in my possession, I was safe. He knew if they wanted to get their hands on the bearer bonds, things needed to be done my way.

After a long silence, I thought that the German would eventually come around to my way of thinking and agree that we had a deal, but instead he insisted that Tamas and I leave the room and go on with our other business, and that he would get back to me once his final decision had been made.

My heart sank, as I walked away frustrated. Feeling that this shit was getting too heavy for me.

CHAPTER 24
Big Money

Walking away from the meeting, we didn't have a clue what was going through the German's mind. Still trying to digest the details of what just happened I tried to figure out if I'd played it right or wrong. Was I too pushy? If so, that's how I needed to play it and show them they couldn't walk over me.

"How do think that went?" asked Tamas.

"I really don't know to be honest, I'm not even sure if they will get back to us," I replied with a disappointed tone in my voice. Even if the German did come back to me in agreement, this was going to be a tough ride. He was hard work and the realisation that the world I was living in now was different to what I'd known before was hitting home. There were no more games, and this was some serious shit I'd got involved with. We went back to our room to find George relaxing. Oh, how I wished that was me at that moment. I'd not been able to sit still for a second since this whole thing started and sleep was a thing of the past. My mind was constantly racing at a hundred miles an hour, putting myself under pressure. However this panned out was entirely down to me and how I handled every decision.

Running the meeting over and over in my mind I wanted to go and start the whole thing again.

"Would I have played it differently?" I asked myself.

But it didn't matter now! There was no other choice but to be patient, put my pride aside and wait.

After my meeting with the German, J was expecting a call with an update on how it went. Having to update him every two minutes was pissing me off. It was me who was in the thick of it all, so they would just have to wait until I was ready with some news.

Everything went quiet in the hotel, and we didn't hear a word from the German for a few days. Although we were staying in the same hotel, we didn't cross paths, not even once. I knew where he would be, sitting in his smoke-filled room every day, poisoning himself, smoking his stinking cigarettes.

Although keen to get on with the deal, I wasn't going to rush him and would wait for as long as it took. He wanted what I had, and he would need to come and find me once his decision had been made. There was no way I'd be chasing him, regardless of who he was. My confidence was at an all-time high and I was thriving on being the man in charge.

Finally, the German was ready to meet again. We were called to see him back in his den of death as before. Dread filled my veins at the thought of opening the doors when we arrived outside his room, knowing the stench that was waiting inside. I wasn't wrong, as we entered the room, he was sat behind his desk puffing away. This place made me feel sick to my stomach. But without having time to think, and after only stepping one foot through the door the German instructed without hesitation:

"I want to buy ten bearer bonds."

Totally lost for words, I remained silent. At last my pieces were aligning, and it was time to move up in this world.

Replaying his words over in my head, he had agreed to take more bonds that I could have ever imagined, 10! Finding it difficult to focus, I managed to calculate that the amount of money we were talking was 3 million dollars! Having to remain calm, I tried to hide my excitement, but I couldn't fucking believe it. This would certainly help me redeem myself after the mess with the Greeks. If this deal could be finalised, the London Boys would be extremely impressed, and more doors would open for me.

"Sounds good to me," I replied after composing myself, hiding the excitement in my voice.

Our conversation continued, and we discussed the cost of the deal for him. He pushed his luck and kept trying to bargain for a cheaper offer. It was a long process, but we got there in the end and reached an agreement. I'd need to confirm the details with the guys from London before we shook on it. Although I was the point man for the operation, I didn't carry any weight when it came to making final decisions.

We agreed that he would hand over 2.5 million euros in cash as used notes. That was going to be some size of fucking money bag! A bag I couldn't wait to get my hands on.

Once all the finer details had been discussed, we left the meeting with an agreed deadline for the cash to be received. It surprised me that he didn't ask to see the bond again but was grateful because I only had one in Germany with me.

Then my mind started to race. How the fuck was I going to get hold of the other nine bonds? The German couldn't know I only had one bond with me, but I knew there was no way the London Boys would simply hand over another nine bonds without any assurances. I needed to see the cash, and fast, before I'd be able to organise transporting the other nine bonds here.

Being involved in this world had taught me the art of patience, so when the German said that it would take him two days to organise the money, I was okay to wait. But as two, three, then four days passed my impatience began to show.

It came to the fifth day and there was still no word from him. I felt like a sitting duck waiting in the hotel for the cash to be delivered, not sure what to do as J was breathing down my neck for an update. Day six came and still no cash, I had to make a move.

I couldn't just storm to the basement and demand the money, that would just be crazy, but I'd had it and felt like he was taking the piss out of me now. I decided that if day seven came, and there was still no cash, then that is exactly what I'd do!

For now, I had to try and take my mind off everything, and in a bid to blend in with the people who were staying at our hotel, and not to draw attention to ourselves, the three of us decided to take a walk. I don't know how George and Tamas felt, but for me the walk was a great escape. It was a relief be able to drift off into my own little world for a while.

As Tamas strolled ahead of us during our walk, I noticed that George was hobbling. He was a private man and I didn't want him to think I was prying but had to ask him if he was okay. He had an embarrassed expression on his face when he turned to look at me, but he continued to tell me he had a hole in the bottom of his shoe, which I found strange.

"If you've got a hole in your shoe then why don't you just buy a new pair?" I asked, unable to understand why he would continue to walk around with a hole in his shoe. It just didn't make sense to me.

That's when he began telling me how he lost all his money. He had around 2 million pounds in the bank just over a year ago but lost every penny in a huge VAT scam. Someone had tricked him, and he'd lost everything. He was such a friendly, trusting guy, and I could imagine that whoever had ripped him off knew that too and that's how they got away with it. I felt my blood boil as I listened to George's story. It made me angry to think that someone had taken advantage of his good nature. So, what you are telling me is you are broke?" I asked concerned.

"I live in a tiny flat that Tamas kindly sorted out for me Mike, and at this exact moment the only money I have is the 10 euros in my pocket!" He replied with a weary look on his face. My heart went out to him and I did not want to embarrass him any further, he'd been through enough, so I stopped talking.

As we continued to walk, I remembered the shoe shop in the village, which was so ironic. In this tiny village there were only two shops and one of them was a shoe shop.

Turning to George I asked him if he would come with me to the shop so that we could get him new shoes. He never said anything, but simply nodded, embarrassed that he could not provide for himself.

As we arrived outside the shop, he put his hand on my shoulder.

"Can we keep this between ourselves please?" he asked.

"Don't worry of course we can my friend" I replied, giving him a firm pat on his hand that was still on my shoulder.

He had been through enough and I wasn't about to embarrass him further by sharing his secrets with anyone.

After picking out a perfectly polished brown pair of brogues that he liked, and I'd paid for them, we were ready to head back to the hotel. It gave me a sense of pride being able to help George. He was older than me, and this was probably one of the hardest things he'd ever had to do, but he had to put his feelings aside to accept the shoes from me.

"Thank you my friend. This may seem like a small thing to you, but it is a huge deal to me," he said gratefully.

"Don't mention it mate," I replied with a smile.

This act brought our friendship closer and I knew he would never forget what I'd done for him that day.

When we got back to the room, I lay on my bed for a while thinking about how easily life can change from one day to the next. The future is uncertain, and you need to make the most out of every opportunity that comes your way. My thoughts made me even more determined to achieve what I'd set out to do.

CHAPTER 25
Crossing Borders

The monotony of being stuck in the hotel made me want to leave, but something was keeping me there. I couldn't walk away without knowing if the German was going to come through for me and come up with the cash. It was a tense time, sleeping with one eye open at night, unsure if his armed guards would burst through the door at any minute to try and steal the bond from us. There wouldn't be anything to stop them! Maybe I'd seen too many action movies in my time, but I created a thousand scenarios in my mind that always ended with me being shot in the head. Maybe it was the paranoia that was killing me, being cooped up in this place for so long.

The next morning, I woke up with sheer determination. Today was the day to confront the German to find out what the fuck was happening, enough was enough! My heart raced as I stormed along the corridor towards his smoking room, but there was no turning back.

"Have we got a deal or not?" I demanded.

Bursting straight through the doors unannounced and promptly sitting down across from him at his table. I never even let him say a word and continued to tell him how frustrating it was for us to sit around and wait, without any form of direction from him. We weren't prepared to do it any longer and wanted answers. When I'd finished what I'd come to say, I looked him straight in the eyes, waiting for his answer, half expecting his guards to grab me by my neck and throw me straight back out of the room. To my surprise they just stood, motionless, watching me.

"No bond, no money! I need proof that you have what you say you do!" He answered.

Why did he have to wait until now to throw a fucking spanner in the works? I needed to think fast on my feet and find some middle ground for us to work with. He needed proof that the bonds existed, but how could that happen without putting myself in danger? Think, think!

"Fuck it," I thought to myself.

Sick of these cat and mouse games, without even giving it a second thought,

"Okay, you want proof, I'll show you proof!" I replied.

And with that I pulled out the Andy McNab book and clenched it tightly in my hand, slammed it hard on the table in front of him. He watched me intently opening the book to the page where I'd hidden the bond, before pulling it out and shoving it right under his nose.

"There's your fucking proof, now stop messing me about!" I demanded.

It took all my effort to control my angry, shaking, hand. I'd probably over stepped the mark, but I'd had enough of the bullshit.

He looked at me with a shocked expression on his face, and it was plain to see that nobody had ever spoken to him like this before. He paused for a moment before telling me that he needed to ensure that the bond was legitimate; as he took a magnifying glass out from his desk drawer, took the bond from me and held it against the light. The room fell completely silent, and I watched his every move.

After he'd finished analysing the bond he stood up from his chair, took his phone out of his pocket and made three phone calls. He spoke in German, so I didn't have a clue what the fuck he was saying. His expression remained serious as he paced back and forth across the room. What was happening? The suspense was killing me!

Once he'd finished his calls, he put his phone back in his pocket before explaining that he would need to take the bond away for one of his contacts to analyse it to confirm its legitimacy.

"I will bring it back to you the following day!" he added.

The man had some balls! There was no other possible explanation for him to casually suggest that I simply let him take the bond. He must have thought I was a fucking idiot, there wasn't a chance the bond was going an inch out of my sight! My life was attached to that piece of paper and if it was stolen, I'd be as well planning my own funeral. The German was oblivious to this being a life or death situation for me.

"That's not possible! Can't you bring your contact here to check it's authenticity?" I asked agitated. but trying my best keep my cool, not wanting things to escalate and end up in a situation that we would both regret.

"No, I cannot," he stated, preparing to walk out of the room.

He was nearly at the door and I wasn't sure what to do to stop him. I didn't have a counter offer but couldn't let him walk out. There was no plan for this situation and he was playing this poker game a lot better than me.

I asked everyone else to leave the room, so we could talk in total privacy, and to my surprise he agreed. With just the two of us in the room, I had his full attention. We both needed honesty from each other.

"Okay, I'll agree for the bond to be taken to your contact on one condition, I go too!" I said.

"Where we're going, it's not the type of place that you want to be!" the German replied, with a chilling look in his eye.

He was obviously trying to scare me into not going, but like I'd told him before, where the bond went, I went! I'd already risked my life by just being here with him. What other option was there? There was nothing to lose.

He went on to explain that the place he needed to go was very dangerous, across the border in Poland, a place called Zagan.

"How will we get there?" I asked.

He explained that it would be a long car journey, but there would be no need for concern about border control because they would have already been dealt with.

"I'm good to go!" I replied confidently, without hesitation.

I'd rather die protecting the bond, than have the London Boys hunt me down for being careless. This was the only chance of completing a deal with the German and I needed a result.

The details were arranged, and it was planned that we'd leave the next day at 5pm. With a firm hand shake I left the meeting with the bond back in my possession. It was time explain the plan to Tamas.

Tamas and George rushed into the room as soon as I'd returned from the meeting. After explaining the plan, they both reacted in the same way.

"Are you fucking crazy? They are going to steal the bond, kill you and then bury you in a field!" said Tamas.

I put a hand on each of their shoulders in a reassuring manner.

"Let's just take a gamble guys! We need something to work or the London Boys are going to top me anyway!" I replied.

They both sat in silence for a minute, not knowing what else to say because they knew that I was right.

After chatting with them more, they reluctantly agreed that I had to go. To be honest they probably gave up trying to convince me otherwise because my mind was made up and there wasn't a thing they could say to make me change it.

Tamas asked George to leave the room for a moment. He wanted to speak to me in private. As soon as George had left, Tamas closed and locked the door behind him. I thought it strange for him to lock the door, but quickly realised why. He reached to the back of his waist band and pulled out a hand gun.

"Fuck me, I never knew you had that with you!" I gasped.

"Did you think I'd come here unprepared?" he replied sarcastically.

"How did you manage to get it here?" I asked.

"I have my contacts!" He replied with a little wink.

Stepping towards me, he placed the gun in my hand, keeping his hand on it as well. Before letting go of the gun he looked at me.

"Do you know how to use this?" he enquired.

I immediately pulled the gun away from him, released the magazine, checked the rounds, cocked the gun, cleared the chamber, inserted the magazine back into the gun and applied the safety catch.

"Fucking right I do, I've been to Goker's house many times!" I replied confidently and we both laughed.

Tamas was a good friend of Goker's too and had been to the range with him many times.

I was grateful to Tamas for giving me the gun. It was protection if needed, and it gave me reassurance to get on with what had to be done.

CHAPTER 26
Russian Roulette

Bang on 5pm the next day, I was picked up by one of the guys in a black Audi, it was very discreet. I was half expecting to be blinded folded on route to prevent me seeing where we were going.

I got into the car feeling confident, knowing that the gun was tucked in my waist band if it was needed. I expected to see the German in the car, but he wasn't there. Maybe he thought he was too important to grace us with his presence. It was just me, one of his bodyguards and the driver in the car. As we drove there was an air of tension, which made me feel a little uneasy.

We had been driving for about three hours, with hardly any chat. I'd no idea where we were going. It looked like we were going to no man's land. Bare land was all that could be seen for miles and I didn't know which direction of the country we were heading towards. We'd crossed the border without using passports as the German had said.

Arriving at our destination, it became apparent why the German had said that Zagan was no place for me. We were in a dark, earie run down town. It felt like a risky place to be. There were only three of us, and if anything were to kick off, we weren't going to be a hard match for anyone. The bodyguard had a gun, which made it a little safer, but I wasn't sure if he was there for protection or to shoot me himself. Surely, they were smart enough to know that I'd be more valuable alive than dead, as it was me that had access to the rest of the bonds. That's what they ultimately wanted. I'd seen greed change people in the past and it was a mystery to me how money could make people behave in a different way, causing then to make rash decisions.

Nobody knew where the fuck I was, neither did I for that matter. Feeling my heart begin to race I reached around to my waist band to check the gun was still in position. Just feeling the butt of it was enough to bring a smile to my face.

"Bring it the fuck on!" I thought to myself.

When we got out the car, I walked tall, a man on a mission.

We walked through a mobile phone repairs shop, which looked more like a shanty than a shop. There was no order and things were everywhere. It was dull, dingy and there was a stale, fusty smell, which made me feel sick.

Heading through to the back of the building, we came across a guy, dressed in holey clothes. He was dirty and looked like he hadn't washed in about a week. He was sitting watching the television, but as soon as he saw us, he mumbled what I assumed was a hello; he must have been expecting us because immediately he asked for the bond. Surely this guy didn't have a clue about bonds? Look at the state of him, how could he? Reluctantly handing the bond over, he tried to walk away with it. I gently pulled him back by his arm.

"Where the bond goes, I go," I said firmly.

He seemed surprised, but this wasn't a negotiation. I followed him though into the next room and the bodyguard stood, with his weapon ready, covering the doorway. Sitting down on an old chair his detailed analysis of the bond began, using some sort of powder to test and examine its hieroglyphics. I stood watching, not taking my eyes off the bond for a second. It was a lengthy process and it seemed to take him ages to finish his authentication. All that interested me were his findings.

When he'd finally finished, he simply handed me the bond back, without saying a word, which made me even more impatient.

"Are we good?" I snapped.

Shrugging his shoulders, as though he didn't give a fuck, he turned to speak to the bodyguard. Arrogant prick, I wanted to punch him in the face. I'd been brought to the middle of nowhere and he wasn't even going to give me the courtesy of telling me the results from his tests. Maybe he'd been ordered to only speak directly to the German, or maybe this was the time he was going to give the bodyguard the nod to put a bullet in my head. I'd not go down without a fight and putting my hand on my own weapon, ready to pull it if needed gave me a sense of control.

But nothing happened. Their conversation finished, and the bodyguard gestured to me that it was time to leave.

Walking out of the shop a feeling of unease washed over me. I could hear the bodyguard scuffling behind. It sounded as though he had drawn his gun. "What the fuck was he up to? This prick's not about to put a bullet in my head."

Within a split second, my gun was out, and I'd turned to face him. We stood holding each other's deadly stare, guns pointing at each other's head. Neither of us daring to break eyes contact. As adrenaline pumped through my veins, I watched a single bead of sweat roll down his forehead and drip into his eye, but still he never faltered. Either one of us could have blown the other one's head off with one squeeze of the trigger and there was no room for weakness.

"What the fuck are you doing! I screamed at him.

"You pulled your fucking gun on me, what did you expect me to do?" he snarled back at me.

The two of us stood, guns drawn, neither one of us backing down. The guy that had been authenticating the bond stood in the doorway, completely still, scared for his life.

After what seemed like an eternity, he finally spoke

"Guys calm down this is just a misunderstanding. No-one needs to get hurt here. Just put your weapons away."

"Were you told to shoot me? I questioned the bodyguard.

"Definitely not! I only pulled my fucking gun because you did!" he replied.

We both realised it had been a mistake.

"Okay, we lower our weapons after three, agreed?" I instructed him.

"Okay" he replied with a shaky voice.

"1,2,3," I counted, and we both lowered our weapons together. We could finally breath again!

"It sounded as though you had pulled out your gun and in the heat of the moment I over-reacted. I'm sorry, now can we get the fuck out of here?" I asked, tucking the gun back into my waist band, glad that I'd not had to use it this time.

He agreed, and we left the shop, heading straight to the car. Once we were back on the move and the moment felt right, I asked for confirmation that they were happy with the legitimacy of the bond.

"We will see!" he replied coldly.

Probably because of what had just happened inside the shop. The journey back to the hotel seemed so much longer than the journey there. My mind raced with thoughts about what would happen next. Was this deal going to go ahead, or was I going to have to tell the London Boys I'd fucked up again? The uncertainty of not knowing was doing my head in.

As soon as we were back at the hotel, I was summoned to the smoking room immediately. At least the wait was over, and I'd find out the outcome tonight. There would be no restless night thinking about it. My life was hanging in the balance here.

Entering the room, I expected the German to have his poker face on as usual and talk shit but was shocked when he came straight to the point.

"It's good!"

He was looking directly at me as he reached out his hand to shake mine. This was the first time I'd seen any happy emotion in his face. His eyes were bright, which could only mean one thing, a positive result!

He continued talking and told me that the cash would be here within twelve hours. He'd been dragging his feet for more than a week now, so I found it hard to believe, but when the money arrived, all the waiting would be worth it. I was over the moon.

This was really happening, I'd kept my cool and pulled it off. I was soon brought back to earth with a bang remembering I'd only one bearer bond in my possession and he wanted ten. What a fucking dilemma! How could I get the bonds here in time? Telling him that they weren't here wasn't an option. His bodyguard would probably have shot me there and then. With only twelve hours to go to produce the ten bearer bonds, I was fucked. He had the cash, but the bonds were in another country and I'd no idea how to fix it.

Getting back to my room there was an immediate knock at the door. It was Tamas

"Thank fuck you're okay. How did it go?" he asked.

"Mate, it was pretty dodgy, but it all went well." I replied.

I talked him through everything that had happened and could see that he was excited by my news. Big money was about to land in his lap, but then came the blow.

"He's looking to buy ten bonds and the money will be here tomorrow. The only problem is, I've only one in this country. When he finds that out, he will think we are fucking him about. He won't be a happy man and I'm sure there will be consequences to pay," I explained.

"Fuck, fuck, fuck! Can we not get the London Boys to get a flight over and bring the bonds with them so that they are here by tomorrow?" Tamas asked panicking.

"No! J and I need to be together to open the safety deposit box. We are the only two authorised signatories," I replied.

Tamas's face dropped, as he sunk into the chair, disappointed.

"Anyway, there is no chance the London Boys would agree for me to take another nine bonds, especially when we haven't even seen proof of the money yet!" I added.

"So, what are we going to do?" Tamas questioned.

I didn't have the answer and felt totally deflated, taking a deep breath.

"We will just have to wing it." I answered.

"Wing it! Are you fucking crazy Mike? How can we do that?" he asked worriedly.

"Let's just see if the cash turns up tomorrow first and then we will take it from there." I reassured him.

"Okay, okay" he said with his head in his hands.

After a long silence he stood up to leave, but before leaving he stretched out his arm to me

"Gun!" he instructed.

That showed me he was worried. He wanted it back for his own protection.

"I'll keep it until tomorrow, in case I need it," I replied.

With a simple nod, he turned and left my room with his head hung low.

I was left alone with time to think. Could the German really be trusted to produce the money? Was he taking me for a ride? I entertained the idea of flying back to the U.K, but wasn't sure if it would spook him, so decided against it. Even if I flew back, I'd have to convince J to come with me to sign over another nine bonds and get back to Germany within a twelve-hour window. That was never going to happen! I'd convinced the German that I'd ten bonds in my possession, not believing that he'd come up with the cash. This game of Russian roulette was ready to blow up in my face!

CHAPTER 27
Dirty Cash

Tonight, it was time to plan my move for the next day's meeting. There were no bonds as promised and this had disaster written all over it. If only something would happen that meant we had to put everything on hold that would give me time to fly back to London and return with the bonds.

Sitting alone with my thoughts, a call came through from my contacts in Turkey. They needed me back to sign some documents and to check progress with the new company accounts that were being set up. Feeling like everyone was trying to get a piece of me, I was under immense pressure from all parts of the world and thoughts of why I'd got involved with this in the first place kept creeping in like the darkness. It was a long night spent tossing and turning trying to work out a plan in my mind.

The next day after a rough night and little sleep, there was a bang on the door,

"The money is here, but the German wants to see you first!" One of the bodyguards growled at me through the door.

Fuck! I wasn't expecting this so quickly as I'd still not worked out what the fuck to do. He'd honoured his end of the deal and come up with the cash, but I didn't have the fucking bonds. He is going to go mental when he realises that they are not here as I'd promised. Tamas was right, winging it didn't seem like such a good idea now that it was time.

"Okay, I'll be there in half an hour!" I shouted back at the bodyguard.

As soon as he'd gone, I jumped up to find Tamas, to tell him the news. Both mine, and Tamas's emotions were all over the place, knowing that there was only one bond. George, unaware of the truth, was totally buzzing. This deal was more important to him than any of us. This was his chance to find his feet again and not rely on Tamas to support him.

"This is the start of the good times guys!" he said, bursting with excitement. Oblivious to the fact that we were short of nine bonds.

Tamas and I looked at each other trying to hide the truth from George, knowing exactly what was at stake. We needed to come up with another plan between us. Knowing that if the situation went wrong and the German wanted rid of me, they would need to remove me from the hotel first and take me somewhere secluded, I handed Tamas back his gun. My decision was to go into the room unarmed. We agreed that Tamas would be my eyes outside of the room and if he saw me being dragged away, he'd do whatever was needed to intervene. It wasn't the greatest plan but it's all we had.

It was time for my meeting with the German. Feeling adrenaline pumping through my body.

"Let's fucking do this!" I said to Tamas.

"Good luck!" he replied wearily.

"Ah who needs luck? I'm Mike Carr," I nervously joked.

With a thousand thoughts bombarding my mind about what would happen next, I walked into the smoking room, with no idea what the next twenty minutes would bring. The book was clenched in my hand, with only a single bond in it.

"Sit down my friend" he gestured, pointing to the seat in front of him.

"I've something to tell you before we go any further," he continued, with a sincere look in his eye. One I'd not seen before.

"I think you are one of the bravest and most honest men I've ever had dealings with, so I feel it is only fair that I'm honest with you," he said, clasping my right hand in between both of his.

131

"I haven't been able to organise the cash as promised. I gave you my word, and for this I'm truly sorry."

I could feel the anger boiling inside me and tried to stand up and storm out of the room before I ripped his fucking head off, but he still had a grasp of my hand and pulled me back into my seat.

"But what I do have is…"

He paused, reaching under the table before handing me a large black sports bag.

"250,000 euros, and I'd be truly grateful if this would let me have just one of the bonds in return. This is only temporary however, and I'll be in touch when I have the rest of the cash in place for the other nine."

You fucking dancer! This couldn't have worked out any better than if it was planned. Taking the bag from him I opened it to look inside. It was filled with countless bundles of used notes. I'd never seen this much money before. We'd got away with it! The cash was in my hands and he didn't have a fucking clue that I only ever had one bond in the first place. He had shown me that he was a man that could be trusted after all. The best of it was he still wanted the other nine bonds. Luck was on my side today.

Calmly, I opened the book and placed the single bond on the table.

"I'm disappointed and expected bigger things from you, which is the only reason I've spent so much time here and put up with all the bullshit. But I will allow you to take this single bond as a sign of goodwill and to cement us working together in the future," I said.

"My friend, I'll not forget your patience and will look forward to doing business with you in the future. When you return to my country you will return as my guest," he said sincerely.

We had a brief chat about what would happen next and we exchanged contact information. I picked up the bag and we left on good terms. As soon as my feet stepped through the door I could relax. That was too close for comfort!

I could see Tamas at the far side of the corridor and felt proud that he'd stood by his word and that he had my back whilst I was in the room. It would have been easy for him to have fucked off, taking himself away from danger, but he hadn't. He rushed over to me as soon as he caught sight of me.

"What happened in there? I've been shitting myself out here waiting for you!" he said, with a harassed tone in his voice.

"Tamas, my friend, never under estimate me! I told you everything would work out!" I replied with a wink.

He laughed and slapped me on the back as we headed back to our room, as I explained what had happened on the way. Once the door was shut it was straight on the phone to London to organise where to drop the cash off. The location that was arranged was on the way to the airport. There was no need to hang around any longer, so we packed up and left quickly. What a day it had been! Tamas, George and I headed to the airport, glad to be seeing the back of Germany. What we had endured over the last few weeks was made a little easier with the small cut of the cash we were given. It certainly wasn't a life changing amount, but it was enough to keep us going. George's cut would certainly go a long way in helping him get back on his feet.

I headed back to Istanbul because there was business that needed to be attended to, whilst Tamas and George headed back home. It was sad to say goodbye to them. They had been good company in the last few weeks but having the company accounts in Turkey up and running was crucial at this point, so I just had to get on with it.

Being the Director of the company, the responsibility fell to me to sign all the paperwork in person, and it was up to me to pick up the fake passports and company accounts. The time had come to get back into the bigger business. The type of business that was going to bring life changing money, the reason I'd got into this in the first place.

Once back in Turkey I had time to go and chill with Goker for a while. On my first night back, we went to a huge barbeque he was hosting for his family. It was so good to see them all again and being with them gave me a sense of normality.

I was only with him for a few days, and after work was completed in Turkey, I headed back to the UK to meet up with J. He was in a buoyant mood and told me that I'd impressed the London Boys and they were happy to see some progress. They were also glad to see some money coming in even if this was just a drop in the ocean compared to the amount of money the real deal would bring. I'd come to understand how these guys worked and they were always right no matter what. They weren't going to make it easy for me. I was a means to an end for them, someone had to do their dirty work, but if I got what I wanted that was all that mattered.

During my chat with J he told me that the London Boys needed me to do something for them before heading back to Turkey again. It was obvious by the tone in his voice that there was no room for discussion. What the hell was it? They were beginning to piss me off. Who the fuck did they think they were? They didn't own me!

CHAPTER 28
Man Mountain

5 grand for a days' work, I wasn't going to knock that back. This business was unpredictable, and with that came the uncertainty of when money would come my way. If an opportunity arose, I was going to grab it.

J's words were still ringing in my ear

"The Boss Man wouldn't risk losing you."

This gave me a sense of importance in his world. It wasn't in my nature to turn away from a job, even if I'd no idea what was involved. The London Boys knew I had balls, and most importantly, they knew they could trust me. I'd do anything they asked but my only limit was becoming involved in the bullshit world of the drugs scene, that just wasn't me.

It did cross my mind that whatever they wanted me to do could be a test. A way for them to see what type of work I could handle. The fact was I'd no idea what the job was, so there was no point guessing, I'd just need to wait to find out. There wasn't another option but for me to take this job and get it right to build their trust.

J gave me a burner phone, which was the norm with this lifestyle and I wouldn't have expected anything else. He told me not to contact him until the job was finished. The phone already had a number programmed into it and he instructed me to call it as soon as I arrived at Kings Cross Station. The number was for the guy who would be the lead contact for this job and it would be him that would give me my next instructions from there.

With everything set, I jumped onto the train heading to Kings

Cross. This was the kind of shit that excited me. A bit of the unknown, laced with a bit of danger! The anticipation of meeting someone I'd never met before, and thoughts about the job, were running through my mind. Would it involve violence or guns? I couldn't wait to find out.

Arriving at Kings Cross, I took out the burner phone from my pocket and called the number, not knowing what to expect when dialing. There was no way of predicting who was going to be on the other end of the line. A guy with a very distinctive cockney accent picked up. I wasn't surprised by his accent because that had been one of the only things J had divulged about the job, the guy I was meeting was a Londoner.

There was no chat and he got straight down to business. He told me exactly where to meet him. Ditching the burner phone, I headed to McDonalds across the road from the station as he had instructed. He already had a description of me from J, but I knew nothing about him.

Crossing the road from the station, I waited for a few minutes, watching every person that approached me, wondering if it was him but no-one stopped. Surveying the hordes of people around me, I spotted a fucking huge black guy who was walking in my direction:

"That has got to be him." I thought to myself.

He was a man mountain! As he approached, he didn't take his eyes off me, which made me certain that he must be the guy I'd been waiting for. My instincts were right, when he was close enough, he stretched out his arm to shake my hand, introducing himself to me as Big Marco. His name suited his build perfectly.

"I'm wee Mike," I joked as he towered above me.

"Good at least this guy has a sense of humor." I thought to myself when he began to laugh.

He was a big fucker with a shaved head. His large, status gold watch, caught my eye as the light hit off it. He obviously liked the bling. Big Marco was probably in his early 50's but looked younger. He looked strong, as if he could smash through someone with just one punch. His old school London gangster attitude made me smile and the more we spoke, it became apparent that he was a man who demanded respect, without being a prick. If you showed him respect, then the same courtesy would be shown to you.

Marco was friendly but direct with what he had to say. I liked that about him and knew that we would get along. I was grateful that he wasn't someone who was up their own ass. I'd worked with enough of them over the last while and couldn't be fucked working with anyone else like that. He was a refreshing change to the people I'd been dealing with.

"Now that we have met, let's get to work," he stated, as we walked away from the street corner, battling with the swarm of people walking towards us.

I still wasn't sure what the job involved but followed his cue. Even though there were a lot of uncertainties about the whole situation, meeting Big Marco had put me at ease. I wasn't sure whether he knew I had not been briefed about the job and would have expected to have been given at least some sort of idea about what was going on by now. It was frustrating, but my only option was to take his lead and go with the flow.

We knew nothing about each other and we didn't really have much to say to each other at first. We both attempted to make small talk, which felt a little awkward at first. I took the opportunity to ask about his watch and was surprised when he told me that his wife had bought it for him for their anniversary. I would never have expected him to be married.

As we continued to walk, he told me that we were heading to a small nearby pub so that we could discuss plans in detail.

The pub was busy and had a traditional feel to it. We chose to sit in a small alcove for a bit of privacy. After a couple of pints, a chat about football and other shit, we got down to business.

"This is going to be a nice clean bank job involving dormant accounts Mike," he stated casually.

I didn't know what the fuck dormant accounts were. He went on to explain that the job was planned to go ahead the next day.

There was no point in bullshitting him, so I told him the truth. This kind of job was a new concept for me and I'd never heard of dormant accounts before.

He went on to clarify that dormant accounts are ones that have been termed dormant because a person has died and there is no clear evidence that the deceased has relatives to claim the accounts contents. He further added that these kinds of accounts are flagged up to the bank due to there being little or no activity on them. I was interested to find out where he was going with this.

"So, what happens to the contents of the account once it has been termed dormant?" I asked curiously, before taking a sip of my drink.

Big Marco explained that the money in the account would be held for seven years. Once the seven years had passed, and if nobody had come to claim what was in it, then the money would be transferred to a government department fund. He wasn't sure what the government did with the funds from there. In short, the contents of the account were going to disappear. The account holder was no longer around to benefit from the money, and there was no family either, which meant the government would receive the lot.

Our plan was for me to pose as the person whose account was dormant. I'd then visit the bank to withdraw all the funds. No-one was going to be harmed in this process and if we didn't do this, then the funds would end up in the government's pocket anyway. I shook Big Marco's hand and we agreed the deal was on.

CHAPTER 29
Number 3

The job sounded like it was going to be a piece of piss, easy money. I couldn't help feeling a little disappointed when finding out it was going to be another job involving paperwork. I was looking forward to getting my hands dirty and being involved in some action but couldn't complain, at least it was going to bring in some cash. Big Marco ran me though the next stages of the plan, stipulating exactly how things needed to happen. I'd need to have a different identity. All my details would need to match those of the account holder and would have to include photographic ID. Once the ID was sorted, I would need to get hold of other documents that supported my new identity. Marco had all of this in hand and was going to source everything to make my new identity seem legitimate that night. I'd become Mr. Johnathon Whitehouse, who was 15 years older than me. It would be important that my appearance supported his age when going into the bank. My look would need to represent my character and boots, jeans and Fred Perry weren't going to cut it.

I'd be allocated a spotter, as expected and he would be their eyes and ears throughout the whole job. Marco assured me that he was there for my protection and that he'd been instructed by the Boss Man that under no circumstance should anything happen to me. They were protecting me as their asset, which was a good sign. Trust in this business was just a word. The reality was that nobody trusted anyone, which was the best way to be. The London Boys were the ones holding all the cards and they knew it.

Marco told me that they had insider information. I didn't know to what extent but knew that the information they held was the basis of the scam and without it there would never have been a job in the first place.

Marco gave me specific instructions about how to handle myself in the bank. All the chat and preparation had built my excitement and I couldn't wait to get on with it now. There was uncertainty about how believable my new identity would be to the bank, but I was determined that I'd pull this off.

During our preparation my instructions were to approach teller number three once inside the bank. It didn't matter how long the queue was, that was the only teller that could help me, and I'd need to wait if I had to. The description of the girl that would be waiting at teller three was detailed and I'd been given her name. This was a precaution, in case there was a changeover in staff during my time of entering the bank. The teller was obviously the inside mole. The job was going to be easier than I first thought. With the teller on the inside, what could possibly go wrong?

I was to make a withdrawal of two bankers drafts, each of the drafts being valued at 50 thousand pounds. I'd have expected it to be a lot more, but after thinking about it realised that it would have been reckless of us to withdraw sums that were any larger at one time in case it raised suspicion.

Marco explained the drafts would need to be drawn up and if it took some time, I shouldn't get spooked. Blending in and appearing as a regular customer was key. It was about having the balls and confidence to front up to whatever was thrown my way.

Even though we had the teller on the inside, I expected that she probably wasn't the only one that would be helping us. A teller wouldn't have the clearance needed for this job. There was undoubtedly someone higher up the chain involved.

Although confident in the job, the responsibility lay with me to ensure that everything ran smoothly, and I couldn't afford to mess this up. We had to ensure the protection of our source inside the bank. This was never a one-off job and it wouldn't surprise me if this had been done many times before. Our insider couldn't be burnt at any cost. She was far too important to the London Boys.

It was the day of reckoning. I ran through the plan repeatedly in my head until I was certain I'd nailed every detail. My patience was tested as I waited for confirmation that everything was good to go in the bank. We didn't want to jump the gun and chance fucking it all up. Once the signal was given and we had the all clear, that was my queue to move in and organise withdrawal of the money.

Marco knew more about my alias than me, so he gave me further information that might come in handy. When entering the bank, I was to become Mr. Whitehouse from the Isle of Wight. The real Whitehouse had been dead for about four years now, but the bank was oblivious to that fact. His account still had active direct debits on it so there would be no suspicions raised with my request to withdraw money. I had a feasible story if anyone questioned me. I'd been using various other bank accounts for my day to day financial business, which is why there hadn't been as much activity on this account.

It was time, time for me to put Mr. Whitehouse's cap on. I was a little wary walking towards the bank but as soon as my feet were inside there was a sense of calm. I knew the spotter was watching out for me and help was on the inside. This should be a walk in the park. My chosen outfit consisted of dark glasses and a tweed jacket, which suited my more mature appearance. I believed that everything was going to play out exactly as we wanted. We had planned everything to the last letter and there was no doubt that we could pull this off without any hiccups. I walked up the escalator to the upper level and looked around. The sheer size of the bank amazed me, this was a place of wealth that was for sure. There were bank workers beavering away in their glass panelled offices and I wondered if one of these workers was an insider. I'd confidence that nobody in the bank would have any reason to disbelieve that I was Mr. Whitehouse. The spotter would be watching my every move and he was probably in the bank already.

My role was spelt out for me and I couldn't do anything to deviate from the plan. If that happened, then this could jeopardise the whole operation. It was arranged that once I'd finished and had the drafts in hand, the spotter would approach me. He would identify himself to me on exiting the bank and then we would proceed together to meet Big Marco. That's where the handover of the drafts would happen, totalling £100,000 and I'd walk away with an easy £5k.

Approaching the top of the escalator, I was focused on finding teller number three and there it was, the big, bright red, number 3, high above a queue of people. This was it!

CHAPTER 30
Playing the Role

This was going to be even easier than I'd thought because there was a separate queue for each teller. I calmly walked to teller number three, as planned. The person behind the booth screen wasn't as I'd imagined. A sweet and innocent Asian girl looked at me, she certainly didn't look as if she would be involved in this kind of world, but that's what made her the perfect cover. No-one would ever suspect her.

Thinking about my own appearance I imagined that others could easily mistake me for a criminal, with my bald head, physique and tattoos, but today I hoped I'd got it right and would be in and out of the bank without any suspicion at all. Always being an over thinker, my mind never stopping for a minute, constantly trying to work shit out, 24/7, was my thing. Today was no different as my thoughts began to drift about why a girl like this would get involved in this whole situation. Wondering whether they were forcing her into this, or was she just like me, in it for the money and the thrill? I'd never know the answers to my questions but I'm sure she had her reasons. The queue was very short, it only took a few minutes before I was next to be served. Confidently, stepping up to the booth "Good morning," I said with a smile.

Obviously, I'd never met this girl before, but knowing that she was part of the setup, made me feel a certain affiliation with her. There was a hint of recognition in her eyes when I told her my name, but she gave nothing away.

The sooner we got business out the way, the sooner I could get my ass out of there.

"Good morning," she replied in a soft and friendly voice. Working in the bank, it was her job to be friendly. Her poker face was flawless, she treated me no differently to the other customers in the bank and she remained calm and never faltered once. Glancing up for a moment I caught sight of a cluster of security cameras, which momentarily made me feel uneasy. But I steadied my own uneasiness, of course the bank was going to have every inch of the floor covered by CCTV. Speaking to the teller, I explained that I needed two 50 thousand pound bank drafts from my account. Following bank protocol, she asked for my identification documents, which I'd prepared for and handed her my passport. She didn't look at it in as much detail as I'm sure most of the other tellers would, but that didn't matter to me. We both knew the reason for me being in the bank.

After filling in a few pieces of paperwork, she explained that it would take five minutes to process my transactions as it would need to be authorised, and then the bank drafts would need to be printed. To keep up appearances, remaining calm I nodded to her that it would be fine, and I'd be happy to wait.

"Help yourself to a tea or coffee Sir, there is a small seating area up there to your left. I'll call you when your drafts are ready!" she said.

Declining her offer, I told her I was in a hurry today in hope that this would speed up the process. There was no need for me to be in the bank any longer than was necessary. I was a ticking time bomb and needed to get out quickly. She stood up from her seat and walked away to complete my request, disappearing into the back with my documents. All that was left for me to do now was be patient and wait for her to return. It was in her hands now and time for her to do her part of the plan.

Whilst waiting, I had a look around to see if I'd be able to pick out the spotter from the crowd of people in the bank, although I'd no idea what he looked like. It was a simple game to keep my mind occupied, whilst waiting for the time to pass. This was never going to be very productive, because if I was able to pick him out then that would have meant that he was doing a shit job. I'd find out soon enough what he looked like once we left the bank.

I was distracted by my game, so hearing a voice call out the name Mr. Whitehouse loudly from behind the counter made me jump. Back to reality, it suddenly dawned on me that it was a man's voice that I'd heard! Why had teller number three not come back? What had gone wrong? Did they find out that the documents were forgeries?

Finally, I stopped my thoughts racing and asked myself would they be as courteous if they had worked out what was going on, not very likely! I'd have been surrounded by armed police by now. Taking a deep breath, I told myself to chill the fuck out. Remaining calm I approached the man to listen to what he had to say. Walking hesitantly towards him, my mind turned to the detailed exit strategy plan we had discussed before going into the bank. This wasn't as we planned though but I didn't panic. I was smart enough to figure out what to do next for myself.

Finally getting control of my thoughts, I heard him call out my cover name again and people in the bank were starting to look round.

"Yes," I answered finally.

He continued to talk as I approached the desk and realised this wasn't an ambush, everything was going to be okay. He introduced himself as an investments mmanager and went on to explain the reason that he wanted to speak to me. His words were just noise to me, but to be polite I nodded when he asked for a few minutes of my time so that he talk thorough some information with me. His bullshit chat wasn't of any interest, but I'd have to play the game to keep up appearances.

I'd never really asked Big Marco many details about Whitehouse's file, thinking that I'd just be going into the bank, speaking to the teller briefly, getting the drafts and leaving. That was foolish because now I'd have to chat to this investments manager blind, with very little information about who Mr. Whitehouse really was. I'd only been concerned about working on my appearance. I should have declined the offer to speak with him, which would have been the sensible thing to do, but there was a part of me that wanted to make the spotter sweat a little and send a message to the London Boys that I was in charge.

The investments manager told me that he had noticed that my account had minimum activity on it for the last few years. Thank fuck that he didn't ask me to offer a reason. There was an awkward silence before he went on to explain that in the period of inactivity on my account, a couple of things had changed. He stated that one of the policies, that were part of my package, had matured six months previous.

"So, what does this mean for me?" I enquired.

I'd not really concerned myself with the details of Mr. Whitehouse's life before, but now things had just become interesting and I was keen to find out more. Feeling more settled it was time to play the role and have a bit of fun.

He explained that the bank was interested in changing the terms of my account. They wanted to move my current account over to a higher interest account, which would be more beneficial to me. Throughout our conversation it was difficult to concentrate but thank fuck this hadn't gone tits up.

I made my excuses and told him that I'd no time to change accounts today but would consider the upgrade and speak with him next time I was in the bank. Being a typical salesman, he tried hard to convince me, which pissed me off. I just wanted out of there, but he wouldn't let it go, reminding me that I still needed to wait for the drafts to be completed and changing my account would be quick.

"You can kill two birds with one stone," he stated with a cheeky smile on his face.

Just as I was about to lose my cool, teller number three walked back into the booth. It was a relief to see her. At least now I could leave, but my relief was short lived

"Sorry Sir I'm just waiting for my manager to finalise your

paperwork. Your transaction will be completed within the next 10 minutes."

Our eyes met, and she gave me a little nod, which was her indication to me that I should continue with the investments manager. This was a total ball ache and not part of the plan. I'd no idea how Big Marco would react if I deviated from what was agreed but if the girl, said that it was okay, then surely it couldn't do any harm. I was meant to be blending in after all. She gave me a little reassuring smile as she went into the back office and left me with him again.

"Okay let's make these changes then," I stated.

A smug smile spread across his face as though he had won a victory. He could think what he liked the truth was this was a way of keeping him silent and getting him out of my face before I punched him.

I'd been given a phone from Big Marco, which had a prepared message in it and if things went wrong all I needed to do was press the send button and the spotter would know I was in trouble. He would then do whatever necessary to get me. With this situation under control and feeling confident that I'd be able deal with a pain in the ass salesman without having to call for back up the phone stayed firmly in my pocket.

CHAPTER 31
Extraction

The dynamics of the situation changed slightly, as the investment manager ushered me away from the tellers' booth into a private room without giving any pre-warning. Confident in the paperwork I'd provided because the teller had given me the nod, I wasn't concerned and happy to go along with the change.

The room was just next to the tellers' counters and had a glass front, so it was possible to see what was going on in the banking hall. Still vigilant, I looked inside the room before entering, double checking there weren't armed police waiting to ambush me. Once certain there was no-one inside I walked in, taking a seat closest to the door.

After listening for what seemed like hours to him talking pish about banking, it was a relief when he changed the subject. He took me a little off guard when he began to talk about the times he'd visited the Isle of Wight.

"I've been there more than once. It's a lovely place." he stated. I'd never been before so never said anything to steer the conversation further but simply nodded with a smile to look interested. I remembered Big Marco saying that the Isle of Wight was where the real Mr. Whitehouse had lived. Realising that he wasn't going to relent, I thought it best to play along. At least it would make the time pass quicker if nothing else.

Getting lost in a made-up story I told him that a couple of miles up the road from the airport there was a big white hotel that belonged to my brother-in-law. He seemed interested and my story grew arms and legs as I continued to tell him things that weren't true. I'd always been a good talker and it was better than having to listen to him.

After I'd finished talking, he passed over the paperwork that needed signed for my new account and went on to explain that my investment would be increased by 3% moving forward. Not really giving a fuck I made comments here and there to feign interest. Listening to him drone on, watching the huge hands of the clock tick round on the wall, I just wanted out of there now.

"You won't regret this Sir," He added.

Which I'm sure he only said for effect.

I had become so caught up in business that I'd completely forgotten about the spotter. He had obviously been watching every move but didn't really know what was happening. He was in the background, clueless as to why I'd been taken into the side room but knew that it wasn't part of the plan. It was his job to protect me if there was any deviation from the plan. The scene that was playing before him wasn't looking good and he had to think fast.

The spotter was under strict instructions that nothing should happen to me. I was a valuable asset to the London Boys and shouldn't be put in any danger. He knew they would blame him if I was put in any danger. He needed to do whatever it took to get me out of trouble and would be kicking himself for letting me go inside the room, without knowing what was happening. In his mind he had to find an extraction strategy without involving anyone else. If he alerted the others this would have created an even bigger issue for him to deal with. They would have directly assumed that he couldn't do his job. I'm sure he didn't want to find out how London Boys dealt with those who couldn't do their job properly.

He needed to get me out of the room by any means necessary, even if it meant revealing his identity. Walking straight to the room that I'd gone into with the Investments Manager, he knocked on the door. I'd never met him before; that was only meant to happen once the banker's drafts were in my possession. The Investments Manager opened the door and asked if he needed any help. The spotter never spoke, looking straight past the Investments Manager and directly at me, with a hint of urgency in his eyes. He was a slim Asian gentleman wearing a suit.

"Hey sorry pal, do you have a blue five series BMW?" he asked me directly. There should have been a better plan in place.

Everything felt very awkward, but it was obvious that he needed to get my attention, so I played along.

"Yeah that's my car," I stated with hesitation, not understanding what the problem was.

"Something has happened to your car," he stated.

I asked him if he was sure it was my car, in hope that he would get the hint that everything was okay with me and there was no need for his help. He went on to explain that another car had crashed into mine and that my wife, who was in the car, had asked for him to come and get me.

"Could he not have come up with a simple story." I thought to myself.

The best lie would have been simple. He simply could have said that somebody had run into my car. Why the hell did he have to create another person? What if the Manager insisted on coming out of the bank with me to help and there was nobody there? I stared at him angrily, wanting to punch him. He was going to fuck this up. I'd never even sent a text to let him know he needed to get me out of there. The stupid cunt!

He insisted that my wife needed me. This was his exit strategy; a way for me to excuse myself from the bank, but there was no fucking need for it.

"Thank you, I'll go as soon as I'm finished here," I stated.

Wanting him to fuck off, I tried to give him a look that confirmed everything was under control and he should let me handle it, but he wasn't taking the hint. Leaving the room, would mean leaving without the drafts, which would be a waste of both our time.

He wasn't giving up and was now causing a scene. He continued to say that my wife might have been injured. He wasn't taking no for an answer. I understood that he was trying to get me out of perceived danger. It was best for me to go outside with him and explain as it was beginning to look as if I didn't care about my imaginary wife. Staying in the bank any longer would arouse suspicion.

"Is she badly hurt?" I asked.

It wasn't an Oscar worthy performance, but I tried my best to look concerned, waiting to hear what the spotter's ridiculous response would be.

As I stood up, the manager was looking at us both, he was unsure what to say or do.

"I'm not sure about the extent of her injuries. There are other people with her. Once she gave me your description, she asked me to come straight in to find you," he replied.

At least his story was believable to some extent. If there had been a real accident there would have been a scene outside the bank. There was no wife, no car and certainly no accident so I had to get out of there quickly in hope that the manager didn't follow and realise that the whole thing was a set up.

Stepping out of the office, the manager pulled me back. I could see a look of concern in his eyes.

"Do you know this guy?" he asked me with a hint of fear in his voice.

He looked genuinely concerned for my safety, but I convinced him I'd be back immediately after checking that everything was okay with my wife.

My thoughts turned to teller number three. Where was she? A long time had passed, yet she hadn't come back with the banker's drafts. My attention was brought back to the manager as he warned me not to follow an unknown gentleman out of the bank because it could be dangerous.

"I'll be right back. Thank you for your concern for my safety but everything will be okay" I reassured him, walking through the door.

The spotter was impatient. He was already well away, and I had to walk quickly to try and catch up with him. What was his rush? Maybe he was adamant that I leave with him because he had some inside knowledge. My plan wasn't to leave the bank but to meet him near the stairs, explain everything was still on track and I was only taking care of regular business. Then all I'd need to do would be go back for the 100 grand!

I looked around to see where the spotter had disappeared to, but he wasn't in the banking hall. I'd lost him when the Manager pulled me back. He couldn't have gone very far. Just about to step on the escalator, I spotted him at the bottom. Why he was in such a hurry? If there was any danger, surely, he should be right by my side.

He was pissing me off now and behaving like a fucking amateur. We might have had a difference of opinion about what constituted danger, but his job was to keep me in sight and he'd made a shit move.

Coming down the escalator I presumed that he would be waiting for me outside. He needed to start behaving more rationally. In his mind he probably believed he was saving my ass, but the reality was, if he didn't chill the fuck out, he was going to mess the whole plan up.

Stepping outside the bank, he rushed straight in front of me. I tried to speak to him but could see he was scared shitless. I'd no idea why, as far as I could see we weren't in any imminent danger, which went back to the question, what did he know? In a total panic he shouted for me to run. The panic in his voice spooked me and I spun around to look at the door to the bank to see if someone had followed me.

"Run, fucking run!" he screamed again before taking off down the street. Luckily the street was empty at the time, so he didn't draw too much attention to us. The coolness and calmness that I was trying to portray inside the bank went in a second. I was unsure what to do so followed his lead and ran after him.

We ran through the streets together before I took a different route. If someone was following us it would be best to split up. We'd arranged a meeting point if something went wrong so I headed straight there.

The Travel Lodge beside Kings Cross Station was my destination. Running through the streets, I took off my jacket, hat and glasses. If anyone was following me then it would make it more difficult for them to identify me. People and shops passed in a blur as my running pace quickened. I was in deep shit, I could feel it. What the fuck had we done?

CHAPTER 32
Miscommunication

I needed to calm down and get control back, the fucking spotter had totally spooked me. He better have a good explanation for this! What the hell was going on? I was slap bang in the middle of this but couldn't figure out what had happened.

Could he have handled this situation in a different way? Was he just doing his job? Or was he just a total idiot that had bottled it and we were running away from a 100 grand because he was a pussy. I started thinking about what Big Marco would say and even though he was a chilled-out guy, there was no way of predicting how he would react when he found out that we'd messed up.

I looked back over my shoulder a couple of times to see if anyone was following me but there was no-one. We'd jumped the gun. For fuck's sake, what a mistake to make! My heart was pounding running down the street. I slowed to a walk before darting into the tube station. The sweat was running down my back. For a second the joker in me was happy to be getting a bit of workout. It was the first I'd trained in weeks, but that was short lived as I began to try and make sense of what had just happened. I was unable to get my head around the fact that we had fucked up this simple plan.

Sitting in the tube station, the cold realisation that I'd left documents in the bank hit me. Fuck, the passport, which had my picture on it. I'd put myself at risk and could easily be identified now. If I didn't return to the bank they'd investigate further, and it wouldn't take them long to figure out my passport was a forgery. I had to try and put it out of my mind for now, my priority had to be to get back to the rendezvous point where Big Marco would know what to do next.

Stepping off the tube, I wondered where the spotter had gone. He better be switched on enough to come back to the meeting point, then at least he could explain what the fuck happened back at the bank. The tube journey had given me time to catch my breath, but my adrenaline was still pumping, as my anger boiled inside at the stupidity of the spotter walking out of Kings Cross Station.

Room 264 of the Travel Lodge was our meeting place. Drawing closer, I felt hesitant about going in and for a minute thought about turning around and going back to the bank. There was still time to go back and fix this mess. If only I had stood firm with the spotter, maybe the outcome would have been different now.

Looking at the numbers on the door, 264, I stood for a while before knocking. Big Marco was the face that welcomed me to the room. I could only just see past his huge frame and there was someone else behind him.

His expression was that of a pissed off man. He wasn't happy to see me.

"What the fuck's going on?" he demanded answers.

I walked into the room without saying a word and sat on the bed, taking a minute preparing the very long explanation. The words were on the tip of my tongue and as I was about to speak when there was another knock on the door.

The spotter sheepishly walked in and stood next to the bed with his arms folded. The sight of him fuelled my anger. Things were about to kick off!

As soon as Marco had shut the door my anger erupted, shouting at the spotter.

"You're a fucking idiot! Why the fuck did you get me to leave the bank?" I yelled.

It was unlike me to lose it like that, but he should have assessed the situation properly and wouldn't be sitting in this mess now. The spotter shifted nervously on his feet, shitting himself about what Marco would do to him.

"When you disappeared into that room, I had to get you out man! Big Marco would have kicked the shit out of me otherwise." he mumbled.

The more the spotter spoke the angrier I was becoming. Unable to stop myself, I threw a punch at him hitting him square in the jaw. Lifting my fist to throw another jab at him, Big Marco intervened, jumping in between us and pulling us apart. As the three of us struggled, a phone began ringing. Everyone suddenly stopped to search their own pockets to confirm who's phone it was.

It was Big Marco's, he answered cautiously, not expecting a call. After a brief conversation with the person at the other end of the phone I could see his expression change and there was hint of relief on his face.

"It's the teller," he relayed to us.

We all sensed the same relief as he did that she was calling. It was only possible to hear one side of the conversation. Big Marco explained to her that there had been a miscommunication and that it was being handled. Whilst he spoke, he paced around the room, making it difficult for us to catch all the conversation, so we waited for him to hang up.

The teller informed him that everything was okay at the bank, and the plan could be salvaged, but there was a problem. She needed me to be back in the bank within the next five minutes. Then I'd be able to walk out with the two fifty thousand pound drafts as we had planned.

We were still determined to make this job a success, no matter the cost.

"Mikey, you should head back to the bank," he ordered.

I was totally up for going but knew it would take me about 40 minutes to get back as I explained to Marco. He called the teller straight back to ask her if she could stall the process because five minutes wasn't going to cut it.

The fact that everything was still okay at the bank only fuelled my anger towards the spotter. I started shouting at him again, he truly was a fucking idiot. I was annoyed at myself for not taking control when we left the bank in the first place and just taking off after him. He should have waited for my signal and not been so quick to react.

I was still shouting at the spotter when Big Marco slapped him hard in the face, which stopped me in mid flow. That was embarrassing, to get slapped like a little bitch. A punch would have been acceptable, but a slap was for a pussy in my eyes. "Mike's in charge! You should have waited for his cue!" he stated casually.

We had all been involved in the finer details of the plan and we all understood that Big Marco oversaw the operation. All problems should have been reported to him first before making any decisions, protocol had been agreed. The simple press of a button on the phone would have sent the text and the spotter would have known I was in trouble. His instincts had been wrong, causing a hell of a lot of drama for no reason.

I didn't feel sorry for him in the slightest, Big Marco had given him what he deserved. This was a disaster that could put me in jail. It was his responsibility and he had to face the consequences, whatever they would be!

CHAPTER 33
Cross Roads

"Mike do you want to go back to the bank?" Big Marco asked.
He hadn't confirmed if the teller had agreed if we could have
more time for me to get back to the bank or not and I still
wasn't out of the door, time was ticking away.
After we had bolted from the bank my thoughts had changed
and my confidence in the plan had taken a knock. Being
approached by the investment manager at the bank had
resulted in a fuck up and it wouldn't be as straight forward as it
was supposed to be anymore. The 100 grand was ours for the
taking, but maybe my return visit wouldn't be as easy as the
teller thought It would be.
I was at a crossroads and this was a big decision to make. No
matter how much we all tried to downplay it, everyone was
looking at me to decide, and it needed to be right now. time
was up and there was no more thinking time.
The teller gave the green light and assured Marco that even if
my arrival was a little later than expected it wouldn't matter. It
was down to me now. Feeling sick to the stomach I'd made my
decision and that wasn't to go back. Marco wasn't going to be
happy, but it was too risky.
The whole operation had already been compromised and it
would have been crazy to go back to the bank immediately.
Marco looked pissed off, as expected when I told him my
thoughts. Reminding him of the bigger picture and that the
London Boys wanted a clean job, he understood, especially
now that this job was a far cry from that.
"This is a shitty job Marco, I'm sure you'll agree with me!"
I stated.

I'd learnt that the London Boys didn't like wasting their money and if we fucked this up, and put their money at risk, then I'd be in deep shit. Silence lingered in the room for a while before planning our next move.

"You get the fuck out of my sight, I'll deal with you later!" Marco scowled at the spotter. As he walked out with his head hung in shame, Marco proceeded to shout that he'd cost him 100 grand. Emotions escalated! There was a lot of money at stake. Once the spotter had left, I sat on the bed expecting to be next in Marco's firing line.

"You've got a valid point man. We can't afford for you to get burnt doing a shitty job, the Boss Man would kill me!" he stated. It felt like admitting defeat, not going back to the bank, although Big Marco understood me. Admitting defeat is not something that I took lightly and didn't want to justify my decision, but felt I owed Marco an explanation.

"I've got the balls to do it but can't afford for this to go wrong. We have the deal with the bonds to think about." I explained. After a short conversation we both got a better understanding of what each other was thinking and knew that it was down to the spotter that we weren't sitting with the two banker's drafts in front of us now.

"It is better to walk away and be ready to fight another day." Big Marco stated. He added that it would be foolish for us to walk into a fight knowing that there was a high chance that we could lose. There was movement close to the door that made both Marco and I turn around. The spotter hadn't left!

"Why the fuck you still here? I told you to leave." Marco snapped.

Before anyone had the chance to react, Marco stormed over to him, punched him hard in the face knocking him out. He fell back onto the floor and never moved for a few seconds as he lay unconscious.

"Let's go get a pint. I've had enough of this shit for one day." Big Marco said. He had a calmer demeanor, as if the punch had help release some tension.

"When I get back, you better not be here!" Marco said, nudging the spotter, as he was coming to, with his foot as he walked out of the room.

It was a short walk to the bar. We ordered the first round of drinks, trying to forget the problems of the day. Then out of nowhere Marco brought me back to reality with a bang.

"You do realise that they still have the fake passport!" he reminded me.

I wanted to forget the whole day, but the bank having my fake passport created a huge problem for me. That was my fault and the spotter couldn't be blamed for this mistake. Although my real name wasn't on the passport, my picture was used. This meant I'd be easily identified.

Marco explained that because I'd not returned to the bank for the drafts, they might run checks on my passport with more detailed scrutiny. If they did that they would be certain to find out my passport was a fake, which had the potential to fuck up the bearer bonds job. I couldn't afford for this to happen and had to do something quick.

The bank would easily put two and two together and their next call would undoubtedly be to the police. Through facial recognition the police could easily find me. What an idiot I'd been, why didn't I think about getting the passport back before leaving the bank?!

No-one could save me from this situation, it was down to me to fix it. Marco was sympathetic, but his priority was the London Boys, not me. I was on my own and knew it.

"You could go back to the bank and get the passport" Marco stated after a long silence.

I looked at him, feeling a sense of déjà vu. We'd already had this conversation and it was agreed that it would be too dangerous to go back without knowing what the situation was inside the bank. We were going around in circles.

"Do you think it will be as simple as it sounds?" I asked.

Without even answering my question, Marco was straight back on the phone, calling teller number three. He was on the phone for a couple of minutes before hanging up.

"It's safe to go back to the bank. That's if you've still got the balls," he said looking right at me with a smug smile.

He was testing me. Not wanting to fall into his trap, but also not wanting to look like I was backing out either, I sat and thought for a moment. Maybe it would be as easy as he made it sound. All that had to be done was convince the manager that the accident that the spotter had described was the truth. My story could be that I'd left to take my wife to the hospital and organise to have my car fixed. Surely that would be easy enough. There was no other choice but to risk it. The bank had my passport and if the police got hold of it, I'd be fucked anyway.

Without any more thought I dialed the banks number and asked to speak to the manager. Once he was on the other end of the phone, taking a deep breath, I confidently told him my bullshit story. It worked, he appeared to believe my lies and we arranged an appointment for me to go back into the bank. When the phone went dead, doubt about whether this was the right move or not started to creep in. What if he didn't really believe me and he too was lying. This could be a ploy to get me back into the bank for the police to be waiting for me! What if he'd already checked my documents and found out that I wasn't really Mr. Whitehouse, but some chancer trying to make fast cash? My head was buzzing with thoughts but there was no other way. I had to go back.

CHAPTER 34
Back in the Game

Big Marco agreed that this was my best option. It was best for him too because if I managed to convince the manager at the bank and pull this off, I'd be returning with 100 grand. No-one was going to say no to that.

Marco arranged a car for us. Our first stop was the shops. After binning my hat and jacket when doing a runner from the bank earlier, I needed to buy new ones.

Everything was riding on me and I'd be on my own this time, which was my preferred way of working. There was no need to rely on anyone apart from myself and there wasn't the chance for another spotter to fuck things up this time.

After the shops we headed straight to the bank. There was no need to waste any more time. The sooner we got there the sooner it would be over. As we pulled up at the at the bank I jumped out of the car, finding myself questioning my decision once more, feeling as though fate was constantly being tempted and it was only a matter of time before fate smacked me in the face. I stood outside the car for a minute, taking my time to get everything straight in my mind.

Taking a deep breath, I began walking towards the bank. It was time to fix the damage that had been done. It was only a few steps to the front door of the bank. After repeating to myself that this was going to be a piece of piss, there was a new-found confidence in me.

I took the escalator; the bank was busier than it had been earlier, but it never fazed me. Choosing not to queue at the teller's desk, as I'd done before, I headed directly to the managers office, watching the look of disgust on people's faces as they noticed me.

Once at the door I knocked loudly and walk straight in. The manager was sitting behind his desk with his head buried in paperwork. He remembered me straight away and there was a glint of pity in his eyes. I replayed my made-up story again that I'd told him on the phone, keeping it short and to the point, wanting to be in and out as quickly as possible.

"Is your wife okay?" he asked, genuinely concerned.

I told him that it wasn't anything serious, just a bit of whiplash and she simply needed to rest and try to forget what had happened. After a brief chat he left the office, stating that he wouldn't be too long. He was just going to pick up the banker's drafts. There was an air of calm and no signs of him being anxious. Any nerves that I had before entering the bank quickly disappeared.

It wasn't a long wait, before he returned with the drafts. It was nearly over, and I could finally be done with this fucking job once and for all. The finish line was in sight at last. It felt as though I'd been running around in circles the entire day.

"I just have a couple of forms that you to sign Mr. Whitehouse and then you can get back to your wife," he said with a smile. I briefly look at the forms, scanning over them quickly before signing them. It was goodbye to Mr. Whitehouse after this.

It felt good when the manager handed me the two bankers drafts, but they were not my priority at that moment. As soon as my passport was firmly in my grasp, that's when I felt the relief. A huge weight was lifted from my shoulders. I'd been lucky to get away with it this time. If I'd only been able to walk out of the bank with my passport, that would have been a good enough result for me. It was over, and I was done. My identity was safe, and I'd not been compromised.

Leaving the bank, I headed directly to Kings Cross Station again. There was no crazy spotter around this time. The way it should have been done in the first place.

Big Marco was still at the pub where we had agreed to meet.

Walking through the doors of the pub I could see his smile beaming from across the bar. I'm sure he thought I'd not make it back.

"How did it go man?" he asked.

Without saying a word, I simply handed him the envelope containing the drafts.

"Is this what I think it is?" he asked with excitement, holding the envelope, looking at me.

"Open it!" I said calmly.

He opened the envelope and looked inside. Without saying anything, he stretched out his hand in my direction, giving me the biggest handshake. He was a strong man and he shook my hand with such force it felt as if he could pull my arm out of its socket.

"You have some balls on you wee Mikey," he laughed, letting go of my hand. He was thoroughly impressed, and this was a great result for both of us. I'd managed to secure their money and all without compromising my identity. In reflection, yes, I'd made 5k that day, which may have looked like easy money from the outside. But I questioned whether the risks taken to earn it were worth it!

After my shit day, I decided to take a short break from business but remain in London, waiting. The job remained at the back of my mind for a while even though it was over. Forgetting about the fuck up and moving on to other things was difficult but it had happened, and it couldn't be changed.

My thoughts turned to the spotter from time to time. I'd no idea what the fuck happened to him and didn't dare to ask Marco what the London Boys did to him. Big Marco and I became friends and we remained in touch even although the bank job was over. We worked on other plans together, but that's a story for another day.

After taking a break, it was time to meet up with the London Boys again, to discuss our next move with the bonds. Meeting with them wasn't ever something I looked forward to but was more of a necessity.

Although we ended up with the banker's drafts, Marco and I agreed that it would be best to keep what happened that day in the bank between ourselves and that the London Boys didn't need to know all the details.

Walking into the hotel where I'd arrange to meet the London Boys, the bad feeling in the pit of my stomach started as it always did but reminding myself that they needed me more than ever now was enough to help me settle down. I'd finished a couple of successful jobs for them now and their confidence in me to pull off the job with the bonds must be at an all-time high.

Being very distinctive characters, they were easily spotted standing at the bar in the hotel. They looked at each other and began laughing the moment they saw me.

"Well that was a shitty job you had with Big Marco?" One said smugly.

I took the fact that they were laughing as a positive sign and joined them in their laughter.

"Tell me about it! I've had better days," I joked, before continuing to explain that the spotter was a fucking idiot who almost blew the deal but chose not to say much more about what happened after that.

"Well you have a huge fan in Big Marco. He has been on the phone telling us how fucking amazing you are", one of them said sarcastically.

"Yeah, and you know how fucking amazing", I thought to myself, sitting down and ordering a whisky.

CHAPTER 35
Unpredictability

Surprisingly the London Boys were sound with me, which was a bonus. It could have been a hell of a lot worse. They could have easily put some of the blame on me for the mistakes that had been made with the dormant accounts. To be fair we got the job done in the end, so that was a result. I would have to buy Marco a drink for having my back.

This is a strange game and you can never really know what's going on in anyone's mind. The main thing was they were praising me for the job that I'd done so it was all good. I wondered what it would be like to get into the minds of the London Boys for just a minute so that I could see exactly what they were thinking. How many times in life do we say that? The fact is, regardless of what they were thinking, they fucking need me now.

I'm too deep in this shit to change direction. The spotter was brought in to handle the bank deal solely to ensure that I wasn't compromised. He took a huge risk during the job to ensure that my identity remained anonymous which proved how important I'd become to them. Even if his actions nearly fucked the whole plan up! I'd been the only one that had the balls to take the bonds. For that fact alone, they would keep me around. With that thought at the back of my mind it put me back on track. Mike Carr was the man that was going to make everybody rich! I'd been the only one willing to take a risk that nobody else would. They had a lot of connections in the underworld who could have helped but it was me that was going to make something of the opportunities I'd been given.

I was the key that would open the door to making millions of pounds. A commodity that the London Boys had invested in. They'd put a lot of time, money and trust in me, but now their frustrations were mounting as all they could do was wait for their return. I'd proved that I had the balls to get the job done the minute I'd taken the bonds from the Boss Man.

I'd earnt their respect and the way they treated me was different in comparison to the others in the team. I'd become their most valuable asset for the task at hand and results needed to be delivered. The possibility of the job falling apart was never a thought in my mind because if that happened the tables would turn on me very quickly.

They trusted that I'd not cheat them out of their money and that I'd keep to my end of the deal, delivering what I'd promised. I was a man of honour, one who would keep his word and they could see that in me. My resilience is what I think they admired the most. Getting a knock never kept me down and I'd always come back fighting harder.

Once conversation about the dormant accounts had been dealt with, we moved onto the bigger deal at hand, the bearer bonds. Things were moving slowly, but that was expected. We had to ensure that everything was considered as there was no room for fuck ups. We had a detailed conversation about what the next stages of the plan were, ensuring that we were all on the same page.

It was agreed that the best move for me now that the dormant accounts job was over, would be to head back to Istanbul the following day. My flight had already been booked. It would be good to get away from the London Boys and the pressure they put me under and back to Goker, where life was much calmer, and I would be around my Turkish family.

Walking away from the meeting, I felt done in, mentally and physically. The lifestyle I'd been living over the past few months was taking its toll. I headed to my hotel room at the airport that the London Boys had also organised and took some time to look back, reflecting on everything that had happened up to this point.

Some space away from it all for a while was exactly what was needed. It's true that solitude is something that should be relished, but being alone creates room for overthinking, and I'm a master of that. As I lay on my bed staring at the ceiling of my room, my mind wouldn't stop racing. Unable to settle, I got up from the bed and walked towards the mirror hanging on the wall. I stood looking at my reflection staring back at me, thinking to myself

"This is your time, time to smash this job and get everything you had ever wanted."

I'd started this journey as an amateur and had grown into a pro. In the beginning, as a wee hard man from Whitfield, no-one would have believed it if I'd told them where I'd been in the last couple of months. If someone had told me a few months previous that this is the world that I'd be part of at this point in my life I'd never have believed them either. Involved in the real gangster world, traversing countries, part of a huge international crime involving bearer bonds!

CHAPTER 36
Honour

What is it that they say about a new day? Well, I was
fucking buzzing waking up the next day, believing I could take
on the world. Starting the morning with an espresso, nothing
was going to bring me down from the high I'd woken up on.
Today it was time to head back to Istanbul; a new day, a new
start, a new dawn and it felt so good.

My flight to Istanbul was stress free and nothing could dampen
my mood. Even the crying babies around me didn't piss me off
as much as they usually did. I didn't know what to expect once
I'd arrived, but whatever it was I'd be ready to face it head on.
Ataturk airport was busy when we landed. Having to wait for
the guys to pick me up I spent my time people watching.
Getting lost in a world of wondering what they were at the
airport for; it was a good distraction.

Goker arrived in the Range Rover, which was odd because he
usually picked me up in the old Clio to keep a low profile. They
were very excited to see me, more excited than I'd seen them
before. Goker's brother was also in the car today. It had been
a while since I'd seen him last. He spoke better English than
Goker, which made it easier for us to have a conversation. On
the car journey, I began to wonder why things were different
and what was going on.

"You are going to meet a very important man today Mike,"
Goker stated. It was as if he could read my mind.

I asked him if he had anything to do with the bonds, but he
shook his head.

"For the next two days there will be no talk about the bonds," he said, whilst smiling.

I was confused about what was happening but was happy that I'd not have to think about the bonds for the next few days. This would be my first time to chill properly for a long while. It was a scorcher of a day and the sun was splitting the sky. We drove to a little back street, just off Taksim Square. When the car stopped at our destination, the guys jumped out and shouted for me to follow. We walked into a small shop that was bursting at the seams with immaculate men's wear, where they introduced me to an older gentleman.

"Meet Atuk, he is the best tailor in the whole of Turkey," Goker stated with pride, as he shook Atuk's hand.

"We have come here today to get you your very own suit, my friend" said Goker.

I had never owned a tailormade suit before, and the thought of having my own made me feel important.

Atuk shook my hand and welcomed me to his shop before showing me to the fitting room, just off to the side of the shop floor, where he began to take my measurements. He was very meticulous and took his work seriously. As he worked, my curiosity was getting the better of me, so I asked him what the suit was for. He was in on the secret and told me to wait, all would become apparent.

Once Atuk had finished and they had discussed all the finer details in Turkish, it was agreed that we would return to the shop to collect the suit the next morning. Once we'd collected the suit we'd head off to another destination, I had no idea where we were going. They were enjoying the secrecy and refused to tell me the location. It was frustrating not knowing, but I'd need to wait until the next day to find out.

That night, we stayed in Goker's flat, just off the Square, which would ease the movements for the next day. We spent a quiet and non-eventful day chatting and relaxing, but that is exactly what I needed. My thoughts continued to wonder about why I needed a tailored suit. It must have been for something important. A suit so expensive wasn't going to be for just hanging out with the guys.

The next day we returned to the shop where Atuk was waiting patiently for us. He ushered me to the fitting room, where my very own suit was hanging. Once dressed, I stood smiling at myself in the long mirror, at how smart I looked. It was made from luxurious light grey fabric and the stitching was flawless. Atuk had done an outstanding job and had tailored it to perfection. Goker and the guys cheered and clapped in approval when they saw me. After thanked Atuk, it was time to go. Goker was still being very tight lipped about where we were going as we climbed into the car, which made me question what they had planned for me. It did cross my mind for a second that maybe they had planned a wedding ceremony. I wouldn't have put it past them!

We drove off, out of the city centre to a lavish hotel. It was only a short journey and as we arrived, I could see around twenty gentlemen lined up at the entrance to the hotel, each of them dressed in the same suits. I guessed that they were waiting for us.

"Please don't tell me that you've got me a wife in there," I said, whilst trying not to smile.

"Brother this is more important than any marriage," Goker replied, half laughing.

Once in the hotel we entered a huge ballroom. The high ceilings were stunningly decorative, and a huge crystal chandelier hung in the centre. The room was dripping in gold and filled with finely dressed people. At the back of the ballroom there was a stage which had three throne-like chairs sitting grandly on top of it. Goker guided me through the crowd and up onto the stage where he asked me to take the centre seat, whilst he sat beside me.

"Very few westerners have had the privilege of being where you are today!" he stated.

I still didn't understand what was going on but gave him a smile and remained quiet.

"Today we are going to welcome you into the Brotherhood," he added proudly.

I was taken aback, I'd heard them talking about the Brotherhood so many times before and knew how very important it was to them. They considered anyone that was part of the Brotherhood as family. Today they were making me part of their family. It was an honour that I truly did not expect. Goker went on to explain that only the head of the family could bestow such an honour and I'd need to follow his lead when he arrived. I promised not to let him down, as I wondered why he had chosen me.

An old, but strong looking man walked up onto the stage. The whole room stood up as a mark of respect for him. The ceremony, a secret family tradition, details of which were never to be divulged, lasted half an hour. I was bound not to disclose the proceedings and swore I'd never dishonour them by speaking about the ceremony.

During the ceremony, the head of the family handed me a plaque containing the family coat of arms, which had an inscription on it,

"You are now part of the Brotherhood and will be protected wherever you may dwell on this land, throughout the world."

"Welcome to the family my brother," he said placing his hand on my shoulder.

I felt tears welling in my eyes and was completely honoured and proud. This was a gesture that I'd never expected.

A barbeque was their family tradition to bring everyone together, so it only seemed fitting that after the ceremony this is how we celebrated. There must have been over three hundred people present when it was time to serve the food. I was continuously hugged by members of the Brotherhood as we enjoyed our lavish meal.

The head of the family didn't stay for long. He did attend, which showed that he respected me. It was such a great honour. Goker took me aside and explained that it was the strength of our friendship that had encouraged him to request that I become part of the Brotherhood. He added that he'd seen the real me, a man of loyalty with no fear, willing to help others. He also went on to explain that with any Brotherhood, there were rules that needed to be adhered to.

"We are an army surrounding you. You are a man that can fight his own battles but know that if you're at a point in life where you cannot, then we will be there for you."

I understood Goker's words to mean that the Brotherhood would be there in the darkest of situations and that I should never misuse the family's trust or loyalty to me.

CHAPTER 37
A Night to Remember

We had an amazing night celebrating, eating, and drinking Raki. I wanted to tell everyone back home about the celebrations and the great honour that had be given to me, but that wasn't possible. I respected the family and the Brotherhood and would never disrespect them by divulging their family secret. It was a surreal day, surrounded by so many people, yet I'd never felt so lonely.

The party continued as a group of us headed back to the villa. "So, what have you guys got planned for tonight?" I asked. They were the life of the party and there was never a dull moment with them around, so I expected them to have something up their sleeve.

They looked at each other and started grinning. One of them told me that it was meant to be a surprise, but I pestered them until they finally gave in and told me what the plan was.

"It is party time in Istanbul for you tonight Mike," they told me. A VIP, guest only, party had been organised in my honour. They went on to explain that they had invited a few of my friends over from Kyrenia. After the days I'd just endured, I needed to have a good time and a laugh. These guys were my friends and knowing that they had put in so much effort just to make me feel good, made me feel on top of the world.

"Oh, by the way Lilly has been asking for you." one of them said whilst laughing. Everyone else in the car quickly joined in the joke.

"For the last two days all she has been asking is when you would be coming back with her passport?" He continued, and even more laughter erupted.

Lilly was a hot Russian girl who worked in one of the restaurants. She never wore any jewellery and wore minimal make up, but she was a stunner and totally fancied me. They said that she was just trying to get a passport from me, but I convinced myself she genuinely liked me. She was an absolute delight to be around, friendly, and you would always find her laughing. She would go out of her way to help anyone and we'd become friends during my numerous trips to Istanbul. Whatever the guys were insinuating about Lilly, I knew the truth, but laughed with them and joined in on their joke.

Being back in Istanbul, I felt at ease and could let loose without fear of being pulled up for it. These moments were priceless. I was with guys that could be trusted and who looked out for me. On the plus side, it was always good to see Lilly, but feelings of guilt crept in because Jenna and I had been drifting further apart.

When we got to the villa, it was the aroma from the food that hit me first, such a welcoming smell. We headed directly to the back yard, where people had already started partying without us.

Sancar loved cooking, so when I saw him at the barbeque it didn't surprise me. His passion for cooking is something that you wouldn't expect from him. Gangsters and cooking weren't stereotypical that's for sure. He had been slaving away at the barbeque all day. The grill was something that every man loved to work, and he'd perfected the art. Being a great host, he'd even marinated the beef and chicken the night before. The banquet he'd prepared was amazing. There were tables laden with delicious food in the yard.

Sancar and Goker had a friendly rivalry when it came to cooking, and it was funny to watch them compete, to see who could make the best barbeque. On this occasion, Goker had stood aside and given the honour to Sancar, well that's how he perceived it anyway. For them it was an honour to be the chef.

174

In all honesty, if I'd to choose a winner between them both, I genuinely couldn't. They were amazing chefs and the food they served was to die for.

Sancar remained at the barbeque grill next to the pool, when I walked into the yard. He was wearing his chef's hat, and nothing was going to take his attention away from what he was cooking. Picking up a drink, I walked around to say hi to everyone.

As I looked up after taking a sip of my drink there he was, larger than life, my Turkish brother Goker. We embraced each other like true brothers, before sitting down to chat like there was no-one else in the yard. After chatting for a while, he said to me

"Go and mingle with your guests, we will chat more later."

Standing up, I paused to look around for a second to take everything in.

"This is the fucking life!" I thought to myself.

It was so good to see all my friends there, it made me happy, something I'd not been for a while. There were some new faces that I didn't recognise. In my life back in Dundee I could only have imagined experiencing something like this. It wasn't about the barbeque but the atmosphere. Nothing in Dundee could compare to this, it truly was a different world. No matter how many times I was exposed to this world, there was always something new that I'd never seen before.

We were all sitting by the pool in the sweltering heat; the villa was luxurious; there was even a big screen TV by the pool. This was a great place to forget about the world for a second. The TV was playing music videos, people were dancing, eating and laughing. Out of nowhere Sancar walked right up to TV to change the channel. It made me laugh out loud when he put their favourite TV program on. People started to boo him jokingly.

"It's only for half an hour, then I'll put the music back on!", he shouted back at them.

Their taste in TV programs was shit and they never deviated

from what they loved watching. Their favourite show was about the Turkish mafia. They tried to convince me that I'd learn to love it too, but it wasn't happening. They were living the mafia lifestyle already and it didn't make sense to me why they were interested in watching others live the same lifestyle as they did. I sat and watched with them for a few minutes but couldn't take it any longer.

"This is shit!" I laughed.

"Anyone want another drink?" I asked, standing up to go and get another, leaving the guys to enjoy their show.

This party is exactly what was needed; it was a completely laid-back day. We talked about nothing in particular and no-one mentioned the bearer bonds. We drank, ate and had a good time. I flirted with a couple of girls as music was playing, and even tried to dance although it's not my strong point. Alcohol has a funny way of making you think that you can do anything, it made me think I was fucking Patrick Swayze. A couple of the girls were taking a dip in the pool and some of the guys decided to join them.

I didn't want the night to end. Nights like this were the best because they helped me forget about my responsibilities, even if it was just for a while. Money didn't take a breath, so neither could we. Tomorrow would bring me back to reality, but tonight I was taking a well-deserved break from it and was going to enjoy myself.

We stayed up partying until the early hours of the morning. We ate so much, but hardly even made a dent in the banquet Sancar had prepared for us. It was brilliant, all of us together again. I could see it in the guy's faces that they needed this escape just as much as me.

It's every mans' dream to wake up with beautiful women surrounding him. Well sometimes dreams do come true and that's exactly how I woke up the next morning. Opening my eyes, I was greeted by a beautiful oriental girl and a stunning Turkish girl, naked, entangled into me. Today was going to be a good day, no-one could ruin this for me. I woke up with a sheepish smile on my face remembering how we'd ended up there. The previous night was one for the books and one the guys and I'd be talking about for a while. Did they have as much fun as me?

I left the girls in bed, they stirred, but covered themselves up and went back to sleep. Wishing I could have stayed in bed with them for the whole day, I headed to take a shower to help get rid of my hangover, standing under the water for ages just letting it beat down on my head, replaying the events of the night before. It was time to get ready to tackle the day ahead and all it had in store for me.

CHAPTER 38
Strategically Planned

I was spending a lot of time in Turkey and needed to learn more Turkish. I knew enough to get by but wanted to be part of the conversation and not feel like an outsider. The guys tried to include me in their chat, but sometimes they would revert to speaking their native language for ease. It didn't happen often but when it did, I wished that I knew what they were saying and hated sitting confused, wanting to be in the thick of it.

I'd bought a little notebook to help me with my desire to speak Turkish. Whilst learning, the pronounciation was the tough part for me, especially with my strong Scottish accent. I sounded funny and didn't quite have it right, but at least I was trying. I'd learnt most of my Turkish so far from watching their shit TV shows and I'd also picked up a few words from chatting with the other guys.

It was now time to get back to the grind stone. We had planned a meeting in the lounge area of the villa. Last night had been a good break and with it brought fresh ideas about how best to move forward with our plan for the bearer bonds. All work and no play truly wasn't our way of doing things. My overthinking had stopped for a while and I was ready to suggest ideas, without questioning them. My mind was clear, well that was apart from the guilt I felt about the previous night.

We were served breakfast in the lounge. Most of us were nursing hangovers and not everyone arrived on time for the meeting. We didn't have a heavy work load that day and we called it a paperwork day, which we laughed about. I was expected to head out to pick up a passport, with a false identity of course, and then go to the bank to start the process of legitimising the fake companies. We had reached a pinnacle point in our plan and this made everything real. We were really going to do this and there was no turning back.

I played out the day in my mind so that I'd everything clear. Things needed to go my way today, without any issues. My cover story was finalised. I was a broker of foreign currency and a bond broker. This would be how I'd present myself to the bank. My appearance wasn't that of a broker, but I'd need to act like one and sell myself otherwise this would be a none starter. I'd confidence in myself to manoeuvre my way through anything. Today was only about setting up a bank account and there was no real heavy shit. It would be a piece of piss even with a hangover.

Everyone had a role to play but mine was crucial. I was the face that would be seen, and it was my ass on the line if anything went tits up. This job was more organised than the dormant accounts; we'd sat at the table planning the whole operation meticulously without missing a single detail. We discussed the strengths of foreign currency and bond brokerage. My knowledge needed to be detailed about my new career so that I'd be believable if questioned. Processing all this information in a short time was paramount. There was no question about what we needed to gain from our relationship with the bank.

We weren't leaving anything to chance this time and we went over the plan again and again. I loved working with these guys because of their professionalism. Goker always led the way and he was the one guy that could be truly trusted.

Going through all the possible scenarios and outcomes was a repetitive process, which would have annoyed me on any other occasion, but this was different. I was putting my life on the line for this and ensuring that nothing was left to chance was vital. We were all on the same page when it came to pursuing total perfection.

This plan was well thought out, which made me confident that it would run smoothly. I tried to erase the memories of what had happened with the spotter. There would not be a repeat of that this time, these guys didn't even have a spotter they trusted and believed in me hugely.

Once we were certain that the plan was foolproof, we agreed that we would go ahead with it the next day. We would meet once more in the morning, just to be certain every possibility had been considered. The bank job had taught me a valuable lesson, and nothing would be lost in translation this time. This wasn't meant to be a risky part of the job, but in this world, everything had to be perceived as a risk. Imagine if we headed to pick up the passport and on that exact day the police decided to raid the place. You can never be sure of what each day will bring, that is why we had to put measures in place to ensure that if anything were to go tits up, we had a chance to escape.

CHAPTER 39
Worlds Apart

The first step was to sort out the passport; there was a guy in place that could organise this discreetly. Discretion was crucial for this job, there was no room for error and the passport had to be flawless. I'd no idea who was responsible for sorting it out but was confident that the guys had this area sewn up and no-one would say a word about what we were up to.

Everything was organised, making it easier for us to get access to all the information we needed. Money had been spent on this deal, a lot of money I assumed. This was way out of my league especially when it came to the money; if I'd been doing this myself, the job would never have even got started. Ishvara and Goker were to thank for getting us this far.

I expected that since the guy finalising the passport worked for high-end clients, the pick-up location would be somewhere fancy and inconspicuous but fuck me I'd got that wrong! When we arrived, I couldn't believe it, we were going into a local kebab shop.

It was only me who was to go in, for obvious reasons. I'd been given a code so that the guy in the shop could identify why I'd come. This place was a good cover and I'd never have suspected it to be anything other than a kebab shop. I walked slowly to the front door. The kebab shop was cover for the real business, which was documentation forgery. I'd been given specific instructions about where exactly to go, and everything was just how it was explained.

"Hey, can I get a chicken kebab with a touch of brown sauce?" I asked.

The man behind the counter looked up and gave me a little wink before directing me straight to the basement.

The place was filthy and there was no way I'd buy food from this shithole. Walking down to the basement, the smell was enough to make me wretch. The heat was unbearable, and it was difficult to walk without standing on the crap and boxes of vegetables that were scattered all over the floor. I walked past the freezer, then through a tiny door as instructed. This place was nothing like I'd imagined, but that was the thing about the underground world, you never knew what to expect.

It was as if I'd walked into a different world. There was a huge 12ft oak table with expensive leather backed chairs tucked in neatly around it. Coming through the front door I'd found myself in a rundown kebab shop, and now just down the stairs, into another room, I was in what seemed to be a posh board room. The guy running this place was a genius. No-one would have ever expected this place to be down here.

Looking around I was amazed by the space I'd walked into. It was small, but the transformation was stunning. The location didn't really matter to me, it was what I'd come for that was important. It was good to be out of the stinking kebab shop though. My thoughts began to drift as I imagined the kinds of people that had been down here previously. One thing was for sure, this was a big business that made a lot of money. The money that had gone into creating this place was evident.

I wasn't entirely sure what it took to make counterfeit documents, but the place was full of high-tech equipment; laser printers, laptops, cutting tables the lot. Whatever was needed I was certain they would be able to produce it in here.

I was grateful that the room had air conditioning and was already sweating even though the walk through the basement was very short. It was ridiculously hot down here. There was only one guy in the room, so it seemed obvious to approach him. He stared straight through me and had an eerie look about him. Without saying anything he handed me a document, which I took my time to look over. I started checking that all the details were accurate. Once satisfied that everything was in order, I handed him back the document, which he put down on the table before telling me to come back for the passport in an hour. I couldn't help feeling pissed off that the passport wasn't ready but had to be patient. This was a lengthy process and one that we had to get right.

What was I going to do to pass the time waiting for the passport? I'd been driven to the location by Goker, but he had headed somewhere else to deal with other matters pertaining to the bonds. We'd planned to meet at a different location to pick up the company documents, agreeing that getting the company documents made in a different place was a safer option. It would be too easy for the authorities to trace if all the documents were created in the same place. Spreading the work around to would ensure that if things ever went tits up, it would take time for the police to figure out who was involved. We needed to cover our tracks, making it harder for us to be identified, or should I say me!

Everything we were working on had to appear legitimate and if the documents were to be scrutinised, we had to ensure that the authorities wouldn't find any indication that they were fake. The system in Turkey was well known and it was a fact that a notary needed to stamp and verify all documents. Of course, we had one on our side, everyone has a price, and money can buy a lot in the underworld.

I walked out of the basement and headed to the street not knowing where to go. I wandered around for an hour to pass time before picking up the passport and going to meet Goker. Solitude wasn't a great place for me at this point, the moment I was alone my mind would always begin racing with thoughts. My life had changed drastically. Not one thing at a time either, everything had changed all at once. I'd been so busy, there hadn't been a lot of thinking time but now, wandering the streets, I was doing plenty of it.

The feeling of control that I'd had in my life before was lost. Situations were happening around me and there was no other option but to go with the flow. Getting into this life was my way of doing something different and escaping routine, but what would it take for me to be content?

In the last few months, my life had been a rollercoaster that had taken me from the ordinary to shit crazy. The ride had been unbelievable. The experiences I'd had so far were flashing before my eyes and it felt like a daze. I thought long and hard about whether I'd change where I was now or whether I'd be willing to go back to my old life. There was money in my pocket and I was living in a luxury villa. Things were good for me, apart from all the threats to my life that is. Life could be enjoyable the way it was right now, I just needed to adopt a fuck it attitude.

The heat in the street was unbearable and after checking my watch it was time for me to go back to the kebab shop.

I walked straight down to the basement and into the office. My passport was ready, and as soon as it was in my hand, I began scrutinising it for myself, checking that it looked legitimate. It was well made and certainly looked like the real deal to me. He'd followed our specifications to the letter and all the details were exactly as we'd asked. The passport was a huge part of the plan, so it was a weight off my shoulders having it in my hand. Not wanting to hang around, after thanking the guy who'd produced the passport, I went back to meet Goker.

CHAPTER 40
The Face of the Business

Next on the agenda was picking up the company documents. This was probably one of the simplest parts of the plan, nothing elaborate. We needed documents to make our business look legitimate. They needed to be backdated so that it appeared we had been trading for a while. We needed to show a history of being a reputable brokerage firm that was involved in foreign currency exchange, bond brokerage, property purchases and all the usual business that would be expected. A portfolio like this would ensure our company seemed legitimate to the bank. Our focus was the bonds, and this would be the perfect way to set everything up. Steve was to thank for coming up with the idea.

I'd been to meet the guys organising the portfolio. It was a lengthy process waiting for them, but we knew they wouldn't disappoint. The details about what criteria they had used to get the company details in order were unknown to me. All they had asked in the beginning were certain specifications, and they would sort out the rest from there.

I was excited when we were heading to meet them. There was a sexy girl who worked in the office and seeing her again would perk my day up a little. It was only a short drive, so I didn't have to wait very long to see her and sure enough she was the first person to welcome us when we walked in. Looking hotter than ever today, dressed in a short black skirt with her top unbuttoned enough for me to be able to see her amazingly pert boobs. While I waited for the documents, we flirted with each other. I obviously still had my charm because all she did was laugh as she twirled her hair around her fingers.

We weren't there for long, which disappointed me because I was enjoying the attention she was giving me. I had to go back to the solicitors to pick up some other documents from them. I'd been running about all day and still wasn't finished yet.

It was time to meet up with Goker again to execute the next stage of the plan. On the way to meet him, I don't know why but a bad feeling began in the pit of my stomach. We had all the documents that we needed. Everything else that I'd done prior to this point was preparation. The next stage in the plan was crucial. If I failed at this point, then the whole operation would fall apart. There was no way I could let that happen, everything was riding on me.

Goker was quiet, which was unusual for him. Once he had double checked I'd all the documents that we needed, he seemed to drift away with his own thoughts. We were both nervous and the tension could be felt in the car. This was the make or break part of our plan. Without the high-end bank account set up, we were fucked and there would be no way forward for us.

I was going in alone to the meeting at the bank, but that didn't concern me, it was just the way I liked it. If anything went wrong in the bank, I'd have no spotter or back up.

We pulled up outside the bank and it was show time.

Leaving the car, I faintly heard Goker wish me good luck. I could hear my heart beating loudly in my chest, it was so loud it was deafening. Approaching the bank, the beating of my heart was accompanied by a strange pain in my chest and my collar began to feel tight.

There was a huge, snarling guard at the entrance to the bank. I clocked straight away that he had a gun, but that didn't faze me. The playful part of me wanted to ask him what type it was, thinking to myself that maybe I should start to carry a gun of my own, just in case.

Getting closer to the entrance, glancing back over my shoulder there was no-one there to tell me to go in or turn back, this was all down to me now. The guard was courteous and said good morning to me. He spoke in broken English, but it was his gesture that mattered. My emotions had been all over the place in the car, but the guard simply saying good morning, as if it were just a normal day and I was just any other person using the bank that day, helped me settle.; reminding myself of the job I'd come here to do and was going to do it to perfection, the way we had meticulously planned.

"Morning mate, how's your day been so far?" I asked the guard, in reply to his greeting.

His response was short, but I understood it most likely because he was at work and couldn't be arsed to chat with every customer. My head was now in the game. Passing security, I headed to the reception, with my head held high. All that was left to do was convince the bank that I was the person on the passport in my pocket. I'd done it before but was under no illusion that the stakes were higher this time.

At the lobby I took a few minutes to compose myself before walking over to the customer service desk. I was smartly dressed, with the look of an important business man, but that wouldn't matter if my chat couldn't cut it. Looking confident and talking like I knew my shit was most important. There was no room for any mistakes, my life was at risk for this.

"Do you speak English?" I asked the lady at reception. Not wanting to struggle to get by with the little Turkish I spoke.

"Yes sir, what can I do for you?" she answered politely.

After explaining I'd an appointment, she asked me for my name. For a split second I almost gave her my real name, but luckily, I stopped myself before messing up the whole operation. She directed me to the branch manager. The closer I got to his office, the greater my belief in myself became. No matter how much I'd dressed for the occasion, my appearance was nothing like a broker, but my knowledge had to convince the manager that I was a reputable broker. You needed to have balls of steel to get through business in this world and my confidence in being able to pull this off didn't falter.

I'd been through the plan meticulously, cramming all the details. I wasn't going to mess up by forgetting minor details. With all the facts and adding a bit of charm, I was going to put my salesman hat on and convince the Manager to go with my proposal.

Standing at the manager's door, I rehearsed the plan one final time knowing I'd be able to handle whatever was thrown at me. He was expecting me; the appointment had already been pre-arranged, but I'd still need to be on my toes and not lower my guard, even for a second, until it was a done deal.

A lot was riding on my success and the expectation was for me to leave the bank with the account set up. If things went wrong, the simple fact was what we were doing was fraud, with a minimum of 15 years in jail. Fifteen years was a life time, so whatever happened I needed to get the job done and get out without raising any suspicion.

The bank was so hot, and the pressure was rising. I could feel sweat dripping down my back and wanted this to be over so that I could get out of there. The time for thinking was over and it was time to get on with the meeting. What is the worst that could happen? Time for cocky confident Mike.

CHAPTER 41
Easy Money

I walked into the office. There was a short, fat, Bank Manager sat slumped in his chair behind a huge desk. Our appointment had been pre-arranged, so he greeted me by name when he saw me. Last week I'd been Mr. Whitehouse, this week it was time to be somebody different. I had to be on the ball to keep up with all these new identities and couldn't afford to make a mistake. He offered me a seat across the table from him.

"Would you like something to drink Sir?" he asked politely.

"Some chi would be great" I replied.

"Great I'll just get my assistant to bring some through," he said, walking towards the door and summoning her with a click of his fingers.

On the way back to his seat, he took the business documents from me to check that everything was in order, whilst remaining very attentive towards me. He knew how to multitask, looking at the documents, but making sure he never ignored me.

I felt like royalty; he kept asking if there was anything he could do for me. It was a good feeling being treated as though I was important and settled into my role easily, enjoying the attention. The more attentive he became, the more I believed this was going to be a walk in the park. It was his job to make new clients feel good, especially those who would bring big money to the bank. With my new persona, that is exactly what I promised to bring, or so he thought. He'd have brought me anything I'd asked for at that moment because he knew I'd make a lot of money for the bank from this transaction. Looking over the documents, he asked me a couple of questions. I answered every one of them with confidence and was on point with every answer. The knowledge I'd gained over the last few months about bonds was certainly being put to good use. After his questions, he took a couple of seconds to look at the documents in silence. I felt a single bead of sweat run down my spine.

"The intention is to deposit bearer bonds into the bank, which would obviously have added advantage to you," I explained. When he realised the value of the bonds, I could see his eyes light up as I continued to explain that because bonds were discreet, his high-end clients would appreciate this kind of business.

"It is a risky affair." he stated.

"No-one has ever made any money by being careful." I replied. He continued to ask many more questions, but I was ready with the answers. Giving him comprehensive insight into the world of bearer bonds, which I could see by his reaction, he appreciated. Being very knowledgeable was key and using bank jargon was going to win him over. He really knew his stuff and there was no way to bluff my way through. Listening to myself, even I thought I sounded very convincing. If it was me on the other side of the table, I'd have trusted everything that came out of my mouth. The bank was just another pawn in this game of chess, which I was planning to win, no matter what it took.

It was my thought that he would give me an answer there and then as to whether he was authorising the account, but that was me being too ambitious. I'd spent an hour in the bank, which to be fair wasn't very long considering the number of questions that were asked, but he wasn't prepared to commit yet. That was until he had carried out his diligence on all the documentation.

Frustrated that there would be no answer today, I was grateful that our meeting hadn't been a waste of time and could see that I'd peaked his interest.

"You have given me a lot to think about. Let me get back to you in ten days with my answer," he said, standing up to shake my hand.

I walked out of the managers office feeling as though the meeting had gone better than expected and was chuffed with myself. My gut feeling was that things would turn out the way they were planned. I'd done everything I could have, now it was time to be patient until he got back to me. The plan was coming together, and it was an amazing feeling. The account was going to be opened, I was sure of that, meaning one of our biggest hurdles would be complete.

Goker was there to pick me up after my meeting. We headed back to the villa to brief everyone else about how my visit to the bank had gone. There wasn't much to say at that point and I explained to the guys that we would be expecting word from the bank by the end of the week, assuring them that the bank was interested in what we had to offer, and they were convinced that it would be a good investment. The guys shared my enthusiasm, but we all felt the same, we needed results and not just chat.

The company had been registered with the bank and they were very interested in letting us deposit the bearer bonds. If the bank had suggested lodging the bonds there and then, it would have caused alarm bells to ring. It was expected that they would need to do their homework on me and the company before agreeing to anything else. I was confident that we had done enough in creating our fake business portfolio and wasn't concerned on that front. My identity was airtight, and we'd gone to great lengths to ensure that nothing was amiss.

There was no other option but to wait for a response from the bank. Only then would we be able to move on to the next stage. Arrangements had to be made to ensure that there were samples of the bearer bonds available. The bank would need to see proof to be able to authenticate them. I could have confidence in the bonds and after my trip to Germany and was certain that they were not forgeries. I didn't have to worry about dealing with the bank because this would be a 'legitimate' transaction and they wouldn't pull a gun out on me and steal them like some of my other associates.

Simply telling the bank that the bonds were authentic and expect them to take my word for it was never going to happen, they were always going to have to check them for themselves. The bank was well equipped and could easily determine if the bonds were legitimate. I'd learnt a lot about bonds during my research and found out that there were various points on a bearer bond that needed to be checked to confirm its' authenticity. Some bearer bonds were even printed with deliberate errors on them, which would be used as an identifier. Nineteen different points on the bearer bond needed to be authenticated; we would only get the green light once this process had been completed. We were on the verge of receiving the money we all wanted.

Once the authentication process was complete the bank would automatically credit the company account with 300 thousand US dollars instantly. This was just the first step. The step would be to deposit more bonds into the bank, which would then be insured, which would be an added advantage for us. The bank would then become a base for us to work from; we'd be able to use the bonds as collateral for any legitimate business transactions.

The finish line was in sight and we were getting closer to our goal. We had laid all the ground work and there was nothing else to be done from our end. It was a nerve-racking time waiting for a response from the bank, not knowing what the outcome would be.

With no other business to deal with, we now had a few days to chill out. We could relax a little and have some fun waiting for word from the bank. This wouldn't be like the wait in Germany, filled with uncertainties. If the bank hadn't taken the bait, then they would have said outright there and then.

The guys were excited about having some time off, even if it was just for a few days. We had all been working around the clock on this job to ensure that nothing was left to chance and there was no room for error.

I'm not going to lie, the waiting period wasn't easy, and there is only so much Raki one person can drink. Even the partying got tiresome. Anytime the phone rang I expected it to be the bank. Sometimes thoughts of the police bursting into the villa came into my head, but that was me just overthinking as always and wouldn't be a reality.

By day six the wait was really starting to get to me, I felt on edge. I thought it would have got easier, but it hadn't. Not knowing what was happening was driving me crazy.

When the phone rang finally, I knew it was the bank by the caller ID. Holding my breath for a second; they had called earlier than expected! Was this going to be a good thing? Had their quick decision been because they had found discrepancies in the documents? Overthinking was going to be the death of me.

Taking a deep breath, I answered the call. The entire conversation was a blur but what I did hear was that we had the go ahead! The bank agreed that they would be at a loss if they didn't jump at the opportunity to work with our company. I could hardly believe the words I'd heard! We'd fucking pulled it off!

"You understand that we had to do a background check before we could commit to anything and I'm pleased to say that you were given the all clear," the bank manager stated.

"The next step obviously, is for you to bring at least one bearer bond to the bank so that we can authenticate it," he added.

I told him that it would be arranged at my earliest convenience. Things were aligning for me. They believed the company was legitimate and we had now crossed over to a crucial stage. The bond needed to be taken and left at the bank where they would begin the authentication process. After that it was time to make a shit load of money. I was going to be fucking rich beyond belief.

CHAPTER 42
Fatal Attraction

Everyone was buzzing with excitement; we could see the end in sight, but we remained a little cautious and couldn't let our guard down yet. It was one thing to have someone dodgy look at the bonds in Poland, but it was a whole other story to have the authorities looking at them. This was a ticking time bomb for us and we couldn't afford for anything to go wrong at this crucial stage.

It was hard to believe that I was going to hand one of the bonds over to the bank. This was the biggest risk that I'd ever taken in my life and there was no turning back. So close to the end we could touch it. I could taste the money, which gave me the motivation that was needed to forget the risks involved.

The next step was to meet the federal banker in Northern Cyprus, who Goker had introduced me to and who was going to give me inside information concerning the international banking systems. It was agreed that I'd give him three days to organise everything before calling to arrange our meeting.

I couldn't wait to call the London Boys and Ishvara and give them an update, knowing that they doubted my ability to pull this off from the moment I stood in front of them, all those months ago, but I'd done what I'd promised them.

For the next part of the journey it was time to go back to Kyrenia. My flight was booked for the next day.

Sitting at the airport, was a good opportunity to look over the notes I'd made and learn some more of the Turkish words I'd written down. Wanting to be part of the banter tonight with the guys instead of feeling like I didn't have a clue what was going on.

Sitting going through the words, thinking that no-one was paying attention to me, I muttered the words out loud, not even noticing that there were people around me. Focused intently on getting the pronunciation right. Learning another language wasn't an easy task and the pronunciations were hard to master.

Totally focused, I never even noticed when somebody took a seat next to me.

"Merhaba nasilsin" I said out loud.

Just about to repeat the phrase again, I felt a tap on my shoulder. When I turned around there was an unbelievably stunning girl looking at me with a smile.

"That's not how that's pronounced," she stated, proceeding to tell me that the h was silent.

It took me a second to gather my thoughts because her beauty took my breath away. Her voice was soft and friendly, and I could easily sit and listen to her talking all day without getting bored. Ok, that might be a bit of an exaggeration, but she was a good distraction.

"Thank you. It isn't the easiest language to learn," I said with a cheeky smile, while subtly checking her out.

She was holding a magazine, which she went on to read. I wanted to talk to her more but didn't know what to say, which was so unlike me. For some reason she intrigued me, and it had been a while since I'd felt that way about someone. Racking my brain for what to say, without being creepy, the words that came out were not at all impressive.

"So, what brings you to Turkey?" I asked, feeling nervous but not understanding why.

It was like being young again, trying to tell my crush I liked her. The words coming out my mouth were all wrong, it was so stupid. Why I didn't start by asking her name, I'll never know. For a second it crossed my mind that she might ignore me.

"I was modelling for a photoshoot, but now I'm going home,"

she explained. She truly deserved to be on billboards, she was a sight to behold. I paid her attention but made sure not to stare at her too much. She was probably used to men falling at her feet mind you.

As we chatted, she told me that she lived in Lapta, which was only 20 miles north of Kyrenia, near the villa I was staying in. "Why are you visiting Turkey?" she asked with a smile.

"I'm visiting on business, an opportunity presented itself and I couldn't let it pass," I explained.

"That is why I'm struggling to learn the language, to help me get by," I added.

We talked and laughed until it was time to board the same flight to Kyrenia. I didn't want to say goodbye and was enjoying her company, so made sure we were seated next to each other on the plane. We got on well and enjoyed getting to know each other better. I was interested in her and wanted to spend more time with her. I shouldn't have been pursuing another woman, but it didn't stop me from initiating our conversation.

As we approached Kyrenia, I asked her if she would be willing to meet up with me for lunch once she was settled and was pleased when she agreed to meet up the following day; I didn't expect her to say yes as quickly as she did. Maybe she was as excited to spend time with me as I was with her.

Things weren't going well with Jenna, I'd broken promises I'd made her and imagined she was getting tired of waiting. With a lot on my mind, I'd forget at times that I'd even had a different life before now. Meeting this mysterious girl was a great escape for me.

Jenna would normally have been my go-to when I was feeling stressed out, but right now she hardly believed anything I said. It was hard being in a different country, and the only people I knew were colleagues. There were times we tried to talk about anything other than the bonds, but our conversations seemed to gravitate towards them in the end.

Wound up tight and under a lot of pressure, it was great to talk to someone who wasn't involved in my new life in any way. It was easy to pretend that things were okay, and we could talk about the simplest of things without being cautious. Once the plane landed, we exchanged numbers and agreed that we would meet the next day.

She filled my thoughts on the way back to the villa. I spent a quiet day by the pool and couldn't wait to go to sleep because when the sun began to shine the next day then that would be the day I could meet this girl again.

We agreed to meet at a champagne bar, which wasn't usually my scene, but I couldn't take a girl I'd just met to some dingy bar and wanted to impress her. It was an interesting place to be, but I'd not be making a habit of coming here. None of my mates would have believed that I'd come to a champagne bar. I arrived first, so waited for her with a drink, looking out to the sea. It was a stylish place, full of beautiful people. There was a sea of white sofas, cushions and hanging silks, and a jazz band played in the background. I hoped that she wasn't going to be too fashionably late because I was desperate to see her again.

When she finally arrived, she looked as stunning as I remembered from the day before. Dressed more casually this time, she gave me a peck on the cheek once she got to the table. We talked like we were old friends; no-one would have guessed that we had only just met.

I asked her what kind of modelling she did.

"I've done a lot of photo shoots for different things, but most notably the Pepsi Cola TV advert this year," she said nonchalantly.

She took my Hotmail address and emailed me a link to one of her videos, when she saw the disbelief in my eyes. What were the odds of a guy like me meeting a Pepsi model! I was in awe and it was difficult for me to hide my feelings. We talked for hours and couldn't get enough of each other. It was an amazing night and we parted with a passionate kiss.

CHAPTER 43
Distraction

Getting back to the villa, I couldn't wait to find the guys and tell them who I'd met for lunch.
"Guys I've met the most amazing girl and she's a model!"
After telling them more they realised who I was speaking about and didn't believe me for a second.
"You are full of shit Mike. Where the hell did you meet her?" they asked.
I explained that I'd met her at the airport and she was on the same flight as me the previous day, but they joked that it was my overactive imagination playing tricks on me. Apparently, the girl, Shakira, was a very popular singer in the Turkish charts, and they believed there was no way I'd been on a date with her.
They continued to take the piss out of me as they laughed.
"I'm meeting her again tomorrow, why don't you guys drop by and say hi?" I asked casually, walking away to my room.
It was hard for me to believe that she wanted to spend time with me, but it had done my self-confidence a power of good. A girl who was totally out of my league, wanted to be in my company. I wanted to prove to the guys that we had met and knew that they would be envious of me for a change. Tomorrow I'd show them.
It was difficult to get a sleep that night. But for once it wasn't the bonds on my mind, it was Shakira. She had got into my head. I hadn't realised how lonely this journey had been, until now. Spending time with Shakira brought this to the forefront of my mind.

Waking early enough the next day to watch the sunrise and feeling full of life, I decided to go for a run. Running along the beach was amazing, watching the waves lap against the golden sands, with the cool breeze from the sea blowing in my face. I pushed myself hard and felt strong. It was the perfect start to my day.

The guys were sitting eating breakfast at the pool when I'd finished my run and I sat down to join them. It was good to relax and have a laugh. Things had been busy over the last few weeks. Attempting to read the paper, only proved my Turkish wasn't getting any better. Feeling excited to see Shakira again, I left the guys to their breakfast and went back to my room for a shower.

Once ready, it was time to go and meet her. We were meeting at the champagne bar again and was surprised to see that she had arrived before me this time. She greeted me with a kiss. I couldn't take my eyes off her, she truly was stunning. As we chatted, sipping on our drinks, I asked her why she never told me about her being a famous singer.

"How did you find this out?" she asked.

"When explaining to my mates that I'd met Shakira from the Pepsi adverts they revealed your other hidden talents." I replied with a cheeky smile.

"I didn't want you to be attracted to the things that I've achieved, but for who I am as a person, that's why."

At that minute my phone vibrated in my pocket. It was a text from the guys telling me that they were on their way. They were buzzing as much as me about her. I'd be the talk of the whole group the moment they lay their eyes on her. Replying to their text I told them exactly where we were sitting, in hope that way they wouldn't walk around the place trying to find us and embarrass me.

It was a relief that they never came into the bar when they arrived. They simply pulled up outside, got out of the car, came close enough to see us, looked at us both and waved before getting back into the car, beeping the horn and speeding off.

Within minutes of them driving away my phone vibrated again. It was another text from them asking how the fuck I'd managed to pull that off, which made me laugh. Shakira was oblivious to what was going on.

Spending time with her became the highlight of my day. Feeling happy, but strangely at the same time felt as though I was going to lose in some way. I tried to ignore the feeling and enjoy whatever it was we had. She was easy to talk to and understood ambition. She was smart and not the stereotypical airhead model. It was okay to want more from life and that's why we clicked.

Arriving back at the villa a few hours later, the guys were waiting for me to give them a play by play account of how I'd got so lucky. I joked it was my charm and tried to brush off their questions, but they just laughed and asked for the truth. Maybe I'd caught her on a good day and she was too tired to tell me to fuck off, but I told them that it was just a chance meeting at the airport.

"Well, maybe we should all go to the airport more often." one of them said causing everyone to burst into laughter.

I didn't meet Shakira again for a while after that day but continued to take time out and relax with the guys. We'd loosened the knot a bit after the bank deal had gone through and it was time to have some fun as we waited for the next step.

I'd never spent so much time partying as I did with the guys over the next few days, experiencing a different kind of fun. They partied on a whole new level and you needed stamina to be able to keep up with them. We had huge barbeques, house parties and night outs in stylish clubs. Day times were spent nursing hangovers, and that's how life continued. It was like a celebration every fucking day! The guys called it our celebration of life. Life was too short not to try different things and I enjoyed every second. Fuck knows where they got the time or the energy to plan what we got up to. Every single day we did something new.

One of the strangest rituals they adopted was going out for soup every night at 12pm. It was their tradition which I respected, so went along with it. They made me eat the most disgusting soups you have ever tasted. It became part of their fun, to challenge me with the worst soups they could think of. They thought that I'd eventually give up but didn't and kept coming back. One day they gave me cow brain soup, the next it was sheep's testicles. Back home no-one would have ever drank this kind of shit, but they seemed to enjoy them.

"What ever happened to plain old tomato soup?" I asked, making them roll about laughing.

Eventually the partying came to a stop, and it was back to work. Time to put on my business suit and be ready to face the day ahead. I had an itinerary, and the next thing on my to-do list was to pick up the bond from the safe house. Nothing elaborate was planned for the meeting with the bank. If sending the bond by courier to the bank was an option that's what I'd have done, but the rules were that wherever the bond went, I went!

My nerves were nowhere to be seen and it was my plan for them to remain in hiding. Once I'd been to the safety deposit box and had the bond safely in my possession, between the pages of my Andy McNab book, I returned to the bank. I was in a good mood and happily said "Hi" to the security guard. Walking confidently inside, I headed to the same room I'd met the bank manager in before. He smiled widely as soon as I'd knocked and opened the door. Sitting across the table from him, the spark lit in his eyes the moment the bond was handed over to him. We had to go through some paperwork, which was my least favourite part about this job. Paperwork took too long to complete and for every transaction it was no different.

I handed over the bond, worth 300 thousand, which he gripped tightly in his hand. That tiny document had caused me so much grief in the last few weeks, but now it was about to bring me the greatest joy. The bond would be safe in the bank and there was no need for me to worry about it anymore.

This transaction was all above board. Apart for the forged documents, this was as legal as anything could be. Our meeting went without any glitches and he promised to keep in touch as I was walking out of his office. It was at that moment the realisation hit. If anything was going to go wrong, now would be the time. But I'd no reason to doubt and walked out of the bank as easily as I'd walked in.

Back at the villa the party continued with the guys. We got totally smashed, now we had something to celebrate. The biggest pay day of our lives was about to become a reality, it was in touching distance.

Taking a long drink of my beer and looking at the guys in front of me, I felt very important. This whole plan revolved around me and I was the man of the hour. The most important piece of this game. Although my strings were being pulled by others, I still felt in control and on top of the world.

This was almost over, and it was nearly time for me to move on with other things and start living my life again.

CHAPTER 44
Life or Death

With no other business to take care of in Istanbul, there was
nothing else for it; partying every night and drinking ourselves
into oblivion became the norm. I started to miss the pressure
we had before because then I felt useful and had a reason to
get up in the morning. Don't get me wrong it was exciting to
live the way we were for a couple of days, but it had started to
become monotonous. We weren't as young as we used to be,
and I had to remember that Jenna was back home, even if I'd
done a couple of stupid things in the last few months. The
reality was that I'd been living in a different world but still had a
life and a real future back in Scotland.
Meeting Shakira another two or three times was a good way
to break the monotony of the lifestyle we had been living at
the villa. I always enjoyed being around her and thought that
spending time with her was what I needed. But in all honesty
the feeling of guilt was starting to set in. When we were
together, I felt happy and enjoyed every second we spent
in each others company, but the moment we were apart my
thoughts turned to Jenna and I'd ask myself what the fuck was
I doing.
Spending time with Shakira was a different kind of thrill that
couldn't be explained. Her company was hard to resist. All
the partying and the other girls were not real life. Thoughts of
Jenna would cross my mind a lot of the time and I hated the
feelings of guilt. Thinking about how it would make me feel if
she was back home partying all the time and knowing that it
would drive me fucking crazy, made me a hypocrite.

Becoming tired of life at the villa and knowing that the authentication of the bonds might take a while, I decided that it would be best for me to return to the UK and try to get my real life back on track. I'd hurt Jenna more than could ever be imagined, but she had a forgiving heart and my hope was that she could forgive me. I knew that I'd totally neglected her and didn't want to lose her. The reason for getting into this in the first place was to make money to give Jenna and I a better life. Owing her so much, it was time to show her how much she meant to me.

Explaining to the guys that I'd be heading back to the UK for a few days was tough. They were sad to see me go, especially because we'd become so much closer during my trip. I'd had some amazing experiences whilst in Istanbul but missed home. If any news came from the bank, they would call me straight away, so I'd not miss anything by heading back.

Excited, I called Jenna to tell her that her man was coming home, and we were going to get our relationship back on track. I promised not to leave her side for a second, and we would talk everything over. Hearing the excitement in her voice, she told me that this was all she'd been dreaming about for the last few months and ended the call by saying

"I love you so much babe and can't wait to see you!"

As tough as I am, her words brought a tear to my eye, feeling overcome with emotion.

Once I got off the phone, the realisation about what a fucking idiot I'd been, started to sink in. Allowing myself to be distracted by other girls, especially when I'd an amazing woman like Jenna waiting so patiently for me. It was time to go back to the Scotland and make her the happiest she's been and make up for all the stupid mistakes I'd made.

My flight landed at Edinburgh airport. I hired a car and headed straight home, stopping off at the garage on the way to pick up some flowers. As if that was going to fix everything! Pulling up outside the house, I sat for a minute before getting out of the car. Once at the front door, for a second, taking time to look around me, I felt a wave of contentment wash over me. It was at that moment I knew this was where I belonged.

I knocked the door, not wanting to use my keys because I wanted to see Jenna's face when she opened the door. It opened slowly and there she was, beautiful as ever.

Forgetting the stupid moments with Shakira, this was the girl of my dreams standing right in front of me. My throat seized up as a tear rolled down my cheek. She jumped in the air when she saw me, hugging me and giving me a huge kiss. With her arms wrapped tightly around me, she gently whispered in my ear "I'm never letting you go. I want to hold you for every second that you are here."

It felt good that she was happy to see me, and I wanted to stay in that spot forever, feeling her against me, but she pulled me into the house.

She had every right to be angry at me, but typically Jenna was just happy to have me home. I still hadn't said a word, because to be honest I couldn't. She went to the kitchen and came back with a glass of juice for me. Taking care of me, as she always did.

"Is there anything else you want babe?" she asked.

"No Jen, that's great. I'm just happy to be home." I said wearily. These past few months had taken their toll. Both of us were in denial, pretending that we hadn't been through a seriously rough patch in our relationship. Maybe she didn't care, and she was truly happy to see me after such a long time apart. I was certainly happy to see her.

We sat for hours chatting. There was no hint of anger from her as you would have expected, she was just my Jenna. We were like teenagers all over again, madly in love. Sitting with her made me question why I'd got myself into this in the first place and why I didn't choose to stay with her and make a decent living here. Seeing Jenna smile was worth more than 100 bearer bonds. Then came the dreaded question.

"How long are you going to be home for babe?" She asked softly.

I was in a catch twenty-two situation, wanting to remain in our happy little bubble, but it was a question I had to answer, and it couldn't be avoided.

"Jen, I'm going to be here for about five days and we'll make the most of every minute, I promise. I'll not leave you for a second!" I reassured her.

Continuing to explain that I was waiting for an important call, but we would have time together and hoped that this time would be a start to healing the wounds from the last few months.

"We can fix this babe. Let's just enjoy the time we have together." She replied lovingly.

We went to bed that night, and I'd never felt so close to her. I needed a good night sleep and to wake up without a raging hangover but was also looking forward to spending time with Jenna, without anyone else being around.

The work I'd done over the last few months meant there was plenty of money in my pocket and I wanted to spend it on Jenna. In as much as she was not a materialistic girl, she still liked to have nice things and have a good time. Things were going to work themselves out which gave me a sense of peace.

We planned to go away, just the two of us, for a couple of days. We didn't decide that night exactly where we would go but we wanted it to be somewhere we'd never forget. I promised myself I'd never hurt her again.

We needed to rekindle our spark and get back the amazing relationship we had before I got involved in all this shit, and for me to stop treating Jenna like she was ordinary. What she had put up with, showed me how amazing she was. if the shoe had been on the other foot, I'm sure I'd have given up by now. Jenna was probably the strongest and most forgiving person I'd ever met. Feeling genuinely happy, there was a calmness that I couldn't explain. It was not thrilling, far from it, but it was safe.

Having money and being able to spend it on the people I cared about the most was an amazing feeling. Thoughts of Shakira couldn't have been further from my mind. I had Jenna back and nothing was going to spoil this moment.

"Good night Jen, I love you so much and can't wait to wake up next to you in the morning". I said before we closed our eyes.

CHAPTER 45
Hard Choices

I'd only just drifted off to sleep, when I got a call from Ishvara. I considered ignoring it but knew he wouldn't have called this late if it wasn't an emergency. He had backed me up from day one and without him I'd never have had the chances I did now, so wasn't about to let him down. He was the one that introduced me to this world and had given me a once in a life time opportunity.

I picked up but couldn't understand a word he was saying because he was talking so fast.

"Hey man, slow down. I can't hear a single word you're saying," I stated.

"I've only got one minute. You need to help right now mate!" he replied anxiously.

"What's up?" I asked with a hint of concern.

Wondering what he could possibly want this late at night, thinking that he was maybe pissed and was exaggerating the need for my help. When he explained that he was in deep shit and it wasn't a joke, I believed him. It was the tone in his voice that convinced me he was genuinely in trouble.

He never gave me a straight answer about what was going on; I began to understand, the more he spoke. He couldn't go into detail over the phone, but from what he did say I knew he was in big trouble. Ishvara told me that he was in London and he'd got involved in some business with a group of Jamaicans. The deal had gone wrong and that's why he was calling me.

"There is a gun to my head, and I mean literally as we speak mate. If this doesn't get sorted, they will shoot me." he stuttered.

"What do you need me to do?" I asked, sitting bolt upright in bed.

Jenna was asleep, and I didn't want to wake her, so quickly went into the other room. I was expecting to hear Ishvara's voice, but somebody had already taken the phone away from him.

Ishvara was an easy-going guy and this gangster persona was just a way for him to try and look tough. He was the type of guy that would walk away from a fight if he could. I could only imagine how he was feeling right now, being way out of his depth. He only looked cool under pressure when I was with him and he knew I'd fight his corner.

I'd no clue what the fuck the deal was or how it had gone wrong. All that was certain was that he needed me, and I had to go now! They gave me directions to where to meet them. The person at the end of the phone had a dark voice, the kind you didn't want to hear when you were woken up in the middle of the night.

"If you do not want your friend dead, you better get here quickly, with a way to solve this mess," he stated.

"I'll be there tomorrow, after sorting a couple of things. I replied.

"You have eight hours to get here or you'll be coming to get your friend's corpse," he grunted.

My plan to go into the next room when the phone started ringing, so that I wouldn't wake Jenna, was about to blow up. Now I'd have to wake her and tell her that I had to break my promise and leave tonight. So much for me living a normal life for a few days. Getting a phone call in the middle of the night, which was a matter of life and death, was the last thing I expected. What the fuck had Ishvara gotten himself involved with?

There was no option but to head to London straight away. The voice on the other end of the phone meant business and wasn't going to be messed around.

"We don't give a fuck about your shit. The only reason we are calling you is because one of our contacts has told us that you would be the man to fix this!" he stated.

For a moment I wondered who he was speaking about, but that wasn't what was important right now, helping Ishvara was my priority.

The phone was handed back to Ishvara; I could hear him trying to hold back his emotions and told him to be strong, which probably wasn't the greatest piece of advice in this situation, but it was the only thing I could think of. Fuck knows how I'd have handled myself if it was me in a similar situation. Who would have been my go-to if I was in the shit? Probably no-one. I always dealt with my own mess and got myself out of trouble.

"Please help me Mike. I'll owe you everything." he pleaded, begging for his life.

He asked that even if I didn't want to come for his sake then please do it for his children, which he was saying for the benefit of the guy holding the gun to his head and not mine. Ishvara knew I'd have his back, but what he didn't realise about these types of people was that they didn't give a shit about his family. Even if the guy holding the gun did have a conscience, he was doing a job and probably didn't have a choice anyway. I remembered that his wife had recently given birth to their third daughter. She would have missed out on knowing her dad; there was no way I could leave him there in London alone. If there was anything that could be done, then I simply had to do it and try my best to get him out of this.

"Tick tock," the voice added, before the line went dead.

There were a thousand questions running through my mind, but they wouldn't be answered until I got to London. They sounded serious enough for me to know that their instructions needed to be followed to the letter. How the hell was I going to sort this? These guys weren't fucking around, and this was big time shit Ishvara had got himself involved in by the sounds of it. My next thought was how I'd explain to Jenna that I had to leave? The last thing I wanted was to go back on my word and break my promise to her. Only moments before we'd been cuddling in our bed and now I was going to have to leave and try save Ishvara's life. It all seemed too farfetched and she wouldn't believe the truth, assuming it was just an excuse. Leaving was the last thing on my mind or what I wanted because being with her had made me the happiest I'd been for months.

This was unbelievable. I'd spent the past few hours telling Jenna I'd not leave her side and promised things would be different this time. This was just typical of my bad luck. It felt like I was being punished for all the fuck ups that I'd made. I was trying my best to make things work with Jenna and in the end, this was going to make things worse than ever. Feeling totally torn, I couldn't leave Ishvara to get shot, there was no other option but to go.

I wanted to tell Jenna the truth, or the closest thing to the truth, but how would she understand?

"Baby I'm leaving because my friends about to be murdered." She wasn't involved in this world and I wasn't about to bring her into it.

Walking back into the bedroom, Jenna was sitting up on the bed.

"Who was that?" she asked with a concerned look.

"A guy I work with. He needs my help babe." I said, sitting down next to her on the bed.

She went on to ask what that meant and questioned why he was calling me so late at night.

"I can't go into all the details babe, but I need to go," I whispered softly.

"It's truly a matter of life and death Jen, otherwise I'd never consider leaving," I added.

She reacted as expected, getting angry and demanding to know why. She was obviously confused why it had to be right now. In a perfect world she'd have told me that she trusted me and that she'd be waiting for me to come back. But that perfect world didn't exist and as I tried to hold her hand she pushed me away.

"You told me you wouldn't leave me. What the fuck is going on?" she shouted. I tried to calm her down, but it just made her more angry and upset.

"Who would call you if they were in danger and what could you possibly do to help them?" Jenna shouted, before continuing to say that this was the shittiest excuse she'd ever heard.

"Are you seeing someone else?" she asked with tears welling up in her eyes. I hated upsetting her and never wanted to make her cry. Why did she automatically assume that I'd be leaving because of another woman? Feelings of guilt about Shakira came into my mind, even though there was nothing between the two of us now.

"Why are you doing this to me?" she asked whilst sobbing.

"Who is she?" she shouted at me.

I knew the real reason for leaving, and she couldn't be further from the truth but there was no way of telling her, it would only worry her more.

"Just tell me who she is, and this will be easier for both of us," she shouted. She was beginning to shout louder. I didn't know what to do to calm her down and felt like shit as I tried to make things better but only ended up making her more upset.

Making the mistake of looking at my watch, made Jenna livid.

"So, you obviously don't care about us. Well if that's the case then leave. You've broken my fucking heart," she yelled as she pushed me.

As she sobbed, all I wanted to do was put my arms around her and comfort her.

"How can you just look at your watch when all I'm trying to do is understand you?" she asked.

Jenna had no idea that the clock was ticking and the longer I stayed, the less time Ishvara had.

"Jenna it's not what you think. Please, I'll explain everything later. I'm so sorry babe but I need to go. I'll call you from the car." I said walking out of the door.

At that moment I might as well have thrown our relationship in the bin. It would take a miracle for her to forgive me now. I'd just thrown my relationship away to save my mate's life, what other option was there? None in my eyes.

This was one of the hardest decisions I'd ever had to make. Seeing the hurt in Jenna's eyes that I'd caused. Getting into the car, I looked up to see if she was at the window. She was standing with her hands clasped together as if praying for me not to go.

I wanted to cry, but my emotions couldn't get the better of me, I told myself

"You are a hard man and have a job to do."

I truly loved Jenna and wanted things to work. Once I'd sorted everything with the Jamaicans in London, hopefully she would at least give me a chance to explain everything properly and make it up to her.

CHAPTER 46
Torn Apart

Everything was fucked up; leaving Jenna like that was painful.
I tried to call her a couple of times, but she had switched her
phone off. I left her a couple of messages, but knew that she
wouldn't call me back, especially in the state that she was in.
My messages begged her to forgive me and understand that I
wasn't doing this to hurt her. There were tears rolling down my
face and there was nothing I could do to stop them. Hard man
or no hard man, I couldn't hold my feelings back anymore. It
was becoming difficult to drive, tears filling my eyes making it
hard see the road ahead. I'd never felt so alone and lost in my
life. I'd do anything, if she would just give me a chance to make
things up to her and clear up the mess I'd made. During the
long drive my mind switched to a very dark place.
Feeling unbelievably sad, the only person to blame was
myself. Jenna and I had a great life together and I couldn't get
my head around the fact that it could be wiped away. I'd known
her for the better part of my life, she knew me inside and out,
including all my flaws, but she still loved me. She never walked
away, even when she had the opportunity to, always finding a
way of fighting for us.
Bringing up the kids, all the amazing holidays and great times
we'd spent together, everything was running through my mind.
In that moment I realised that the best days of my life had
included Jenna and our family. I'd fucked things up big time but
couldn't focus on how to fix it and had to focus my thoughts on
how to save Ishvara from the shit he was in.
I was driving down the motorway like a maniac. The Jamaicans

hadn't called me again, so I still had hope that I'd find Ishvara alive. Maybe a little fucked up, but alive at least. Driving whilst in this state was a bad idea. My head was all over the place and preoccupied with my drifting thought. Luckily the road wasn't busy.

Although worried sick for Ishvara, at the same time I was sure that I'd be able to work things out with the Jamaicans. Going into the situation blind, and not knowing exactly what I was getting into, was concerning me a little, but there was a threat to Ishvara's life.

I'd have felt more comfortable if there had been someone with me, but they were very clear that I had to come alone. There was no back up this time. My negotiating skills needed to be on top to get him out of this mess. If I fucked this up, I could forget about fixing things with Jenna, they would probably put a bullet in my head as well as Ishvara's.

The bonds couldn't have been further from my mind right now, which showed me that when it came down to it, money wasn't really what mattered. I wasn't in a good place, sad, lonely and hurt. Still driving, I tried to call Jenna again, but her phone was off. I just hoped that she had stopped crying at least but knew she would be far from okay.

I was getting closer to London, and after a couple of hours finally managed to get Jenna on the phone. I thought she would have been calmer by now, but she was still sobbing her heart out, which made me feel worse about leaving her and made me question the person I'd turned into. How could I leave her when she was so upset?

Why had Ishvara picked me to help him?

"Jenna please, I know I've hurt you, and hate that I've made you feel like this" I said whilst fighting back the tears.

My attempt to try and console her, was having no effect.

"I'm so sorry. I know it doesn't seem like much, but I truly mean it babe," I added.

She was still sobbing, and all I wanted was to hug her until she stopped crying. "Do you still love me Mike?" she asked in between sobs.

This was the worst conversation to have over the phone, but the circumstances didn't give us any other option.

As I was about to answer, she went on to ask if I still cared for her at all. I'd made her insecure and that was the worst thing to have done to her. Putting my phone on speaker, I opened the flood gates.

"You are everything to me Jenna and I love you more than you can ever imagine," I said.

Opening my heart to her and I told her how much I cared and loved her.

"You need to trust me. There is no other girl, it is only you." I reassured her, begging her to believe me, desperately needing her by my side.

"Honestly, I'm going to help someone, but can't give you all the details to protect you," I added.

If I told her exactly what was going on, she would understand, and we wouldn't be going through this, but I couldn't knowingly put her in danger just to save my own ass.

"Just bear with me for the next two months and this will all be over, and we will be living a better life together," I reassured her.

I told her that once the two months were over, I'd be there full time and wouldn't be the on and off boyfriend that I'd been for the last while. Once the bearer bonds deal was coming to an end, I'd have more time to myself and get my life back. I told her that we would make a great life together and that she could count on me.

Completely caught up in the emotion, I hadn't noticed that she had finally stopped crying. She didn't understand the situation, but I appreciated the fact that she was listening to me.

"Okay, I trust you and will wait for you, but this is your last chance. I swear it Mike." she said sternly.

I promised her that I'd be back the next day and we would be able to talk things through properly, knowing that she hadn't forgiven me yet but at least she had agreed to wait for me.

There was no doubt that she loved and cared about me. I felt a huge relief hearing her words.

"Just know one thing. I don't care about the money, houses or cars babe," she stated.

I believed the sincerity in her voice, all she wanted was me. We had the best times of our lives without money. All she needed was for us to go back to how we had been. Jenna wanted us to be honest with each other, without all the secrets I'd been keeping. It hurt her knowing that I wasn't letting her in.

This was progress, we weren't yelling at each other, but talking, the way we had always done before. I felt happy and sad at the same time. Talking had put a couple of things into perspective for me and now I could get on with saving Ishvara's ass.

There was hope for me and Jenna and I'd not let her down this time.

"I'll call you back as soon as I can Jen," I said softly.

"Be safe babe," she said, before hanging up the phone.

I really needed to hear those words. She had just given me my hopes and dreams back.

CHAPTER 47
Second Chances

I was glad to have another chance with Jenna and there was no way I was going to blow it this time. There was a feeling of guilt still left but knew it would fade away in time. I wasn't expecting to feel good because it was me that created all this shit. My thoughts drifted to how I'd make things better and my initial feelings were money. Those thoughts were quickly dashed remembering that money was the root of our problems. I needed to start thinking about spending time together, rather than buying things for her to forgive me.

There had been a heavy burden lifted from my shoulders, even though I'd not worked out all the answers. Things might not be completely fixed but we had made some head way and that was good enough for me. I had to put Jenna and our relationship at the back of my mind for now, because the only thing I could be focused on was dealing with Ishvara's situation.

Driving like a maniac, with no clue what I'd be walking into once arriving in London, I wished I'd some idea what had got Ishvara into this mess. It was probably a safe bet to assume it would be something to do with money. The clock was ticking, and they had been too quiet for my liking. I'd expected at least a couple of threats along the way but had heard nothing.

With only about an hour and a half before arriving in London, my phone began ringing, and the caller ID showed it was Ishvara. I answered, putting it on speaker so that I could keep driving and speak to him at the same time.

"Where the hell are you man? You only have one more hour to get here," he said. I could sense that he was panicking.

"I'm almost there, relax, just give me an hour and a half," I replied.

"You don't get it mate. They are serious about killing me!" he added, close to tears.

"I'm on my way Ishvara," I reassured him.

As I was about to say something else, the phone went silent. The Jamaicans had taken the phone away from him.

"This is not a courtesy call you prick," the guy snarled.

"You have an hour." he stated, with a dark calmness.

They were beginning to piss me off and make me angry. These guys were dangerous, but I'd passed giving a fuck. I wasn't Ishvara and they weren't going to intimidate me.

"Listen, I've been driving for the past seven hours. You will just have to fucking wait until I'm there. I can't get there any quicker," I snapped.

I expected him to go nuts on the other end of the phone, but he didn't. He made it clear he wasn't happy, before agreeing that they would wait. I didn't scare easily and wasn't afraid to stand up for myself, or in the mood to be treated like shit either, especially after what had happened with Jenna.

After eight long hours, I was finally at the destination where Ishvara was being held. It was show time. Pulling up into the car park of a rundown Beefeater, which was attached to a Travel Lodge, it looked exactly as they had described over the phone.

They told me that once I arrived, I'd find a silver minibus parked up. The car park was only half full, so it didn't take long for me to spot the minibus under a huge tree in the dark. Getting out the car and approaching the minibus, I could feel my heart begin to race with adrenaline. Ready for them, I banged hard on the door until it was opened. Climbing into the back of the ten-seater, Ishvara was inside terrified, with his new "friends".

There were eight huge, mean looking Jamaican fuckers in the back. One of them had a gun pressed into Ishvara's stomach. My first thought was if this was going to kick off I didn't stand a chance against these guys, being completely outnumbered.

"Great of you to finally join us," one of them said sarcastically. I recognised his voice from the phone calls, so assumed that he must be the Boss Man.

"Your friend is still alive as you can see and I'm sure you want to keep it that way." he added.

He went on to explain that 200 thousand pounds had gone missing and Ishvara was responsible for it, which was hard to believe. Ishvara liked to show off, but he would never mess with anyone else's money.

"It wasn't my fault" said Ishvara nervously.

He looked calmer than he had sounded on the phone. Probably because he had me there now fighting his corner. He added that he needed to get in touch with a contact and that the money wasn't lost, just on route and these guys had over-reacted.

"They just need to be patient with me Mike," he stated.

The Jamaicans began laughing. They laughed hard, as if Ishvara had said the funniest thing they'd ever heard. I agreed that his explanation was weak and would have been pissed off too if that was the only explanation that he'd given me. The minibus quickly fell silent again.

"On route! What, for ten fucking days?" the Boss Man snarled.

My phone began to ring, at the worst possible moment. I ended the call, but whoever was trying to get hold of me was persistent. It kept ringing time and time again, checking the caller ID I saw that it was Jenna. Why she was calling? What was so urgent? There was no way of answering the call now, so she'd just need to wait.

We continued our conversation, thinking Jenna had given up trying to call, but my phone started ringing again. It was starting to irritate the Jamaicans and she wasn't going to give up until she spoke to me.

"Give me a minute, I have to get this," I said, pressing the receive button whilst getting out the back of the minibus.

The Jamaicans were already annoyed, and this was probably going to make the situation worse, but if I didn't answer, Jenna might have changed her mind about giving me another chance.

"Hey Jen, what's up? Can I call you back?" I asked.

She was already on the offensive

"Who the fuck is Shakira?" she snapped, before I'd even

finished speaking.

I thought about hanging up straight away and pretending that my battery had died but knew that would put me in even deeper shit. This is the last fucking thing I needed right now. There wasn't time to explain this to Jenna.

My heart sank. How the fuck did Jenna find out about Shakira? Should I be honest with her? The truth would come out in the end but when opening my mouth to tell her, I denied any knowledge of her.

"I've no idea who Shakira is, Jenna," I stated, hoping that my voice portrayed confidence because she'd know straight away if I was lying.

"Since you don't know, let me tell you who she is." she said with an angry, sarcastic tone.

I'd fucked up by lying, but how did she know? Why didn't I just tell her the truth?

Jenna went on to explain that she'd been speaking to Shakira via Hotmail messenger, pretending that she was me.

I'd forgotten all about the Jamaicans. There was no-one else except me and Jenna at that moment. My mind was racing, what could I possibly say now to minimize the damage I'd caused by lying?

Jenna told me that Shakira's name had popped up on the computer.

"When a girl's name pops up on the computer, wanting to speak to your fiancé in the middle of the night, you become fucking interested in who they are." she shouted.

"Speaking to her myself, she told me, without realising it, what was going on!" she added angrily.

She explained that Shakira had been reminiscing about the time we'd spent together at the champagne bar and how much fun she had during our dinner date.

"We talked a lot Mike and I found out a few things about you that's for sure." she snapped.

I tried to speak but Jenna told me to shut up. She'd never spoken to me like that before in the whole time we'd been together.

221

"If you were hoping to keep talking to her, don't worry, that won't be happening again. She already knows that you're engaged," Jenna shouted.

I thought that Jenna would break down in tears at any minute, but she didn't. I'd never heard her this angry before.

"If she was anywhere near me right now, I'd kill her." Jenna threatened.

"What was it Mike? Was it because she is younger than me?" she asked.

I wanted to explain that it wasn't about her and I'd just needed someone to talk to. We'd drifted apart and didn't speak the way we used to. I wanted her to know that I'd never try to replace her with Shakira. There was so much to say, but this wasn't the place. Feeling myself sinking, this was all happening at the worst time. I was truly fucked.

"Jenna please understand that my plan was never to hurt you," I whispered.

CHAPTER 48
8 Hours

One of the big fuckers banged down hard on my shoulder from behind.

"Are you fucking here or what?"

I asked him to give me a second and I'd come back inside. Jenna wouldn't accept my apology right at that moment, but I had to try and smooth things over until we got home, and I'd be able to explain to her properly.

"Are you with her now? Is that why you had to hurry away?" Jenna asked. I could hear the hurt in her voice.

At that moment the Jamaican snatched my phone from me, hung up, switched it off and put it in his pocket.

My blood began to boil. What the fuck did he just do? I totally lost the plot. That was my only hope of trying to calm Jenna down. She now thought that I'd left to be with Shakira, and that I'd hung up the phone on her.

Furious, a red mist came down over me as I swung my right fist, which landed hard, smashing his jaw. Following with another five or six rapid punches to his face, before we were pulled apart by the other guys. They threw us both back into the minibus and explained that we had more serious shit to deal with.

As I sat in the minibus and calmed down my mind was filled with thoughts of Jenna and how the hell this mess was going to get fixed. I'd drifted away from what was going on around me and wasn't even concentrating, until someone tapped my shoulder.

"I'm sorry, are we boring you?" one of them asked.

"Sorry, I'm just a little preoccupied. What were you saying?" I replied sarcastically.

He turned to look me right in the eyes.

"You do understand we are going to shoot Ishvara don't you?" he threatened.

I nodded, of course, I'm not a fucking idiot. Needing to pull myself together and try to fix this situation, I had to put Jenna to the back of my mind for a second, no matter how difficult it was.

They were dragging this out and my patience was wearing thin. We'd been in conversation for about three hours before any agreement was made about how Ishvara's situation could be fixed. I just wanted to get the fuck out of there.

It transpired that Ishvara had been involved in a money laundering scam with the Jamaicans and there was some outstanding money due. Ishvara assured me the money was on its way and they agreed to give him seven days to deliver the money. The responsibility was put on me for ensuring that the money was delivered and if it wasn't it would mean a bullet for both of us. These guys weren't fucking about, and they meant every word. Not really thinking, I agreed to their terms just to get us both out of there.

Once they agreed we could leave, the guy who I'd punched offered me his hand, to which I obliged.

"No hard feelings mate, but that was a very important call." I explained.

He gave me a nod as he handed me back my phone.

Ishvara was shaken and needed to lean on me to walk. I helped him into the passenger seat. I started the car and pulled away, knowing that this was going to be a tough drive home, feeling mentally and physically fucked.

"Thank you for saving my life. I owe you big time." Ishvara stated.

"Don't mention it. If you deliver their money, we are square." I replied.

Driving away, Ishvara knew without me explaining, that I didn't want to talk. My priority was to speak to Jenna. Turning my phone back on, there were about five messages from her, each one was worse than the previous one. She was shouting and crying at the same time, furious, thinking that I'd hung up the phone on her. She told me that she never wanted to see me again. I hated her thinking the reason my phone was off was because I was with Shakira.

I thought Jenna believed me when I'd told her the reason for me leaving was to help a friend in danger. If she thought I'd lied about that then she would never believe a single word from now on.

I considered taking Ishvara home with me, as proof of the truth, but Jenna may have believed that he was covering for me. They had never met each other before so why would she believe the word of a stranger? I was sincerely sorry for fucking everything up but I'd no idea how to show her.

Ishvara fell asleep quickly; the events of the day had undoubtedly drained him. If only I could have fallen asleep and woken up to realise that all of this was just a horrible dream. If only I'd ignored Ishvara's call, none of this would have happened. Don't get me wrong, I was glad to save his life but wished it didn't have to be at the expense of my relationship. Running through my mind what to say to Jenna, I knew that whatever I did say it wasn't going to be good enough to erase all the pain and hurt I'd caused. I tried calling her, but she had switched her phone off again. I left messages, begging her to call me back, but stopped after the fifth message, deciding that it was probably best to give her space to find it in her heart to listen to me. The radio was my only distraction whilst driving. Ishvara woke up just as we were arriving back in Scotland. "Let's go for a drink mate. You just saved my life and we must celebrate." he said.

I wasn't in the mood for celebrating and just wanted to get home and sort things out with Jenna. It surprised me that he didn't want to rush home to his wife and children. That would have been my first stop if I'd just stared death in the face.

Still adamant that he was going for a drink, I dropped Ishvara off at a local bar and told him to have enough fun for both of us.

My life was totally messed up. I'd got myself here and didn't know how I'd get myself out. All I wanted was a chance make some decent money and have all we'd dreamed of, but the money didn't matter anymore. It was the last thing on my mind. Jenna's words, "If we are together, the money's not important" kept ringing in my ears.

Why hadn't I listened to her? She was being honest, but I'd not been honest with myself. I'd lost the most important person in my life and it was only now that I realised how important she was to me. Being so invested in making money, I'd forgotten to be part of her life.

I'd driven straight back to Scotland. It had been a 16 hour round trip and I was exhausted. As soon as the car was parked, I rushed into the house. It was silent, but I went straight to our bedroom. Jenna wasn't there. My heart sank as I checked every room in the house but couldn't find her. Panic filled my veins, trying to call but her phone was still off. Where could she be? I called continuously, until it was pointless, and I finally gave up, exhausted, falling onto the bed.

CHAPTER 49
Moving Fast

I woke up the next day still fully clothed. As soon as my eyes were opened it was straight back to trying to get hold of Jenna, but it was futile. Feeling lost not knowing where she was.
I finally got in touch with her three days later and was relieved when she told me that she was okay. Thinking that time apart might have softened her, but she was still angry and all we did was fight for the next two days. We couldn't find a way to work things out and it was killing me. I knew that I'd pushed her to her limit but didn't want to give up on us. I asked her if we could meet up and talk, but she wouldn't, telling me that she would think about it.
A call the next day meant it was time to go back to Cyprus. This had been one of the worst weeks of my life. Not being able to explain to Jenna what had happened with Shakira, I felt leaving now would destroy our relationship forever.
"Jenna, I have to leave again, but I'm coming back for you." I explained, knowing that my words didn't mean much to her at that point and she was still angry with me.
"It is over. This is the end for us Mike." she replied, trying to hold back her tears.
I couldn't believe what she was saying. Surely, she never meant it? We were meant to be forever. But she couldn't forget the last couple of days. I'd caused her too much pain.
Refusing to give up on her, I had to finish what I'd started and went off the phone convincing myself that she didn't mean what she was saying and that we weren't over. Never more had I wanted the deal with bonds to be over. I wanted my life

back and to forget about everything that had happened in the last few months.

My flight was the following day and as soon as I arrived back in Cyprus, I went straight to the villa. The guys knew nothing about what had been happening back home, and how fucked up my life was right now.

They were relaxing and playing volleyball in the pool. The double patio doors were opened, and I stood watching them for a minute. No-one noticed me for a while until Sancar turned around. Catching sight of me he threw his hands in the air in excitement and shouted to everyone that I was back.

"We've fucking done it brother." he said as he walked towards me.

"The bank has authenticated the bond. A letter was sent to the company address to confirm it." He continued.

Everyone stood silent by the pool for a second, trying to take in what he'd just said. Sancar had waited for me to return before he told us the news. This was what we'd been waiting for. Everyone began cheering, hugging and giving each other high fives. All our work had paid off, the excitement was electric. As the mayhem was going on around me, I drifted away, zoning out and not hearing anyone. If I was to compare the feeling at that exact moment it was like being back in the ring, seconds before a big fight.

My head was buzzing with thoughts. We were touching distance away from making almost one million pounds. Outwardly I remained calm, but inwardly I wanted to explode. We were going to be rich and have everything we'd ever wanted. It made me feel like a different person and that I could do anything, including get Jenna back. Now it was time to see the real fucking me.

I was shaken out of my day dream by Goker. He had his big huge hands on my shoulders.

"You've done it brother. You've actually done it." he said, with what could only describe as childish excitement.

"Yes we have bro. We so fucking have." I replied.

We all knew there was still work to be done, but realistically, it was just formalities.

I'd need to arrange for the rest of the bonds to be taken to the bank. Sancar explained that the bank had given me three days to finalise the transaction. Speaking to the London Boys had to be my next priority to tell them what was happening.

Calling J, we spoke in code so that if our phones were being tapped then nobody would have any idea what we were really discussing.

"Hi mate, good news. The bank has completed all the paperwork for the villa you wanted me to buy. We will need to arrange the money transfer." I said, with a hint of smugness in my voice.

"What? Really?" he questioned.

"Yip, all cleared." I replied.

There was a short silence.

"When can you make it back here?" I asked J.

"I'll get the first flight out tomorrow." He answered.

I needed to tell Ishvara the good news but decided to wait until the deal was done before telling him. I wanted to be certain of the timescales for the job to be finalised. This came at a perfect time and would help him out big time with his little problem with the Jamaicans.

The next few hours were busy arranging all the details. After I'd finished, Goker handed me a thousand euros and told me I'd done a good job and deserved to go and have a good time.

It would be good to let off some steam and relax before having to be on the go the next day. I remembered that the Scotland game was on that night, which would be the perfect distraction. Knowing the guys would be partying tonight, I didn't really want to stay in the villa. It was hard to say no to the guys once the alcohol started flowing and tomorrow was going to be a big day for me.

To be polite I invited the guys to come along with me to watch the game, but they weren't interested. As I'd imagined they were going to hold a barbeque and have a few drinks. Leaving them to it, I was glad to have some alone time. Jenna was still on my mind and it was going to take me a while to figure out what I'd do next. A lot of that would be dependent on the deal with the bonds. We were only days away from this being over, not months anymore. With a thousand euros in my pocket, tonight was about trying to relax and forget about everything.

I went to my room to freshen up from my flight, before heading down to the local bar. Watching the game on one of the big screens, I was sitting alone, downing more drinks than I could count. After chatting to a couple of English guys for a while during the game, they invited me to eat with them. To be honest their banter was a good distraction.

We met a couple of other guys at the restaurant who also joined us. We ate, laughed and drank until it was time for the restaurant to close. We agreed that the bill would be split equally between all of us, so I handed over my share to one of the guys.

Suddenly out of nowhere one of the guys snarled

"Hey, why are you refusing to pay? Everyone else has paid their share."

He was looking directly at me. I thought he couldn't be talking to me, so ignored him.

His next mistake was pointing at me and accusing me of trying to get a free meal from them. We began arguing, which I wasn't in the mood for, so was going to walk away, but he kept on pushing my buttons. He really was starting to piss me off.

"You think you're tough wee man? Well let's settle this outside." I challenged.

A couple of his mates tried to calm him down. They could see how drunk he was and how pissed off he'd made me and knew this wasn't going to end well if we went outside.

"Come on, let it go." they urged.

But the prick didn't seem to care and kept trying to wind me up. I tried to keep calm, but he wasn't interested in settling this. Although drunk, I knew that I'd easily kick the shit out of him. We were in the middle of a crowd of guys that had surrounded us. He moved around, trying to throw punches at me, which I easily took or avoided. He was a fucking pussy. I'd had enough and after only hitting him twice, I knocked him out. He hit the floor hard, smashing his head on the pavement.

I needed to get out of there and fast, before drawing any more attention to myself. If the police, or even worse the army, showed up I'd be in deep shit. I needed to steer clear of any trouble, especially now that the bond had been authenticated by the bank. Being arrested would compromise the deal being finalised.

The fight should have been a sign for me to go straight back. Me being me I headed to a local nightclub instead for another couple of drinks before getting bored and heading back to the villa.

Walking back, I began to think about how stupid I'd been for getting into a pub brawl at this crucial stage but laughed it off. Nothing had gone wrong luckily, and the little prick deserved it anyway.

At the villa, there was no-one in the pool area, which surprised me because they knew how to party hard and it was still early. I wasn't ready for bed and stayed in the living room for a while, continuing to drink. Only a short time had passed before Sancar come down the stairs. I didn't even notice him until he tapped me on the shoulder. He could tell I'd not been myself since coming back and there must something on my mind, but he never asked. He sat with me and we chatted for a while, before telling me that it was time for me to go to bed. I remember thinking that he was a wise man.

"Mike, we are going to be very rich soon." he said, before disappearing back up the stairs.

CHAPTER 50
The Time Is Now

I dozed off on the patio that night, too drunk to even think of going to sleep in my bed. Waking up to the feeling of the sun beating on my head. I turned around to escape the heat and almost fell into the pool because I didn't realise I'd fallen asleep in the hammock.

It was a beautiful day, but with a bitch of all hangovers, I couldn't appreciate it and wished it was raining. Instantly I started thinking about Jenna and what I'd probably lost. The guys didn't know what was going on and I certainly wasn't going to tell them. I had to stay strong and be the hard man, well at least on the outside anyway. Our personal lives had always been kept at a distance. They knew a bit about my life, but I wasn't ready to start falling apart in front of them.

I could hear music booming. It took a moment for me to realise that I'd been sleeping through the beginnings of a party. The guys were already up and full of energy, planning another barbeque. Where the hell did they get their energy from? This was an ongoing thing with them. It was exciting at first because they lived life like every day was the last day. Right now, it made me resent them because their life seemed perfect and mine was far from it. Little did I know that what had happened to me so far was just the tip of the iceberg and nothing in comparison to what was coming next.

I'd slept until midday. The guys tried to get me involved in the party, but I'd no energy to be sociable today. Still half pissed, I went into the kitchen to get some water. It was the only remedy to cure my hangover. Then it was off to the room I was now calling mine, to go for a sleep, hoping that I'd be able to recover from last night's events. We didn't have any work on until the next day. The only thing for me to do that night was meet J to pick up the bonds. At least I'd have the rest of the day to sort myself out.

The next day I went to the meeting with J. We met in a small British bar in Kyrenia.

"Good to see you mate," were the first words out of his mouth.

"Yeh good to see you too buddy. Glad you managed to get through customs with all the bonds" I replied.

"Well, not all the bonds. The Boss decided not to risk them all in one go. I have just over 10 million dollars' worth with me." J said.

"For fuck's sake J, all the paperwork that has been drawn up with the bank is for the full amount." I replied angrily.

"You know the way it is Mike. We just have to get on with what the Boss Man tells us and deal with any problems ourselves." He stated.

We chatted for a good hour and went through the plan in detail. J explained he would be staying in Cyprus for the next ten days, until the money had cleared in the bank. As I left him in the pub, with a shit load of bonds in my bag, he wished me luck. This was on my head now.

I had to take the bonds to the bank later that day and felt a little cautious although they had authenticated the first bond. This was a huge step, for starters there were over ten million dollars' worth of bearer bonds in the briefcase I'd be carrying into the bank. The realisation of exactly how much money I'd have in my possession made me feel on edge. The bonds were my responsibility until they were handed over to the bank and if anything happened to them, I'd be fucked.

After leaving J, I went to the villa to take a shower, get ready and transfer the bonds from my bag. Hearing the car pull up outside that Sancar had organised, I picked up the briefcase, gripping it tight in my right hand and headed out. Getting into the back seat of the car, the importance of this next hour began to hit home. It was only a short car journey, but it was enough time to ready myself.

Approaching the bank my head was racing. In seven days, the money from the bonds would be available to us. The end was finally in sight, and I promised myself that this would be the last job I'd ever do. I took this journey in search of a thrilling life and I'd had enough thrills to last me a life time.

My appearance spelt importance. I was dressed in a very sharp suit, crisp white shirt and no tie. That would have been a bit over the top. Feeling like 10 million dollars, I wanted this over with, to get my money and get the fuck out of dodge.

I didn't have the same zeal that I'd had when first deciding to get involved with the London guys. Once a visionary, something had changed, causing me to lose my spark. I'd started as an ordinary bodyguard and stood up against guys who were used to money they never even noticed me. Now I was their most valuable asset, and should feel on top of the world, but felt far from it.

I'd a bad feeling about today, I don't know why but something wasn't right. My nerves were getting the better of me, even though the hard part was over and today was just a drop off. My time in the bank would be short, I'd only be signing some paperwork and be out of there, as easy as that.

Walking into the bank, I didn't feel as excited as I'd been on my previous visit. I never even bothered to see if the guard at the door was the same guy as I'd met before. Hearing someone say hello didn't even prompt a response. Knowing exactly where to go, I walked straight past the reception. Heading straight for the manager's office, where he was expecting me. I knocked on his office door. As he opened it, there was something odd about him. It was as if he was waiting for me, but not in the sense that he wanted to see me. He seemed anxious to get this over and done with. Things seemed very suspicious.

I stood at the door of the office for a few seconds, feeling a different uneasy atmosphere. Shaking the manager's hand,

I noticed that it was sweaty and wondered what he had to be nervous about. All he had to do was receive the bonds. On my previous meeting with him he seemed relaxed, ready to give me the world, but this time he appeared to be stressed. He seemed worried, but I wasn't sure if it was just me being paranoid. I'd been paranoid before, but there was something making me feel uneasy.

Maybe my instincts were trying to tell me something, but I quickly pushed those thoughts away. I'd come this far, if things were meant to fall apart, it would have happened well before now. This thought helped relax me a little and I stood tall and proud.

"Nice to see you Mr. Maguire," he said, gesturing with his hand for me to come into his office.

CHAPTER 51
Disaster

With only one foot through the office door, and before I knew what was happening, I'd been tackled to the ground. What the fuck was going on? It all happened so quickly. This was as real as anything could possibly be. With no time to rationalise my thoughts, which was always my downfall, I tried to speak and get up, but the words never came out.

"Stay down", a voice snarled at me, slamming me into the floor again.

Well that's what I thought I'd heard; the accent was too difficult for me to understand. What felt like a gun was jammed hard into my back. I was unable to see who was in the room as my face was being pressed into the rough grainy carpet. Somebody put their foot on my back to make sure I stayed down. There were at least six people in the room, I could hear their different voices. Feeling totally disorientated, I wanted to see their faces, to see who the fuck had put me on the ground like that. Without a doubt it was the police. They were having fun knowing that they had arrested me and there was no way of fighting back against them. The only thing I could do was submit to their wordless demands.

They were being total bastards and I could feel the weight of at least four guys on me. I wanted to fight back, but knew it was a lost cause and there was no point. There was no way to compete with guys who had guns. The weight pushing down on top of me made it hard for me to catch my breath.

No-one had spoken directly to me to tell me what was going on but was able to piece everything together and knew I was in deep shit. Wanting to know who these guys were, but knowing I'd get zero response, I kept my mouth shut.

Struggling to believe what the fuck was happening, trying to set myself free from the choke hold, the thought of running never even crossed my mind. There was no way out, this wasn't a fucking Jason Bourne film, and this was really happening.

Running through everything in my mind, I tried to figure out what had given me away? Maybe I'd been on their radar the whole time. Had they figured out that my identity was forged? I kept asking myself questions, but there were no answers.

I needed to comprehend what was going on. A phone rang, and more conversation followed. I couldn't understand everything that was being said because most of it was in Turkish. Tasting the dirt off the floor, I tried to turn my head, but it didn't make any difference.

The room was absolute mayhem. All the commotion was unnecessary. They already had me pinned to the floor but were obviously enjoying the power they had over me and thought they were big men. There was a lot of shouting and swearing going on. Struggling to turn my head, another one of the pricks kicked me hard in the back. I managed to turn my head enough to see uniformed police officers surrounding me.

All the negative images I'd played in my mind about this job were becoming a reality right here in this room. I'd been ambushed and taken down. I always knew things could go tits up, but truly didn't expect it to happen at this stage. Again, I fought with the idea of trying to fight back. Considering they were all armed and could draw their guns and shoot me in a blink of an eye, I talked myself out of it. What was coming next for me?

I felt afraid for the first time in my life and didn't stand a chance against them with my face in the ground. It was a feeling I didn't like, as it showed weakness. Well out of my depth, I couldn't see a way out. Up until that point they hadn't used too much force with me, but that would all be about to change as soon as they got me out of the bank.

There was a big fat guy, with three pips on his shoulder, rummaging through my briefcase. Remembering the threats, the London Boys had made when I'd first taken the bonds, increased my fear but I couldn't allow myself to think about that right now.

Their guns were drawn, they must have thought that I'd been

armed. One of the guys who saw me looking up, walked towards me and towered over me. Taking the end of his gun, he rammed it hard into my cheek. I thought for a second that he was going to pull the trigger, and, in that moment, I wanted him to, giving me an escape from the misery that I'd be certain to face next.

Then came the consistent punches. A few of them smashing into my ribs, winding me, making it difficult for me to catch a breath. Trying to shield myself with my hands only made them attack me more. I chose not to put up a fight and take the beating they were giving me, remaining silent until I was able to speak to someone of authority.

With each punch they hit me harder and harder. My body was in agony but didn't let them see that. I just needed to endure their beating until it finally stopped.

Once they'd finished, I was pulled up onto my feet and punched straight in the face. The prick that hit me burst my lip, I felt the blood dripping down my face. They had no intention of being civil, they were barbaric, but no-one seemed to care. The bank manager simply stood watching with his mouth wide open. He looked sympathetic to the abuse I was having to endure but that was all he could do. There was no need for all the violence towards me, especially when I'd not put up any resistance.

Finally, they took cuffs out to put on me. They were fucking tight, but no-one gave a fuck. I asked in vain for them to be loosened but was ignored. They dragged me on my feet outside the office; every customer in the bank turned to look at me. The bank was filled with whispers. Would they ever remember my face? This would certainly be a story that they would share with their friends that was for sure.

The police dragged me slowly across the banking hall; they were enjoying their moment and the attention that they were getting. This was probably the most action they'd seen for a while. I think me being a foreigner fueled their rage further and that is why they were being so aggressive towards me. This was going to be a day to remember for all of us. I didn't know whether I'd live long enough to tell the story, but I'd certainly remember it.

Why were they still pointing their fucking guns at me? I wasn't a threat to them anymore being handcuffed. They'd already diffused the situation and if they wanted to prove a point, they'd already done that. This was police brutality at its finest. Not wanting to draw any more attention to myself, I took everything they threw at me.

I'd no idea what was going to happen to me next and didn't have a clue how the Turkish police system worked. In hindsight, maybe I should have considered it, knowing that being caught and getting arrested were a possibility if things went tits up but there was no point thinking like that now and I needed to take whatever was thrown at me next. I felt outside my own body, watching everything happen, with no way of gaining any control.

The policemen were laughing, buzzing with the whole situation. Once we were outside the bank, they shoved me into the back of a police van. The van had a distinctive smell. It smelt like a place where dreams went to die, if such a place existed.

CHAPTER 52
Turkish Torture

I didn't expect my day to turn out like this when waking up this morning. I was supposed to be at the villa right now, celebrating the fact that we were going to be fucking rich. Instead there was no money and I was going to get banged up for this. Still no-one spoke a word of English to me, they continued screaming at me in Turkish. Needing some sense of familiarity and feeling like I was going crazy not having any idea what was going on. All the words I thought I'd learned in Turkish just disappeared. Confused and disorientated, I was alone in this and knew this was a burden I'd have to carry by myself. My mind was racing, and already thinking so far ahead of the situation. Needing to remain calm, I closed my eyes for a second and took a deep breath to help myself focus.

With no idea where we were going, the only assumption was that they were taking me to the police station. Due to the very high speed they were driving, I was being thrown from side to side in the van. Why were they driving so fast? I didn't understand the urgency but at least they had stopped fucking shouting at me.

They continued the conversation between themselves. It was the longest drive I'd ever been on. Not wanting to know my fate once we got to our destination was the worst thing. The drive was probably only ten minutes, but it felt like a lifetime.

They never read me my rights as they cuffed me and didn't serve an arrest warrant when taking me into custody. There was something wrong with the way they'd arrested me, but I was unsure if the same laws applied in this country as they did back home. The whole situation had blown up into something much bigger than it was. I wondered how long it would take for them to send me a British representative and after hearing a couple of stories about the Turkish prison system, I didn't want to believe everything they said was true. Being insignificant meant that my extradition would probably take time.

Sitting in the van, I had time to reflect. My life wasn't all that bad before deciding to become involved in this world. It was my desire for more and thinking I could set myself up for life, even with the risks involved, that had got me here.

I'd created this fucking mess and didn't know how to clean it up. Was it all worth it? If you asked me the same question a month earlier it would have been a definite yes, but right here and now it was a different story. Turning back the clock to the first meeting in London was an option. Where I'd been asked if I was certain about taking the bonds. My answer would have been to turn around and walk out the door.

I was an international criminal now. I'd traversed boundaries which brought with it serious shit and consequences. The magnitude of my crimes was unimaginable. I was in the country with a false passport, which would be the first thing they would prosecute me for. I was certain that news about my arrest would have already reached everyone else that had been involved in this job, and they would inevitably be looking for ways to distance themselves from me.

I was going to jail and there wasn't a thing that could be done about it. I'd been in a juvenile detention centre before, but this was a man's jail. The time I'd spent in there would be child's play compared to this, but jail was a better option than facing the London Boys. Having just lost 10 million of their money, there was only ever going to be one outcome to that!

I was on the verge of losing my mind. Options were limited and I'd either spend the rest of what was left of my life in a Turkish prison or get shot by the London Boys. If only I'd just remained Ishvara's bodyguard, I'd still be dealing with people who didn't pose any threat to me and I'd never have been tempted by the money. There was no way to turn the clock back now.

I'd been so confident in myself, proud, and wanted to prove that I could do just about anything. I should have just shut my mouth and been content with my life. I'd have been in my own home right now with Jenna; it was a simple, but perfect life. I needed Jenna more than ever and wondered if she would pick up the phone if I called her with my one call. Feeling in another world, not knowing what was going on, I wanted to be numb. There were so many questions. I'd let her down, even when she told me that she didn't care about money. If only I'd stayed to prove to her that we were meant to be together, instead of making the decision to come to Cyprus.

The van suddenly came to a halt, which brought me back to reality. The doors were flung open and I was grabbed and pulled out of the van. The shouting began again. Why were they being so fucking over the top? They already had me, and there was no way for me to escape.

Playing everything over in my mind, I thought that maybe we'd become too complacent once we heard back from the bank. But there was no we anymore, there was only me.

This was it for me, prison. We were met by a huge, white, solid metal gate. A small side gate was opened, and I was pushed through, still cuffed. They were still using excessive force, with no way of breaking free I'd no energy left to fight against them. Breathing was becoming increasing difficult with every punch they landed on my ribs. I was visibly struggling but they didn't give a fuck. The blood was still dripping from my lip where I'd been punched in the face back at the bank. They were treating me like an animal.

As we approached the charge desk, the guard began to speak to the desk sergeant in Turkish. I hoped that at least now I'd be treated with a bit more respect. Finally, my cuffs were removed. I rubbed my hands to try and get some life back into them after the cuffs being so tight. They then demanded that I strip. I'd no idea what had happened to the briefcase after it was taken from me at the bank, as they hustled me to the ground.

The desk sergeant wasn't friendly in the slightest, and he relieved me of everything in my possession, before taking me back to where I'd been asked to strip. They were being absolute fucking wankers, trying to show their authority and embarrass me. I was ready to snap when they searched me, before marching me down to an ancient cell with grey bars, forcing me inside.

The room wasn't fit for human habitation. It was disgusting, and the smell was horrendous. There was a concrete bed with no mattress, just a dirty cover and a hole in the floor to shit in with only a few squares of toilet paper.

Struggling to breath, I felt like the walls of the cell were closing in on me. I needed to get a grip of myself before losing it all together.

"Keep calm." I told myself.

The less attention that was on me the better. I couldn't afford to fall apart in here. Sinking onto the hard concrete bed, sitting for hours staring into space, solitude wasn't good for my mind.

A guard walking past, heading to the other cells, distracted me from my daze.

'Excuse me!" I called out to him.

I needed to know what was going on, but he ignored me, so I called out to him again. He ignored me again and it became apparent he didn't give a shit what I had to say, the fucking prick.

For my own sanity, I needed to figure out a plan to give me some clarity. Wondering whether a British attorney would be best and when I'd get my phone call. I battled with the decision of who I'd call to bail me out, if things ever progressed that far. My only thought was Jenna, hoping that she'd find it in her heart to forgive me. I couldn't call anyone connected to the bonds as that would be too risky.

I hadn't seen anyone for a while and had no idea what time it was. Then someone came through the door to give me a cup of tea and some type of stale bread. If this was the shit I was going to be fed, I'd die in here, not able stomach it. Even the

243

rats I was sharing my cell with turned their noses up at it.

"Hey, could I talk to someone about my arrest?" I asked.

Again, being ignored as they walked off, I banged the metal bars in frustration. The way they were treating me was bang out of order. Being held in jail, not knowing what the hell was going on was driving me crazy, I needed answers. Maybe they were treating me like this because they were trying to break me. What more did they want from me? They had the bonds and I was locked up. The least they could do was talk to me.

It was getting darker outside and I tried to get some sleep, which was impossible on the concrete bed. I lay awake for the better part of the night, fearing what the outcome of this would be. One thing was for certain, I was fucked, and it was my fault.

As daylight broke, I hoped that the day would bring some sense and clarity. Grateful that the guards had left me alone in the night because my body couldn't have taken another beating, aching and covered in bruises.

Hearing one of the guards coming, I got to my feet. He handed me a plastic cup of water and another piece of stale bread. At least this time it had a piece of ham on it. I never bothered to speak, knowing I'd only be ignored. Another day came and went and still no-one spoke to me or gave me an indication about what was happening. Days were long in here.

"Are you English?" a guy shouted from a few cells down. He was the first person to have spoken to me in two days. I replied saying I was Scottish but didn't want any conversation past that.

"Why are you in here man?" he asked.

I wanted to ignore him but couldn't handle any more silence.

"Just some bank problems mate," I answered.

Not knowing who he was or anything about him, there was no way I'd give him any more details.

"Are you a bank robber?" he continued to question.

He made me laugh, in a roundabout way I guess he was right.

"No, I'm not a bank robber," I replied coldly.

Then a light bulb moment struck. I could use the conversation to my advantage.

"Do you think that you could get someone to speak to me?" I asked, feeling hopeful for a second, but his reply shot me down.

"They are all bastards and won't speak to any of us." he added.

He never spoke again after that, which made me realise that I'd have a hard time trying to get through to the guards.

"Desk."

A guard appeared as he mumbled again "Desk."

I thought he was talking to someone else, until he repeated it again stopping right outside my cell. He opened my cell door and pointed towards the desk. Unsure what this meant for me, I did as he instructed. The guard left me standing alone for a moment until the desk sergeant had finished what he was doing.

"What is your name? He asked.

Before I could answer, he told me that he'd been through my briefcase and retrieved my passport.

"Your passport is a forgery. What is your correct name? He asked again.

I was about to tell him my name but decided to use this as my chance to be heard.

"Can I have contact with a lawyer, solicitor, or someone from the British Embassy?" I asked.

It was my right to legal representation. I wasn't going to make things easy for them if they refused to treat me properly. They weren't getting my real name until they showed me some fucking respect.

CHAPTER 53
A Hard Reality

This shit was up to me to deal with. The realisation that the police were in no hurry to help me was the kick up the ass I'd needed to accept the fact I was on my own in here. None of my friends had any power to help me. Searching in vain for a way to fix things, the only thought that kept punching me in the face was that I was well and truly fucked.

One of the policemen grabbing me brought me back to reality "Okay, no name, back to your cell." He snarled.

Is that it? Surely, they're going to ask me something else other than my name? Fuck me. They need to speak to me. I need to know what charges I'm facing. Continuing not to give my name would only mean that would drag out telling me what was happening to me. If they ever planned on doing so that is. They'd found bonds worth ten million in my possession. Why weren't they asking me about them? Something wasn't right about this whole situation and it felt wrong. I needed to watch my back, maybe these cunts were going to try and skim some of the bonds for themselves.

They threw me back into my cell, slamming the door shut behind me. Sitting for hours, alone and silent, I kept running things over in my mind again and again. What the fuck went wrong? Where had they taken me, and what was going to happen next?

"Don't piss them off. You will be in deep shit and live to regret it my friend." a voice I recognised said.

The voice went on to say that I should just do what they asked because they could make it very difficult for me in here.

What kind of shithole were they running here? Maybe I should tell them my name as a sign of good faith, and they might give me some information in return. I'd been one of the lucky ones in here so far, the guards had left me alone. My cell was luxury in comparison to some of the others. The one across from mine, which was meant for only two, had four guys crammed together.

The days were long in this shithole, but night times were worse. On the second night I could hear screams coming from another cell. They sounded like a cry for help. No-one could do anything to help and it was torture having to sit and listen. There was no way to know if the cries were from guards attacking prisoners or prisoners attacking each other. The only consolation was that nobody was giving me grief. Every moan or scream would haunt me for a long time to come. Night time was the perfect opportunity for shit to go on, and in the morning it was like nothing had happened. Not a single prisoner ever complained. This was a sign for me not to fuck the guards or prisoners off.

Remembering what I'd been told about the guards being bastards, they would probably still treat me like shit even if they had my name. I'd read somewhere that in foreign jails they can use lengthy pre-trial detention to make you lose your mind. I'd only been here for two days and the place was already doing my head in.

The guards never came near me or offered me food for a long time, I'd almost gave up hope and thought they'd given up on me, but one of them came back and asked again for my name.

"I'm not giving my name until I've spoken to a British lawyer!" I told him

"No name, no lawyer." he simply replied.

As he turned away, he looked at me and sniggered

"We are in no hurry foreigner."

I'd pissed him off by not giving him the answer he wanted but hassling me to give them my real name wasn't going to work. If they wanted to start any of their hardmen shit with me that I'd heard the night before, then they could bring it on. I'd fuck all left to lose now.

Another long night passed without any real drama for me. The only thing that bothered me was my mind, it wouldn't stop for one second. I still couldn't sleep, partly due to the fucking concrete bed. Every hour that passes seemed like a day. Completely frustrated, my mind was going crazy. The routine of prison life wasn't working for me. Waking up, having to eat the shit food they offered, and waiting. Not knowing what you were waiting for made it tough. It was easy to understand how people could lose their mind when they had no idea what was going to happen to them. The mental torture of being unsure of the time, or if you'd ever get out of this place was the worst. How did guys who spend years in solitary confinement survive? It was easy to see why someone would consider giving up in a place like this. I'd only been in jail for three days and I hated it already.

Time moved slowly. There were no windows just blank walls. I'd nothing else to do apart from sit in my cell and think shit thoughts. There wasn't even anyone to speak to. For my own sanity the need to understand how their system worked was driving me. With that knowledge I'd be able to endure my situation more easily. Being in the dark was making me crazy. On the fourth day, two guards came to my cell and dragged me back to see the desk sergeant. I hoped that this time we'd make some progress. The place had already hardened me. In four days, my decision was made, I wasn't going to co-operate with the pricks.

Walking towards the desk sergeant, two soldiers wearing green berets, standing at the front desk, were the first to catch my eye. They were huge and had a mean look about them. They both easily towered above me and I hoped they weren't here for me. I knew that the police were tough, I'd witnessed that first hand, but the Turkish Army has a bad reputation for being brutal. You didn't want to fuck with them, they could easily make you disappear! This had just turned into heavy shit, all because I refused to give the police my name. Obviously used to getting their own way, they'd do whatever it took to get what they wanted, without any reservations. Maybe this Turkish prison wasn't the worst place to be after all. The thought of being in an army prison didn't sit well with me.

The soldiers said fewer words than the police. I was pushed into a dark and dingy room. There was only a single lightbulb hanging from the ceiling that provided a little bit of light. The room was completely empty other that a desk and two metal chairs in the middle of it. I assumed that this was an interrogation room. My head was spinning, what the fuck were they about to do to me.

One of the guards pulled out a chair to sit down. As he pulled it the metal scrapped against the concrete floor creating a piercing high-pitched screech. He pointed at the other chair and ordered me to sit.

I felt completely intimidated, there were two armed soldiers and three policemen in the room who could put a bullet in my head in a split second, but I did well to portray calm on the outside. My hands were shaking, as they handed me a four-page document. Having no idea what it was, flicking through it was pointless, everything was written in Turkish. How the fuck did they expect me to understand this?

"Sign the document." he demanded. To which I refused, not knowing what the document contained. My request for them to translate what was written was only met with aggression.

"You have to sign this document." he shouted in broken English.

"You want out of here? You sign this." he said shoving a pen in my hand and pointing it at the papers.

Of course, I wanted to get the fuck out of there, but at what expense? Where would they take me? I'd be crazy to sign a document blind. Even though this was a desperate situation, there was no way I'd put myself into a worse position.

"If you don't sign this, we come tomorrow and do this all again until you do sign it." he snapped.

If they would just tell me what the fuck it was. What if it was a confession? Even if they had made promises to be more lenient with me in the document, I simply couldn't just sign it. They asked me to sign it again, but my answer was still the same. One of the policemen gave me a hefty slap on my shoulder and bent down to whisper in my ear, "Sign the fucking papers immediately."

He had a chilling evilness in his voice. Looking around the room, I saw two soldiers standing directly behind me with their weapons at the ready and a policeman standing in front of the door with his baton drawn. There was nowhere to go. What would happen if I continued refusing to co-operate with them. I'd never feared for my life before until this moment.

CHAPTER 54
Uncertainty

Knowing I shouldn't sign the document without being able to read it, I gripped the pen tight and scribbled my signature before changing my mind. The document was signed, now maybe they would give me a fucking break. I'd used the name Sean McGuire to sign the papers, the same name that was on my passport. They were so adamant about me signing the documents, they didn't say that it had to be with my real name. My signature was needed on three pages. Once I'd finished, they told me the papers would be sent to a solicitor. The bastards had set me up, and I'd fallen for it. How had I been so stupid and let them get the better of me? The need to get the fuck out of here had made me careless.

I should never have signed the papers and continued to stand my ground. They would have come back the next day, but by that time I'd have figured out what to do. It was stupid to rush in. I kept making mistakes and was starting to give in to their intimidation tactics. My situation was deteriorating and becoming more confusing. I needed a lawyer and quickly, unsure of what was right or wrong and what to do to help myself.

The papers were snatched away from me. One of the soldiers countersigned them, and the sergeant, who was now standing at the door, also signed.

Suddenly everything became clear. The police had just signed my custody over to the army. What the fuck was going to happen to me now? This was deeper shit than I could have ever imagined. I'd just tried to cash in 10 million dollars' worth of bonds and been caught red handed. That could only mean one thing, I'm going away for a very long time. But not in a normal prison, in a fucking Turkish one!

The meanest looking soldier handcuffed me with plastic cable ties. In that moment I knew the game had changed. The army followed a different set of rules. My time with the police didn't seem so bad after all and these crazy bastards were going to do whatever they liked with me now.

The way things had panned out felt unorthodox, and unofficial. Surely this couldn't be legal? One of the policemen entered the room and handed me all my belongings, which they had taken from me on the day I'd arrived. I put my shoes on but carried everything else, before being directed out of the prison.

We headed to the courtyard on the other side of the gate. One of the soldiers kept pushing me in the back as my walking pace was slow. I wasn't in any hurry to go with them. There was a cream-coloured Mercedes parked up waiting for us which they threw me into the back of, still cuffed.

No-one had told me where they were going to take me. I started to think that maybe they were going to hand me over to the Americans, because technically this was a federal crime. Maybe I'd be taken to a maximum-security prison because of the magnitude of my crime. Either way there wasn't going to be a happy ending for me. Sitting in the back of that car, I felt like a shell of my former self, scared, lost and completely vulnerable.

They were exaggerating this crime, it didn't warrant all this attention. Why would the army become involved in white collar crime?

"Maybe it's because of the 10 million dollars in bearer bonds you idiot." I thought to myself.

There were so many questions that I needed answers too.

"Do you speak English?" I asked.

Nobody even acknowledged my question. What was their obsession with silence? It wouldn't hurt for them to say something, even if it was simply for me to shut up. I'd rather that than total fucking silence.

As we drove through the countryside for a while, I spotted signs for a military base ahead. Submitting to the fact that I'd no idea what was going on, I began preparing myself mentally for whatever was going to happen next. No longer in charge of my own fate anymore, it was in somebody else's hands.

My thoughts turned to home. What if I was never able to see, kiss, or touch Jenna again? My family would be devastated if I didn't return. My whole world was falling apart right in front of me. It was a struggle to fight back the tears, not ready to die.

The car began to slow down, which was strange as we hadn't reached the army base yet. One of the soldiers took off his beret and turned around. He was looking directly at me and I wondered what he was doing. Was he expecting a reaction from me because if he was, I was done. There was no more fight left in me.

"Your friend Goker sent us." he whispered, with a smirk.

The words that had just come out of his mouth were difficult to comprehend. Were my ears deceiving me or did he just say that Goker had sent them? This was unbelievable and by far the best news I'd ever received. A wave of relief washed over me, but I wasn't in the clear yet.

Was Goker protecting his interests, or was he truly looking out for his Brother? Had he used his influence to get me out of there because he was worried about the kind of information I could divulge if pressured? Information that could put a lot of people behind bars for a very long time. Suddenly it dawned on me that maybe they weren't here to get me out but get me out of the way. My sense of relief disappeared immediately, and I became suspicious within a second.

"Did Goker send you to help me?" I asked hesitantly.

I was asking if they were sent to get rid of me. Not expecting an honest answer, when he told me to be quiet and that everything would become clear once we got to our intended location, I shut my mouth and did what was asked, keeping my questions to myself.

I wanted to ask for a phone call, unsure of who my call would even be for. But someone had to hear my last words if these were my final hours. Jenna would be my last phone call. I'd tell her that I was truly sorry and loved her with all my heart.

The soldier was no longer interested in having a conversation, that much was obvious, which left me in silence contemplating all the things I'd done with my life. This couldn't be it for me. My promise to Jenna had been that we'd have a better life. I wasn't about to give up on that without a fight.

CHAPTER 55
Protection

It was a long drive, and all the uncertainty made it seem much longer. It took at least another hour before we arrived at the army barracks. The camp was surrounded by a huge twelve-foot fence, which was coated with barbed wire. The gate was secured by four armed soldiers carrying machine guns. No-one was getting in or out of this place without their approval.

Driving through, I saw two recruits being beaten by two soldiers. They were part of a group that were taking part in some sort of physical punishment. There were other recruits being hosed down with what I assumed to be freezing water. The car pulled up outside one of the vehicle hangers and the cable ties were removed from my wrists. When we got inside, it surprised me to see that it had been converted into offices. Everybody I met treated me with respect. I was offered a change of clothes and they disposed of what I'd came with. Still unsure of what was happening, I considered if all this hospitality was a pretence.

"Is Goker coming?" I asked the soldiers that had brought me here.

"No, he will not be coming to the barracks. He cannot be seen to be involved with this situation and must keep his distance." one of them replied.

I was beginning to feel less wary. The upside of being here was that I'd got out of that shithole jail and was being treated better. I didn't know what the soldiers' intentions were but was starting to trust that they had come to help and not get rid of me. I'd worked myself up in the car, which was probably due to being stuck in that prison cell for the last five days.

Being in the barracks reminded me of my time in the army. I missed the routine during those days and the discipline that was instilled in me. It reminded me of the precision we gave to every task we did, and I imagined that the operation to get me here was planned with the same precision.

The soldiers had isolated me, even though they were trying to be kind to me. I understood that they were only doing their job. I'm sure they weren't entirely happy to be part of this situation, but they did what every good soldier did and followed orders. They had given me food that was edible, and that alone made me feel better. Being in prison for the last few days, had given me a lot of thinking time, and it made me see that everything could change in the blink of an eye. Only hours before I was stranded in a Turkish prison but now, in an army barracks, I'd been given new hope.

After three hours on the military base, a finely dressed gentleman came to see me. He could speak English eloquently. Hearing him, gave me a sense of solace. Finally, there was someone who could understand me and bring some clarity. I could have my questions answered at last.

After a short conversation in Turkish with the soldiers, he turned to speak to me.

"How are you Mike?" he asked.

"I've never been so glad to hear an English-speaking voice, particularly one who knows my real name", I replied.

I asked him who he was, but his answer was very elusive.

"I'm a friend of your friend." He stated.

His introduction was very vague, but I never pestered him for more information. I'd learnt to accept whatever was handed to me.

"There was problem at the bank. That's why the police were waiting for you when you got there." He explained.

I was intrigued to know what kind of problem he was talking about but wanted him to finish what he was saying before I began posing my own questions.

"Many strings had to be pulled for me to get you here", he added.

It was apparent by his switch in conversation that he wasn't going to offer any other information about the issue at the bank, which was frustrating. I wanted to know if the situation could have been avoided.

It must have been near on impossible for him to get me out of the police station and under army jurisdiction. There must have been contacts in high places hard at work to make it happen.

"I just want to know what the fuck's going on." I replied.

"The less you know, the better for you!" He responded.

"What happened at the bank will remain an issue for you moving forward, but Goker couldn't leave you to hang Mike." He stated.

His words were the confirmation needed to prove that Goker had done this to ensure my freedom. My concern that Goker needed to get rid of me wasn't justified and now able to think rationally, it was an outrageous thought in the first place. The rollercoaster of being caught and thrown in jail had fucked with my mind.

Goker had contacts in the right places and had managed to pull this off without anyone suspecting his involvement. He truly was a great man, who I now owed everything.

"We need to get you out of Cyprus. It is safer for you that way!" He continued.

I agreed with him completely and needed to be as far away from here as possible. Turkey wasn't even safe for me anymore. The police could have easily come looking for me. It would be stupid of me to stay, because eventually it would come back to bite me in the ass.

Unsure of how I'd escape without being caught, I listened to find out what he had planned next. He continued to explain that once night fell someone would come and take me to a different location. My extraction was already meticulously planned, which was no surprise with Goker behind it. There was no time to waste and we needed to hit the ground running. The next step was to have me sail as a deck hand on a cargo ship the very next day. Sailing didn't require many identification or security checks, so it was the low-key option for travelling and it would be the best way for me to get out of the country. After leaving Cyprus I'd make my way to Gibraltar and on to Calais, where I'd travel on the ferry back to London. It was going to be a fucking long and tiresome journey, but the end justified the means and I'd be back on home soil.

The plan was very detailed and elaborate. Every measure was put in place to ensure that we avoided getting caught. It was going to be tough, but it sure sounded sweeter than sitting in jail for years. The execution of this plan was paramount, if it failed it would put a lot of people at risk. If there was any deviation which resulted in my capture, I'd be back in a jail cell. I needed at least one thing to go my way.

"What will happen once I'm back in London?" I asked.

"You are leaving, which will create a huge mess, but we will clean it up!" He replied.

The London Boys were going to be a different issue. I owed them ten million and had zero to offer to begin to repay them. I may have been on the verge of avoiding years in jail in Cyprus, but my escape was only going to lead me into the hands of a gang that were most likely going to kill me.

The Brotherhood had come through for me in a way that I'd never have imagined, but there was nothing Goker could do to help me with the London Boys. Everything was far from okay, but he had put everything on the line for me for which I'd be forever grateful. I would never have survived years in a Turkish jail.

CHAPTER 56
The Journey Begins

After being given a passport to cross the border on the next part of my journey, and a work identification card to board the cargo ship, I was ready to go. This was going to be the start of a long journey for me and one I never imagined would be possible, but Goker had made the impossible happen.
Waiting to be picked up, my head was filled with doubt about whether London was the best place for me to go. My fate would be determined once I returned and my life would be in the hands of the London Boys. They had the power to decide whether I lived or died and that filled me with fear.
Heading straight back to Scotland to get Jenna and fuck off on the run seemed like a good option, but there were two problems with that idea. The first being, going on the run would mean a life of looking over our shoulder constantly and feeling on edge, and that wasn't the life we had planned. The second being that I wasn't a pussy and would stand and take whatever consequences came from losing the bonds. Even if we did go on the run, with their contacts and resources, the London Boys would track us down in no time, so it would be pointless. I'd escaped one fucked up situation but was heading straight into another.

Once my transport arrived, we headed straight to the port. The driver never spoke much English, but he was going to ensure that I got onto the cargo ship with no dramas. He worked on board himself, which would make things straight forward. The drive down was easy and uneventful. The past few days had been enough of a rollercoaster to last a lifetime.

Our plan was to stay at the port overnight and head onto the ship in the morning. We couldn't risk staying in a hotel that night. Laying low in the car was our only option. Although I tried to get a sleep it was impossible. Thinking every car that pulled up would be there to take me back to jail, but what made things worse was having no idea what would waiting for me when my journey was over.

We spent a long, freezing night in the car. I had fuck all, only the clothes on my back to keep me warm. How the tables had turned. Only a week ago I'd been living the dream with the guys at the villa, but now it felt like I was beginning my journey to hell.

When morning came it was time for us both to board the ship. As I got out of the car, a feeling of dread washed over me. I'd not been sailing very often but the times I had, it'd been a shit experience.

My journey wasn't going to be about luxury. It was a means to an end to get me out of this mess. I'd been given specific instructions that had to be followed to the letter, with no room for any fuck ups. I had to keep my head down on board and not bring any unwanted attention to myself.

The ship was huge and well worn. It had obviously earned the guys that worked on it a good living. When we were boarding, seeing the masses of rust coating the outside, brought doubts in my mind about whether it should be in the water in the first place.

We sailed the Mediterranean Sea for three days, heading towards Gibraltar; I never left the cabin once. Although I'd been taken onto the ship under the pretence of being a deck hand, I wasn't expected to do any work. This was only my cover to use if anyone asked questions, or the authorities were to come on board.

The journey gave me a lot of thinking time and I constantly battled with my own mind, trying to work out what I'd do when arriving back in London. Being alone in my cabin quickly became very boring. I didn't have a phone and wanted so much to speak to Jenna.

The crossing was extremely rough, and I was bashed around in my tiny cabin. There were only two beds inside, hardly big enough for me to lie on without falling off. The small bathroom constantly smelt of piss. It was enough to make me feel sick but at least it was better than being in jail. The cabin was on the upper deck and had a window that looked out onto the water. I'd spend hours watching the beast that was the sea, smashing against the rocks and the side of the ship, wondering if the London Boys would do the same to me.

Things were still shit at home with Jenna and we hadn't had the chance to speak properly for days. I just hoped that I'd get the chance to go home and sort things out with her but there was so much doubt and uncertainty in my mind about my fate or if I'd even make it home at all. This was a dark time for me. Worse than any I'd ever been through.

Getting back to London was the first step in trying to pick up the pieces, but I wasn't stupid enough to think it was going to be simple.

"Oh, you lost our 10 million, no problem, have a nice day." is not the words I'd hear from the London Boys once they got their hands on me, but there was no other choice but to face them. I knew what the consequences were once I'd taken the bonds from the Boss Man's hand. He had made them crystal clear, and it was time to deal with whatever these would be. For the first time, I was worried for my own life.

There was minimal contact with other people whilst on the ship, apart from a few brief chats with my contact who worked on board when he brought me food. I had to be a fly on the wall and remain un-noticed. My mind wouldn't give me a rest and I struggled with thoughts about what would happen when I got back to London. There was some hope that the London Boys would at least give me the chance to explain, and if possible, make amends without putting a bullet in my head the second they caught sight of me. What the fuck were they going to do to me? The uncertainty was killing me.

The Boss Man's words haunted every second, both awake and asleep.

"If you take these bonds out of my hand then they are your responsibility, if the police get hold of them, or if you lose them, then you owe me their value."

Ishvara had been the clever one to walk away when he did. When the Boss Man had said the exact same words to me, I'd been the idiot that replied

"Yes, I'll do it, no problem."

I wasn't feeling like such a tough guy now.

CHAPTER 57
Tough Times

Arriving in Gibraltar was a relief, at least it was a British Colony, and familiar territory. As far as I was aware, they didn't have any information about my arrest back in Cyprus. It was time to separate from my contact at this point and I'd be alone for the rest of my journey.

Goker's contact had given me money back at the army base, which he told me to use for food and a place to stay whilst on the road, but it wasn't much, and there was still a long way to go so I'd need to live on very little. For the next part of my journey I'd travel from Gibraltar to mainland Spain by train and then on to France, where I'd catch the ferry from Calais to Dover. I was exhausted from not sleeping for days and hungry. Not having enough money to even eat a decent meal was soul destroying. London seemed so far away and the thought of what I'd have to endure to get there filled me with dread.

It had been the toughest five days. I tried to focus on getting home but feeling helpless, started me thinking about my life before all of this began. It had been a good life that was easy to maintain, with a good woman by my side. I should have been happy, but instead insisted on chasing the dream. There was no point in rewriting the story in my head, because I'd chosen this path, and no-one had held a gun to my head or forced me to do any of it. This was all on me.

The train station was only a short walk from the port. Sitting waiting for my first train, two guys began arguing right next to me. Within seconds they were throwing punches at each other, shouting and swearing. The two of them had obviously been drinking as the stench of alcohol drifted towards me. This was the last thing I needed, for them to cause a scene and bring attention from the police. Needing to get out of there, I stood up, but it was too late the police were already running down the platform towards us waving their batons. My heart was in my mouth, what if it had been reported that I'd escaped from jail and they recognised my face from wanted pictures? I'd be fucked and straight back to jail, so I quickly turned away from them, and walked further down the platform out of their eyesight.

The two pissed guys were no match for the police and they had been tackled to the floor and handcuffed in no time. Luckily my train arrived whilst all the commotion was going on and I quickly jumped on and took a seat.

On the train I sat motionless, with my head resting against the seat and my eyes fixed to the roof, wishing to be anywhere but here. All I could think about was the London Boys. Would they kill me straight away or take pleasure in kicking shit out of me first? And the battle with my mind started all over again.

The next few days were spent hopping from one train to the next, working my way towards mainland Spain. I'd sit for hours sometimes in stations just waiting. The only thing I could afford to buy to eat was a couple of chocolate bars, sandwiches and water. This was a shit life, so close to breaking point. I'd never felt so alone.

Once arriving in mainland Spain, I headed straight to the ticket office to buy a one-way ticket to France. The train would take me across the border where I'd have to use the passport I'd been given by Goker's contact. At that realisation I stopped and for the first time, took the passport out of my pocket to look at it. Standing in the middle of a busy train station, surrounded by so many people, ironically feeling alone, I stared at the face looking back at me. The picture had been taken right back at the beginning of all of this. I looked young and my eyes were bright and alive in this picture. Catching a glimpse of my reflection in a shop window as I stood right here, right now, I'd aged unbelievably. My eyes told a different story. They were the eyes of a man that had the weight of the world on his shoulders.

The loud piercing sound of a whistle being blown brought me back from my thoughts and I headed in to buy my ticket. There was no queue which surprised me. The guy sitting behind the desk was very overweight and scruffy. He had stains down the front of his shirt, which were probably the remains of his lunch. It was obvious that he hated his job and never cracked a smile once.

The next part of my journey would take me to Toulouse. I had a few hours to wait for my train and found a seat in the station. I watched people rushing around, eager to get to where ever they were going, caught up in their own little worlds. It was a distraction for a short time but then my thoughts returned to London. The closer I was getting, the greater my fear became. It was a darkness that was engulfing me.

About ten minutes before my train was due, I got up from where I'd been sitting and took a walk over to the kiosk. Needing to get something to eat, my stomach ached from lack of food. The only thing I could afford was a Mars Bar. Slowly unwrapping the chocolate my mouth began watering. What I'd have given to be back at one of our barbeques right now, laughing with the guys drinking a beer. The thought of all the succulent meats and fresh food caused my stomach to rumble loudly.

What had happened to the guys? Were they in the shit too? I'd no idea as the last time I'd had any contact with them was just before going into the bank. Hoping that they were okay, I slumped down onto the floor against the wall and put my head in my hands, feeling completely lost and helpless.

The voice on the tannoy told me that my train had arrived. For a moment I considered not getting on it but knew that would only bring more shit my way, so getting off the floor I slowly made my way to the platform. Being pushed in the back by other passengers trying to get on the same train, started to piss me off. What was the fucking rush, we'd all get on anyway. Eventually I got to my seat, sat down, letting out a huge sigh of relief, put my head back and closed my eyes. This journey was beginning to take its toll on me. The beeps sounded for the doors to close and we were off.

CHAPTER 58
Times Up

Listening to the sound of the tracks as we raced along, must have caused me to fall asleep because the next thing I remember is being woken by the ticket inspector to check my ticket and passport. Feeling dazed from my sleep I never even had the chance to worry about showing my passport, he had checked it and walked away before I'd realised what was happening. We must have crossed over in to France.

It wasn't long before we arrived in Toulouse. I must have completely passed out when I'd fallen asleep, sleeping for nearly the full day. That wasn't a bad thing because it meant that I'd escaped my head fucking thoughts for a while.

It was a four hour wait in Toulouse before the train came for Calais, another long wait in the station.

Just as I stepped off the train when we arrived, a guy spoke to me.

"You must have needed that sleep. I've never seen anyone sleep so long on a train before." He said, in a familiar midlands accent.

Turning to look at him, I was greeted by his smile. The guy had long messy hair and was wearing a pair of shorts, and well-worn hiking boots. On his back he carried a huge rucksack that probably held his whole world. He had obviously been travelling for a while.

"It's been a hell of a journey." I said with a little laugh.

If only he knew the full story.

"Where are you off to mate?"

"Heading to Calais to catch the ferry."

"No way, me too. We've got a hell of a wait now though, fancy grabbing a beer with me?" He asked.

He looked like a genuine enough guy and his chat would be a good distraction, so I agreed.

We headed into the first bar and he ordered us a couple of beers.

As he struggled to take off his rucksack, I asked where he had been. I'd been right with my first thought, he'd been travelling all over Europe for the past few months but was now heading home.

"What about you man, where have you been on your travels?" He asked.

I paused for a moment before answering, trying to make up a bullshit story in my mind.

"Ah, I've just been visiting friends in Gibraltar, but lost my fucking luggage, hence I've nothing with me. It had everything in it, including my money." I answered.

"That's shit for you mate. Well don't worry the drinks are on me." He replied with a warm smile.

I liked this guy, he was sound. We spent the next few hours talking shit about anything and everything. It was good to not be on my own, left with my dark thoughts and I was grateful for his company. Hardly having anything to eat for days had made the beer go straight to my head.

The time passed quickly, and it was soon time for us to get the train to Calais. I had to go for a piss before getting on the train, so we said our goodbyes before heading our separate ways. Walking towards the toilets, I noticed a couple that had obviously not seen each other for a while. They threw their arms around each other and held each other tightly whilst passionately kissing. My thoughts immediately returned to Jenna and the realisation that I may never see her again made tears well in my eyes.

Running along the platform, I made it onto the train just as the doors were about to close. It was a quick journey to the port at Calais compared to what I'd been through over last few days.

Once I was on the ferry, it would only be a few hours and I'd be back on home ground. A wave of impending doom washed over me, sending a shiver down my spine.

Boarding the ferry at Calais was a lot different to boarding the cargo ship. This was a passenger ferry and a lot more comfortable. Staff members were so eager to help at every turn, they were enough to make you feel claustrophobic.

I'd been stuck inside a jail cell, cars, trains and train stations for days, so I made my way out on deck, where I remained for most of the crossing. It was good to not feel like a caged animal for a change. Standing at the rear of the ship I watched as France got lost in the distance and finally disappeared from the horizon, ironically as my dream had.

Almost instantaneously my mind returned to London again. I'd be arriving back in Dover in the early hours of the morning, with no phone to contact the guys and no phone number to even call them on. How would I get hold of them? The only option would be for me to make my way to their pub in Gravesend and hope that one of them would either be there, or someone in the pub would be able to get hold of them for me.

Reaching into my pocket, I pulled out the last of my money. All that was left was £2. How had it come to this? I'd done everything that was asked of me. I had everything there for the taking with this job and in the blink of an eye I was standing on this ferry with only £2, making my way back to what would probably be my own funeral.

I paced the ship's deck up and down, feeling empty, until we docked in Dover. Before leaving the ferry, I spoke to one of the staff members who directed me to the closest train station. This would be the final stage of my journey and the need for it to be over was becoming stronger. I'd get the train to Dartford and on to Gravesend. From there, what would happen next would be up to the London Boys, my fate would be in their hands. Dartford was a shit hole and not a place anyone wanted to hang around in, but I needed to get my head together before heading to the pub. These next few hours were going to be my last and I needed to prepare myself for that. Not being able to have a final conversation with my family or Jenna was tearing me apart.

Walking through a park, I came across a small stream. Stopping for a few moments, taking the passport and documents I'd used to get this far out of my pocket. Slowly, I ripped both into tiny pieces, watching them float down the stream, until the water engulfed them, sucking them under. This was what had become of my life, I'd been engulfed by my desire for a better life and it had pulled me under.

"You need to snap out of this self-pity." I said, whilst slapping myself hard in the face.

It was time to face the consequences for losing the bonds. My train journey to Dartford took the last of the money and in a desperate situation I had to jump the final train to Gravesend, bolting as soon as the doors opened. Adrenaline pumped through my body as I ran, running longer than needed. Beginning to recognise my surrounding, I slowed my pace to a walk, knowing their pub was just around the next corner, looking at my watch to see the time and if anyone would be in the pub yet.

Turning the corner to reach the pub, my watched turned 12.13pm and as I put my hand against the pub door to open it, my watch stopped. Time was up, the wait was over.

CHAPTER 59
Facing the Consequences

My heart was in my mouth as I pushed the heavy pub door open, not knowing who would be inside. The door let out a large creak and everyone in the pub turned to look at me, to see who dared enter their territory, as I stepped inside. They soon lost interest, the second they caught sight of me and went back to their drinks.

The barman was serving a customer but gave me a nod in acknowledgment. His face was familiar, the huge slash down the left side of his cheek was something you would never forget. He'd been serving behind the bar before when I'd been here with the guys.

The pub was busy, I imagined that most of the punters were regulars. They were a tough looking crowd, skin heads and tattoos. If things were going to go up in the air, this is the last place you'd want it to happen. These guys looked like they would fight to the death.

With no money in my pocket, I gestured to the barman that I'd go to the gents before he served me, this way I could scan the place and see if there was anyone here that was familiar. To my disappointment there wasn't. What the fuck was I going to do now? The only thing left to do was speak to the barman to see if he could help me out.

Leaving the gents, I could see that he'd finished serving the other guy. This was my chance to speak to him. Approaching the bar brought with it a mixture of emotions, if I speak to him and he can help me then that'd be it for me, no more waiting. The London Boys would be here in no time. If I didn't speak to him and left and he recognised my face, he would tell them I'd been here as soon as he saw them next. Either way I was fucked.

Just as I was about to speak, a hand giving me a hard slap on my shoulder caused me to spin round. At first, thinking it was someone wanting to fight me, my guard was up straight away, but couldn't believe it when I saw J.

"What the fuck Mike! How did you get here?" J asked, completely shocked.

I could tell that he was pleased to see me, but that was probably to save his own ass. I'd imagine that the London Boys weren't too happy with him when he returned from Cyprus without the bonds and with no idea where the fuck I'd been taken either.

"Ah fuck J, I can't even begin to tell you the shit I've been through this last week." I replied.

"I can see that mate. You look like shit." J said with a laugh as he stepped back to look me up and down.

"I'm completely done in." I replied.

J stood staring at me. He obviously wanted more of an explanation than that. I began to tell him in detail what had happened, from the moment my face was being jammed into the carpet back in the bank, to being thrown into a Turkish jail.

"No fucking way. A Turkish jail? We need a drink." J said as he gestured to the barman for two straight whiskies.

Continuing with how Goker had pulled every string possible to get me out and my horrendous journey back. J's face spoke a thousand words, without him even opening his mouth once, as I relived my ordeal. He couldn't believe how lucky I'd been and how I almost certainly shouldn't be standing in front of him now. We'd been standing at the bar for over an hour and I'd only given J a snap shot of what went down.

"Listen man, you know I should be on the blower to the Boss Man straight away, but here take this money and phone. Go get yourself a room at the hotel across the street, get some food and crash out. I'll put him off until tomorrow. You need to fucking promise me though that you won't move from your room. The Boss Man will have my balls if you do a runner." J said.

"Honestly mate, you don't know how much that means to me." I replied.

J owed me nothing, but he was being sound. He could have easily landed me right in it to save his own neck, but he was giving me time. To be fair I'm not sure if waiting another night before getting a bullet to my head was going to make any difference and part of me wished that he'd just phone him there and then, so it'd be over.

J ordered us another two whiskies. As soon as the barman put both glasses down on the bar in front of us, I picked mine up, downing it in one.

"Fuck me. You must have needed that." J laughed.

"You've no idea J" I replied, thinking back, replaying the events of the last week in my mind.

J downed his drink and took the phone back that he'd handed me, programming his number into it. As he handed it back, he told me that as soon as I'd checked in at the hotel, I was to message him with my room number and he'd bring the Boss Man to see me first thing.

I stood without saying anything for a few minutes, staring into space, trying to take in the fact that this was going to be my last night. J had thrown me a small lifeline, but on the grand scheme of things it was fuck all.

"You okay with that Mike?" J asked.

I wanted to scream in his face

"Of course, I'm not fucking okay. Would you be if you were about to get done in?"

But I never, realising that keeping quiet was probably the best thing to do, and simply nodded in agreement.

J's phone began ringing. After a brief conversation with the person on the other end of the phone he hung up.

"Listen, I need to shoot. I've got shit to deal with. You go get sorted in the hotel and remember to fucking message me that room number and we will see you tomorrow. I know we've got to know each other as friends but you need to understand that working for the Boss Man comes first so whatever happens tomorrow just know that it's not personal. You and I both know it's not going to go well for you." He said as he put his hand on my shoulder before turning to leave.

And with that I was left standing alone at the bar. The barman put another drink down in front of me.

"On the house, you look like you need it." he said with a smile. Lifting the glass and raising it in his direction with a nod of appreciation, I downed it.

I'd had enough of this place and needed to be on my own. With J giving me the phone at least I'd be able to call Jenna to make sure that she was okay. Knowing that the conversation with her would be one of the toughest of my life, I headed to the off-license next to the pub for a bottle of whisky before going to the hotel.

Placing the bottle on the counter

"Party tonight then big man?" The cashier asked.

"Something like that mate." I replied.

If only he knew the reality of what tomorrow would bring for me.

CHAPTER 60
The Final Goodbye

The reception in the hotel was quiet. There was no-one at the desk so after waiting a few minutes I rang the bell. It was at least five minutes before a young girl appeared from the back looking flustered.

"Sorry, to keep you waiting Sir. How may I help you?" she asked.

"I'd like a room for the night, please." I replied.

"Certainly, I can get that organised for you. I'll just be a moment." She said as she disappeared into the back again.

"Where the fuck is she going?" I thought to myself.

All I wanted was to get into my room to be able to speak to Jenna.

Another five minutes passes and she appeared again.

"Sorry, Sir, how was it I could help you?" She asked again.

Was she for real? I'd only just told her that I wanted a room for the night.

My patience was starting to wear thin.

"I'd like a room for the night!" I replied, with a little less patience in my voice this time.

"Of course, Sir. Is it a room for one? Would you like a standard or executive room? What about your pillows, what kind would you like?" She asked cheerfully.

"I just want a room with a bed. If you could just organise it for me quickly as possible." I snapped.

Within seconds I felt bad for being rude. The girl was obviously new and trying to do her best.

"Sorry, I've had a bad day and shouldn't have been so rude." I apologised.

"No problem at all Sir. Tomorrow is another day and hopefully it will be a better one for you." She said as she smiled, handing me the key card for my room.

Giving her an attempt at a smile, my thoughts turned to the next day and what it would mean for me. My heart sank at the realisation of spending my last night alone.

The girl continued to talk, giving me directions to my room but I didn't hear her words and only saw her lips moving.

Turning to walk to my room, I closed my eyes for a second, taking a deep breath and gripping the whisky bottle tight in my hand.

My room was on the second floor of the hotel and was the first door off the elevator. It took a few attempts for the key card to work. On the third time of it not working I banged the door hard with my fist in frustration, causing the man in the room next to mine to open his door. He quickly scurried back into his room when he saw the look in my eyes. Realising that he didn't want to fuck with me today.

Finally, the colour changed to green and the door opened. I stepped inside closing it behind me and stood with my back up against it for a few minutes feeling alone, lost and broken.

Moving away from the door, I threw the whisky bottle on the bed and pulled the curtains shut to block out the world.

Slumping down on the end of the bed and staring at myself in the mirror, I grabbed the bottle again, unscrewing the cap and taking a long swig from it. The whisky was strong and burned all the way down to my stomach.

The only place I wanted to be right now was home, with Jenna by my side. Picking up the phone I dialed her number whilst taking another drink. The phone rang for a while and for a minute I thought she might not pick up because she wouldn't recognise the number.

"Hello" she said in her soft voice.

Wanting to say so much, but not knowing where to start, I was unable to speak. A single tear rolled down my cheek, dripping onto the whisky bottle in my hand.

"Hello, who's there?" she said.

"Hi Jen, it's me." I replied, trying to control the emotion in my voice.

"Babe, is that really you? I've been so worried about you." I could hear the concern in her voice.

"Yeah gorgeous it's me. You've no idea how good it is to hear your voice. I've missed you" I continued.

"Where are you? You've not even tried to contact to me for over a week." She said, with a hint of frustration.

"I'm sorry Jen, it wasn't that I didn't want to speak to you, it was just impossible." I replied apologetically.

The last thing I wanted was for her to be angry at me, especially with this being the last time we were going to speak.

"When are you coming home?" she asked hopefully.

My heart broke into a thousand pieces. It felt as though I'd been stabbed in the chest. Tears began streaming down my face. How could I tell her I'd never be coming home? That I'd never be able to hold her or kiss her again.

"Are you still there?" She asked.

"Yeah babe, sorry, I'm not sure when yet. I've still got a few things to sort out." I replied, fighting back the sadness.

"Okay, well let's hope it's soon." she said with disappointment.

"I'll be back as soon as possible babe." I said, knowing that it was a lie.

"Is everything nearly over? I need you back Mike." Jenna asked with sadness in her voice.

"Yes babe it's nearly over." I replied.

That was the truth it was nearly over, for me anyway.

"Promise me that when you come back you won't leave again babe. Being without you is too hard." She begged.

"Babe, never forget how I much love you. No matter what happens you'll always mean the world to me. I'm sorry for everything I've done to hurt you." I replied, beginning to breakdown.

There was a short silence before she spoke.

"The kids have just burst through the door, I need to go but phone me later." She said warmly.

"I love you with all my heart." I said softly, trying to hide my weakness.

And with that the line went dead. Falling back onto the bed I broke down, sobbing into the pillow, unable to control my tears. I'd never felt sadness like this before. I'd always told Jenna that I'd be there for her and I'd never let her down, but I had. I'd failed her and that thought destroyed me.

The next few hours were filled with dark images of how it would end for me, concluding that it would probably be in the middle of nowhere with a bullet to the back of my head. As darkness fell outside the blackness filled my room. The bottle of whisky was my only comfort, but it did not take away the pain.

Laying pissed on the bed, I called Jenna one final time.

"Hey babe. What's up, why are you calling again?" she asked.

"I just wanted to call to say goodnight babe and tell you that I love you before going to sleep." I replied.

My goodnight was really my goodbye.

"Good night handsome, I love you too." She said softly before hanging up the phone.

She has no idea how much I needed to hear those words.

Laying there alone on the bed, it didn't take long for me to fall unconscious with all the whisky I'd drank.

CHAPTER 61
Penance

The sound of the phone ringing woke me up. For a minute I'd forgotten where I was. My mouth was dry, and head was thumping. Still slightly dazed I reluctantly answered.

"Hello" I said, with a groggy voice.

"It's me. We are on our way up Mike." J replied.

In that moment my daze had passed and remembering what day it was, caused me to sit bolt upright. Still fully clothed from the night before I clambered out the bed, smashing the empty whisky bottle as it fell onto the floor.

There was no time to clean it up because just at that moment there was a loud bang on the door. Fuck they're here.

Fear filled my veins, I wasn't ready for death. They banged the door again louder this time. There was nowhere to go, I had to face them. Peering through the spy hole before opening the door I could see J, the Boss Man and one of his heavies.

I'd only just put my hand on the door handle and pulled it down when the heavy booted the door open, smashing it into my face. He was in the room and on top of me in a second, punching me hard in the face and stomach causing me to fall to my knees, onto the broken glass. Before having the chance to defend myself, he kicked me hard in the stomach with his steel toe capped boots. There was a huge crack, and with the excruciating pain that followed, I knew the bastard had broken my ribs.

"Enough." the Boss Man demanded.

The heavy stepped away, allowing the Boss Man to tower over me. He grabbed me by the throat and squeezed hard with his fingers, making it difficult for me to breathe.

"You've got some fucking explaining to do" he growled, pushing me back so hard that I was now lying flat on my back in the glass.

He brought his foot up, stamping hard onto my stomach, pushing down where the heavy had cracked my ribs. I'd never felt pain like it, but never made a sound. They weren't going to see my weakness. I could feel the pieces of glass from the whisky bottle pierce the skin on my back as he pushed down. Blood dripped down my face.

Walking over to the window, the Boss Man pulled the curtains open. The light hurt my eyes. This was some fucking hangover. "Get up and start talking." he demanded.

Slowly I dragged myself up and sat with my back against the bed. J looked on helplessly, there was nothing that he could do to help me. The Boss Man was in charge here and J had to do whatever he was told.

What had happened over the last week flashed before me as I relived the whole thing again, explaining everything in detail to the Boss Man, except for who got me out of the jail. After two hours of interrogation there was no way to read what he was thinking. He'd not shared his thoughts once about what had happened, but simply kept firing questions at me. I couldn't help feeling like he had me on trial.

"So, you simply turn up at my pub and expect what exactly? You know who I am Mike and there's no way you can walk away from losing 10 million dollars of mine. You knew the consequences when you took the bonds from my hand." He stated, with a darkness in his eyes.

"Yeah, that's why I'm here, to face what's coming to me head on. I've never ran from anything in my entire life, and I'm not about to start now." I replied.

The Boss Man shifted on his feet impatiently.

"What I need to know is who got you out the jail?" He asked. Knowing that I was probably off my head, but was fucked anyway

"Just a contact. That's all you need to know." I replied.

For the first time the Boss Man lost his cool, walking right over to me where I sat, pulling a gun out and ramming it into my forehead.

"Don't fuck with me. This isn't a game." he warned.

"You're not going to put a bullet in my head here. There's too many witnesses in the hotel." I replied.

"You're fucking damn right I'm not. Get to your feet." he demanded.

"J get the car." he ordered.

J quickly opened the door and left to get the car.

"You will walk out of here with no drama, because if you don't it's not only your life you'll need to worry about Mike." the Boss Man threatened.

His words sent a shiver down my spine. There was no way I'd put my family at risk. I did as he instructed and walked out the room, into the lift and out of the hotel without saying another word.

J was already parked outside with the engine running. He jumped out as soon as he saw us, opening the rear passenger door. The heavy jumped into the front seat to drive, and as soon as the Boss Man and I were in the back, J slammed the door shut and ran around to the front passenger seat to get in. The heavy had already pulled away at high speed before J had even shut the door.

Fuck where were they going to take me? Maybe I'd been too cocky and should have played it different, but I'd lost all fear and was a dead man walking anyway so why the fuck should I give him Goker's name. My death was inevitable, and there was no chance I'd betray the Brotherhood.

J turned to look at me, I could see the fear in his eyes for what the Boss Man was going to do to me next. The Boss Man stared straight ahead, not speaking. He looked deep in thought. You didn't need to be a genius to work out what those thoughts would be.

We drove for about 15 minutes, before I saw a sign for

Woodhill's Park.

"Make sure you take us deep into the woods." the Boss Man instructed the heavy, who never spoke, but simply nodded in acknowledgment.

The trees got thicker, and it became darker as we drove deeper into the woods. It was an earie place. I couldn't hear any birds singing, which seemed strange. Maybe they knew death was coming.

"Here is fine." The Boss Man said.

The heavy pulled up just next to a huge oak tree.

"Take him out and don't take your eyes off him for a second. J and I have decisions to make", the Boss Man stated, handing his gun to the heavy.

Feeling the muzzle of the gun in my back as I got out the car, the heavy pushed hard, indicating for me to walk forward. We walked about twenty yards into a small clearing amongst the bushes.

"On your fucking knees." he growled.

Slowly lowering to my knees into the dirt, feeling the chill in the air. Looking into the woods, waiting for the bullet, my mind began to drift away thinking about how it had come to this. One decision had brought me to this moment right here, right now. Had it been the right choice? If I had the chance would I go back and choose a different path? The answer was no. I'd followed my desire for a better life and although things hadn't turned out as planned there were no regrets. My fear had lifted, and I was ready to face what was coming to me.

The crack of a branch snapping brought me back from my thoughts. J and the Boss Man stood in front of me.

"Okay, J has confirmed with his contact in Cyprus that you were arrested, and the bonds were ceased. At least I'm certain you didn't try to fuck me over, but you still lost my 10 million none the less. Which brings us to the point we are at now." The Boss Man said before pausing.

"I now need to decide how you will pay for your fuck up. Option one, I put a bullet in your head right now and bury you where you fall, but realistically is that enough pay back for losing 10 million? I'm not certain. Option two, you feel the pain of knowing I'm going to hurt your family before you die."

The anger inside me erupted and before the Boss Man had a chance to say anything else, I looked him straight in the eye "Don't you fucking dare go near my family, they have nothing to do with this. I've done everything you've asked of me from day one. The deal went tits up, not through any fault of mine. I came back to face you like a man so at least show me some respect." I warned.

With that I felt the butt of the gun smash into the back of my head.

"Keep your fucking mouth shut!" The heavy threatened.

"If you're quite finished whining, you might be interested to hear option three!" The Boss Man said sarcastically.

"The fact that you managed to get out of a Turkish jail and all the way back to the UK, shows me that you have some powerful friends. These are the kinds of contacts that would prove very useful to me." He continued, stepping closer.

"Today might be your lucky day! J has convinced me that option three is that best way forward. You owe him your life Mike. This is what's going to happen. You belong to me now and you will for many years to come. When I need you to do a job for me you will do it without question." He stated and turned to walk towards the car, leaving me on my knees.

"We are leaving." he barked to J and the heavy.

Before leaving, J shook my hand

"Keep hold of that burner phone mate. I'll be in touch in a couple of days. Good luck and I'll see you soon." He said.

As he pulled his hand away, he'd pressed a small bundle of bank notes into my palm.

My throat was that dry I only just managed to squeeze out the words

"Thanks, I owe you big time mate" before he got into the car.

Watching the dust from the tyres as the car sped away, I dragged myself onto my feet. The weight of the world should have been lifted from my shoulders, but I didn't feel relief. The thought of walking hours to get out of this place wasn't my concern, it was the fact that the Boss Man had just told me that he owned me. What the fuck was this going to mean for me now?

CHAPTER 62
The Twist

After walking for hours, I finally reached the train station. It wasn't long before the next train to Scotland arrived and I was on my way home. Remembering the burner phone was still in my pocket, I sent Steve a text to tell him what time my train was due in and if he could meet me.

The journey back was completely surreal. Only hours before I'd been playing my own death over in my mind and now, I was on my way back to reality. Thoughts of the events over the past year were enough to keep me distracted, and time passed quickly. Before I knew it, I'd arrived in Edinburgh and was on the final train to Dundee.

Steve was waiting for me in Dundee when I arrived on the platform. He greeted me with huge hand shake.

"How are you mate? Good to see you. Glad to be home?" He asked.

"You've no idea Steve. It's been a fucking nightmare. I'm lucky to even be here." I replied.

Steve looked at me with a confused expression on his face.

"Why what's been happening?" he enquired.

"Let's grab a drink and I'll explain everything to you." I replied.

We went into the pub in the station. It was quiet, and Steve told me to grab a seat whilst he went to the bar to get the drinks.

As I sat waiting for him, it felt good to be home. Even though there was a lot of shit coming my way, being back to what was familiar to me was a comfort.

Steve handed me an ice-cold pint and I took a long drink. It was exactly what I needed after the day I'd had.

"So, tell me what's been happening mate." Steve asked.

I took another sip of my beer before telling him the short version of the shit I'd been through. Steve never interrupted me once but simply sat in silence and listened to me in amazement, finding it difficult to believe what I'd been through. Once I'd finished explaining, Steve looked at me and gave a huge sigh before saying

"Sorry, mate I know you've been through shit, but I've got more bad news for you."

"Fuck I can't handle any more bad news. What is it?" I asked.

"Remember the bond we gave to the Stirling Brokers? Well they have come back to me to tell me it's fake, but the strange thing is when I went to their office to speak to them, it was empty. They've fucked off! I've tried finding them through my contacts but there's no trace. That means the 20-grand retainer, and the single bearer bond, are both gone. Mike I'm so fucking sorry. I trusted those bastards." He said apologetically.

"What the fuck. Does that mean the bonds were fake and worth fuck all? I've put my life on the line for those worthless pieces of paper. I feel sick to my stomach at the thought of what I've been through." I replied.

"This is a nightmare for you Mike." He said regretfully.

I sat for a moment trying to take it all in, when suddenly something came into my mind.

"Maybe that's why those bastards never shot me. They knew the bonds were fake and I never really lost them 10 million!" I said angrily, bringing my elbows up onto the table and put my head into my hands.

"What you going to do now?" Steve asked.

Standing up from the table in a rage, nearly knocking my pint over, I began pacing back and forth trying to figure out what to do next. Like a bolt of lightning it hit me.

"Hang on a minute. The bonds can't be fake Steve!" I said, turning to look at him.

"The German had one of them checked by his contact in Poland, who confirmed it was legit, before he paid me 250,000 euros for it. Fuck my heads bursting with this, I don't know what to believe. What is certain is that I've no choice but to work for the London Boys for the next few years. They are not the type of guys you stand up to and call liars without having solid proof, or a death wish." I said.

"You're going to be working for the Russians and be part of the Turkish Brotherhood. If you were looking for excitement at the start of all this, fuck me you've got it now Mike." Steve said with a subtle smile, before pausing.

"Only fucking you." He stated.

At that we both let out a nervous laugh.

"Mate, thanks for everything you've done and for coming to meet me. I'm done with all this shit. I need time to clear my head so I'm going to go up the road." I said.

"Do you need a lift mate?" Steve asked.

"Na, I'm good. I'm just going to make my own way. but thanks." I replied.

Steve stood up and shook my hand before leaving me alone in the pub.

Sitting back down and taking the phone out my pocket, I dialed Jenna's number.

"Hello" She answered.

"Hi babe, it's me, I'm coming home."